The Asian Vegan Kitchen

The Asian Vegan Kitchen

Authentic and Appetizing Dishes from a Continent of Rich Flavors

Hema Parekh

KODANSHA INTERNATIONAL
Tokyo · New York · London

Distributed in the United States by Kodansha America, Inc.,
and in the United Kingdom and continental Europe
by Kodansha Europe Ltd.

Published by Kodansha International Ltd.,
17–14 Otowa 1-chome, Bunkyo-ku, Tokyo 112–8652, and
Kodansha America, Inc.

First edition, 2007
15 14 13 12 11 10 09 08 07   10 9 8 7 6 5 4 3 2 1

www.kodansha-intl.com

To

Ayesha and Alok
my strength, my love
my dream come true

Contents

Introduction   9

INDIA   13

SOUPS AND SALADS····················· 14
CURRIES AND MAIN DISHES ··········· 18
RICE DISHES ···························· 26
SIDE DISHES ···························· 28
SNACKS ································· 31
BREADS ································· 35
DRINKS AND DESSERTS················· 38

JAPAN   39

SOUPS AND SALADS ·················· 42
MAIN DISHES ························· 47
NOODLES ···························· 53
RICE ································· 56
SIDE DISHES ························· 58
DESSERTS ···························· 64

CHINA   65

SOUPS AND SALADS ·················· 66
MAIN DISHES ························· 69
RICE AND NOODLES ················· 75
SNACKS ····························· 79

THAILAND   113

SOUPS AND SALADS ·················· 114
MAIN DISHES ························· 118
RICE AND NOODLES ················· 121
SIDE DISHES AND SNACKS ··········· 125
DESSERT ···························· 128

VIETNAM 129

SOUPS AND SALADS 130
MAIN DISHES AND RICE 133
SIDE DISHES AND SNACKS 136
DESSERTS 138

BURMA 139

SOUPS AND SALADS 140
MAIN DISHES 142
RICE AND NOODLES 144
SIDE DISHES 145
SNACKS 147

INDONESIA 149

SOUPS AND SALADS 150
MAIN DISHES 152
RICE DISHES 155
SNACKS AND SIDE DISHES 156
DRINKS AND DESSERTS 158

MALAYSIA 159

MAIN DISHES 160
RICE DISHES 162
NOODLES 163
SIDE DISHES AND SNACKS 165

KOREA 167

SOUPS AND SALADS 168
MAIN MEALS 169
PANCAKES AND MORE 174
RICE AND NOODLE DISHES 177

Glossary of Ingredients 180
Index of Main Ingredients 185
Acknowledgments 192

Introduction

I believe no place on earth can compare with Asia as a source of culinary excitement, and the recent popularity of the region's cuisines has proven me right. The simple, complex, spicy, mild, exotic, earthy, and delicious dishes from the entire continent now tantalize the taste buds of food lovers all over the world.

Asian cuisine is ideal for those who care about healthy eating. The spiced food of India is world renowned for its medicinal properties. The Japanese diet guarantees longevity with reduced risk of obesity and heart disease. The Chinese method of quick stir-frying keeps nutrients intact. The Vietnamese, Burmese, and Korean cuisines embrace the health needs of today with the use of natural herbs, soy beans, and spices in their daily diet. Indonesian, Malaysian, and Thai cooking also use a combination of herbs and spices to enliven the most basic vegetables.

Equally important for this book, many Asian dishes are vegan in nature, which allowed me to choose traditional recipes that are traditional local favorites using traditional ingredients rather than substitutions. In fact, only Indian cuisine includes dairy in some of its dishes. (Luckily, the Indian diet is such a treasure trove of regional recipes that it was quite easy for me to focus on the foods that I grew up eating.)

I was born in India to a Jain family. Jainism is an ancient Indian religion and philosophy that is founded on the principle of non violence, and therefore Jains are strict vegetarians. Our diet included an amazing variety of wholesome dishes that were made with a combination of seasonal vegetables, lentils, and pulses- -some simple, some complex, but always tasty. In fact, my grandmother's daily diet was devoid of root vegetables such as potatoes, onions, carrots, and strong flavorings such as garlic. She did not eat anything after sunset and before sunrise. She lived to the ripe old age of ninety and remained healthy until the very end. Today, many nutritionists believe that this is the only way to lead a long and healthy life. Eat early, eat light, and include more vegetables and lentils in your diet.

My earliest memories of food are of the aromas that came wafting from the kitchen each morning as my mother prepared breakfast in our Mumbai home. It consisted of fruit, a hot snack such as dhokla savory sponge cakes, and a variety of dried snacks that we nibbled on with our masala tea. Lunch was a packed hot meal from home that was delivered to our school. Dinner was always a sit-down family meal, with at least two vegetable curries, a lentil dish, salad, chutneys, pickles, and a sweet, always served with bread and rice. Dinnertime was family time, with everyone eating together, and plentiful second helpings of freshly baked chapati bread, piping hot rice, and crispy pappadums. My childhood is full of happy memories.

I was in my second year of college in India when I met my husband, Atul, at a family gathering. He was visiting from Tokyo, where he worked. We got married while I was a still a senior year student, and I remember the first time I flew to Tokyo to get a glimpse of my future life. It was a cold January night when our flight landed at Narita airport. It was snowing, and as far as I could see the snowflakes had made a beautifully soft, white blanket. Everything was pure and auspicious, a perfect way to start a new life in a new country.

One day, not long after arriving, I decided to put on my thick winter coat and walk to the supermarket. My husband came home in the evening to find a box of cereal and milk on the table—that was all I had been able to bring myself to buy. I was in a state of shock after looking at the prices of fruit and vegetables in Japan. After we had a good laugh about it, he told me that I had to stop converting yen prices to Indian rupees. We then went out and brought enough food to fill up our fridge. I must confess though that I almost choked on the melon, knowing that it cost the equivalent of two thousand rupees—which could buy twenty melons back home!

Then came another realization. I could not cook at all. I had led a sheltered life, and all I had done in the way of cooking was to clean some lentils and chop some vegetables on weekends under my grandmother's supervision. In my tiny Tokyo kitchen, I struggled to make sense of my new life; I missed my mother and my home comforts terribly. During my first phone call to my mother, I broke down in tears. She comforted me, assuring me that there was nothing to cooking. I just had to start and I would be fine.

She was right. I found that the smells of my mom's kitchen in Mumbai had remained firmly imprinted in my memory. From the cardamom and ginger in the morning tea to the mustard seeds and lentils in the savory semolina porridge, they were all there, locked away, waiting to be explored and experienced.

After my first month in Tokyo I had to go back to India for my senior year exams. Once there, I hungrily tried to absorb as much about cooking as I could by observing everything and everyone I saw in the kitchen, wherever I went, hoping that everything I saw in that short period would remain with me on my return to Tokyo. The ease with which everyone threw spices and herbs around was fascinating, and in that attitude lay the secret. I learned that cooking delicious food is not about getting the recipe right, it is more about getting a feel for the ingredients and quantities. It is this flexibility that makes cooking a delightful and enriching experience.

My interest in cooking soon led me to expand my culinary boundaries. With both my children attending international schools in Tokyo, I was naturally surrounded by people from all over the world. I found many new teachers. I was never afraid to ask questions and they were always enthusiastic about sharing information about their native cuisines with me. Wherever possible, I asked for lessons in their home cooking. I read every book I could on each cuisine that was of interest. I enrolled in classes for Japanese Buddhist temple cuisine and learned about the Zen vegetarian tradition. When we traveled abroad on family holidays, especially to other countries around Asia, I would haunt local restaurants and pester the chefs. When we returned home, I would immediately try to recreate from memory the flavor and fragrance of the dishes we had enjoyed on our vacation. Soon I realized I had learned a second lesson about what cooking is. It is about respecting a cuisine, its basic ingredients, and cooking methods, while retaining one's own individual and original style.

When I started creating all the new dishes I had learned for my family and friends, my only concern was that they would enjoy the food I cooked for them. I was thrilled to find that they all did. Before long, I was invited to teach at classes organized by the Tokyo American Club. That was almost twenty years ago, and I am still there today, as a teacher specializing in vegetarian cuisine. What started as a hobby turned into a profession, and here I am now sharing my favorite and most popular recipes with you.

All those years ago when I first started cooking, I never thought I would enjoy it so much. For our first dinner at home with ten guests, it took me three weeks to plan an Indian meal. Today, I routinely plan meals for thirty people in three days—of any one of a number of Asian cuisines. And if I can do it, anyone can.

The dishes in this book can be enjoyed by vegans, vegetarians, and by anyone with an interest in healthy eating. Not only will mundane daily cooking be transformed into an exciting experience for you and your family, but the combinations of fresh herbs, spices, pulses, and fresh vegetables will provide immense health benefits.

This book focuses on recipes for dishes that Asian people eat every day in their homes. In my humble opinion, nothing can compare with a meal put together in the comfort of your own kitchen, in the warmth of your home, for the people you love.

Hema Parekh
Tokyo, 2007

India

Food is celebration; food is love; food is hospitality; food is spiritual. Food seeps into every pore of the Indian culture as an expression of emotions.

If that sounds like I'm passionate about my mother country's cuisine, it's because I am. Like the country itself, there is very little that is understated about the food of India. Piquant spices are at the heart of Indian cooking, adding zing, color, and energy. In some dishes, the whole all-star cast of spices makes its appearance. Yet spices are not just an indulgence of the palate; they also impart a medicinal benefit to the food. Cumin is considered a digestive, turmeric an antiseptic, and pepper a lozenge.

If you have ever thought that Indian food lacks variety, I hope you will be pleasantly surprised by the range of dishes on the following pages. The full-bodied spices of Punjabi dishes, such as Navratna Korma, contrast with the subtle spices and coconut flavors of dishes like Kosumalli from the south and coastal regions. If Bengali food of the east, such as Masoor Ki Dal, arrests your attention with its use of the exotic five-spice mix panchphoren, Gujarati food in the west—with dishes ranging from Sambhariu Shak to Khaman Dhokla—can baffle you with its variety.

But all Indian cuisines across the country have a soul-satisfying finale to them: the crackling of mustard seeds in hot oil, meant to be doused sizzling over dals and vegetables, an irresistible invitation—one that I'd like to extend to you—to savor the romance of my country through its food.

SOUPS AND SALADS

Crunchy Red Cabbage Kachumber

Kobi nu kachumber

SERVES *4*   PHOTOGRAPH ON PAGE 85

This is one of my favorite salads: a tasty, crunchy cabbage dish that takes just a few minutes to prepare. A kachumber is a combination of minced or shredded vegetables, usually raw, seasoned with spices and lemon juice. It can be served at room temperature and makes a colorful addition to a party menu.

1. Place the red cabbage, white cabbage, and fresh green chili together in a bowl. Sprinkle with salt, and toss to mix.
2. Heat the oil in a small saucepan, then put in the mustard seeds. As soon as they start to splutter, add the turmeric, asafetida, cayenne pepper, and curry leaves and fry for 20 seconds.
3. Drizzle the oil and spice mixture over the cabbage. Add the peanuts, coriander leaves, and lemon juice. Mix thoroughly and allow to stand for 10 minutes before serving, for the flavors to blend.

2 cups (90g) red cabbage, shredded
2 cups (90g) white cabbage, shredded
1 fresh hot green chili, finely chopped
Salt to taste
1 tablespoon mustard oil or vegetable oil
1 teaspoon mustard seeds
½ teaspoon turmeric
Pinch of asafetida
½ teaspoon cayenne pepper
8–10 curry leaves
1 tablespoon peanuts, coarsely ground
1 tablespoon fresh coriander leaves
2 teaspoons lemon juice

Cumin Seed and Pepper Soup

Jeera rasam

SERVES *4*

Rasam is a light, delicately flavored soup, traditionally served as the second course of a south Indian meal, after the thick, spicy curry known as sambar that is served as the first course. Rasam makes a great hot appetizer, or it can be served over rice with kachumber on the side for a light meal.

1. Wash the lentils and soak for 10 minutes. Bring the 2 cups water to a boil in a saucepan, then put in the lentils. Cover and simmer for 15–18 minutes, over medium heat, until tender. Mash the lentils gently and pass through a sieve. Add the tamarind paste and salt to the strained liquid.
2. For the pepper and cumin paste, heat the oil in a saucepan and add the peppercorns, cumin seeds, pigeon pea dal, and red chili and stir for 2 minutes until fragrant. Add the asafetida then turn off the heat.

¼ cup (45g) split yellow lentils
2 cups (480ml) water
2 tablespoons tamarind paste
Salt to taste

FOR THE PEPPER AND CUMIN PASTE
  2 teaspoons vegetable oil
  2 teaspoons whole black peppercorns
  1 teaspoon cumin seeds
  2 teaspoons pigeon pea dal
  1 dried red chili
  ¼ teaspoon asafetida
  ½-inch (1-cm) cube fresh ginger, peeled and chopped
  2 tablespoons water

FOR THE TEMPERING
  2 teaspoons vegetable oil
  1 teaspoon cumin seeds
  1 dried red chili, halved
  3–4 curry leaves

3. Using an electric blender, grind the pepper and cumin paste mixture with the ginger and water to a smooth paste. Set aside.
4. For the tempering, heat the oil in a saucepan and add the cumin seeds, red chili, and curry leaves. When the seeds sizzle, add the strained liquid from the lentils and the pepper and cumin paste. Bring to a simmer then turn off the heat. Serve hot.

Red Lentils with Coriander

Masoor ki dal

SERVES *4*

1 cup (170g) red lentils
2½ cups (600ml) water
½ teaspoon turmeric
Salt to taste
2 fresh hot green chilies
2 teaspoons vegetable oil
½-inch (1-cm) cube fresh ginger, finely chopped
½ teaspoon cayenne pepper
2 tablespoons fresh coriander leaves

FOR THE PANCHPHOREN
½ teaspoon mustard seeds
½ teaspoon fenugreek seeds
½ teaspoon fennel seeds
½ teaspoon onion seeds
½ teaspoon cumin seeds

* For a quick and easy variation, add 8 whole peeled baby onions to the lentils during cooking, and replace the vegetable oil with mustard oil.

Red lentils have a mild taste and a creamy texture. The panchphoren—a 5-spice mixture from Bengal—transforms these simple lentils into a stunning dish.

1. Wash the lentils and soak for 10–20 minutes. Place the lentils in a saucepan, and add the 2½ cups water, turmeric, and salt. Bring to a boil. Cover and cook over medium heat for 20–25 minutes, until the lentils are tender.
2. Slice the green chilies lengthwise from the tip, leaving the stem end of each chili intact.
3. Heat the oil in a saucepan and add the panchphoren spices. When the seeds start to splutter, add the ginger, green chilies, and cayenne pepper. Stir until fragrant.
4. Add the cooked lentils and a little water to make thinner if preferred. Heat through so that the spices blend in and finally add the coriander leaves. Serve hot.

South Indian Salad

Kosumalli

SERVES *4*

2 tablespoons split mung beans
1 cucumber, finely chopped
½ medium carrot, finely chopped
2 tablespoons fresh coriander, chopped
1 fresh hot green chili, finely chopped
1 teaspoon desiccated coconut
1 teaspoon ginger juice (see page 13)
1 tablespoon lemon juice
Salt to taste
A few cherry tomatoes, halved, for garnish

FOR THE TEMPERING
2 teaspoons vegetable oil
1 teaspoon mustard seeds
½ teaspoon urad dal
½ teaspoon asafetida
1 dried red chili
3–4 curry leaves

South Indian cooking uses a variety of pulses and vegetables, and this salad is distinguished by its vibrant colors and delicious crunchy texture. This is the perfect dish for a hot summer afternoon.

1. Wash the split mung beans, soak for 30 minutes, then drain.
2. In a deep bowl, mix the split mung beans with the cucumber, carrot, coriander leaves, green chili, and coconut. Add the ginger juice, lemon juice, and salt to taste.
3. For the tempering, heat the oil in a small frying pan. Add the mustard seeds and urad dal. When the seeds start to splutter, add the asafetida, red chili, and the curry leaves.
4. Spoon the tempering over the split mung beans, cucumber, and carrot and combine thoroughly.
5. Serve garnished with cherry tomatoes.

Spicy White Lentil Soup

Dal maharani

SERVES *4*

The word *maharani* means "queen," and this mild white lentil preparation is befitting of its royal title. I make this soup at least once a week for my family. It complements a sandwich as nicely as it does a chapati.

1. Wash the split black gram and soak in water for 10–15 minutes. Drain and put to one side.
2. Heat the oil in a saucepan and add the cumin seeds and the onion. Sauté for a few minutes until the onions are soft. Add the green chili, garlic, and ginger, and stir until fragrant. Add the tomatoes and cook, covered, for 1 minute.
3. Add the asafetida, turmeric, cayenne pepper, coriander powder, and garam masala and mix well. Drain the split black gram and add to the mixture. Sauté for 1 minute. Add 3 cups water and salt to taste. Cook covered for 10–15 minutes over medium heat, stirring occasionally, until the gram is tender.
4. Transfer to a serving bowl and serve hot, garnished with fresh coriander leaves.

1¾ cups (300g) split black gram
1 tablespoon vegetable oil
1 teaspoon cumin seeds
1 medium onion, finely chopped
1 fresh hot green chili, finely chopped
2 small cloves garlic, finely chopped
½-inch (1-cm) cube fresh ginger, peeled and grated
2 medium tomatoes, chopped
Pinch of asafetida
½ teaspoon turmeric
½ teaspoon cayenne pepper
1 teaspoon coriander powder
¼ teaspoon garam masala (see below)
3 cups (720ml) water
Salt to taste
2 tablespoons fresh coriander leaves

Garam Masala

MAKES ABOUT *3 tablespoons*

1½ tablespoons coriander seeds
1 tablespoon cumin seeds
1 teaspoon black peppercorns
1 tablespoon poppy seeds
1 small stick of cinnamon
3 green cardamom pods
8 cloves
¼ teaspoon nutmeg
¼ teaspoon mace

Garam *means "hot," and garam masala is easily the most famous and commonly used flavoring in north Indian cooking, for which each family has its own recipe. My mother prefers to dry roast the spices before grinding them to a powder. Freshly roasted and ground spices emit an irresistible aroma. Garam masala is added to dishes in small quantities towards the end of preparation time. Ready-made garam masala is available in supermarkets.*

1. Heat a small pan and add all the spices, dry roasting them over low heat for a minute or two until lightly browned and fragrant. Shake the pan a few times, so that they are evenly browned.
2. Allow to cool, then grind to a fine powder. Store in an airtight jar. Tastes best if used within 1 month.

* The proportions of the ingredients may be varied to suit individual tastes.

Sprouted Mung Bean and Avocado Salad

Mung aur avocado kachumber

SERVES *4*

PHOTOGRAPH ON PAGE 84

Mung bean sprouts are highly nutritious and easily digested. In this salad, velvety avocado combines with the crunch of the sprouts and the red onion to give a contrasting texture. Fresh tomato, cumin, and coriander round out the textures perfectly. My son's favorite salad is an easy variation of this one—Sprouted Mung Bean and

2 ripe avocados
2 teaspoons lemon juice
2 cups (480ml) water
1 cup (100g) mung bean sprouts
1 medium tomato, chopped
1 cucumber, diced
2 tablespoons red onion, finely chopped
1 tablespoon fresh coriander leaves
½ teaspoon cumin seeds, roasted and ground

¼ teaspoon mango powder
½ teaspoon coarse salt
Dash of ground black pepper

* For Sprouted Mung Bean and Fruit Salad, replace the avocado and red onions with ½ apple, sliced; 1 banana, sliced; 1 cup (200g) canned mandarin orange slices; 2 tablespoons ground peanuts, and ½ teaspoon sugar.

½ cup (95g) split mung beans
¼ cup (25g) white cabbage, chopped
1 medium onion, chopped
1 medium carrot, chopped
3 cups (720ml) water
4 canned tomatoes, pureed
Salt to taste
1 tablespoon vegetable oil
1 teaspoon cumin seeds
½ teaspoon cayenne pepper
A few curry leaves, optional
Dash of ground black pepper
Fresh coriander leaves, for garnish

Fruit Salad—and I used to make it for him every day during his high school wrestling season.

1. Peel and chop the avocados, then sprinkle with the lemon juice to prevent discoloring.
2. In a saucepan, bring the 2 cups water to a boil, immerse the bean sprouts in the pan, and drain immediately. Rinse the bean sprouts under cold running water.
3. Mix the bean sprouts with the avocado, tomato, cucumber, onion, and coriander leaves in a large bowl. Season with the cumin seeds, mango powder, coarse salt, and pepper. Serve chilled.

How to sprout mung beans
Although it takes some planning, I like to sprout my own mung beans. Soak a cup (170g) of mung beans overnight in plenty of water. Drain the next morning and place in a bowl. Keep in a dark, warm place for 24 hours. By now, the mung beans will have begun to sprout. Sprinkle some water over the beans and keep covered for another 10–12 hours. When the sprouts are about 1 inch long, they are ready for use. (Note that in winter it will take an extra day for them to sprout fully.) Keep the sprouts refrigerated and use as required. I like the crunch of raw sprouts in my salads, but some people prefer to boil them for 3–4 minutes in salted water before using.

Vegetable Soup with Mung Beans   *Mung dal shorba*

SERVES 4

Split mung beans add a wonderfully creamy texture to this wholesome soup. You can serve it with a salad for a light lunch or it can be an elegant first course for a sit-down dinner.

1. Place the mung beans, cabbage, onion, carrot, and water in a saucepan. Bring to a boil then simmer for 15–18 minutes until tender. Allow the vegetables and cooking liquid to cool. Transfer to a deep bowl and combine with the pureed tomatoes.
2. Blend the mung bean and tomato mixture to a smooth paste, using a food processor.
3. Transfer the blended mixture to a saucepan and bring to a boil. Add salt to taste.
4. In another saucepan heat the oil then add the cumin seeds. Let them sizzle. Add cayenne pepper and the curry leaves and spoon the mixture over the soup. Serve hot, sprinkled with black pepper and garnished with coriander leaves.

CURRIES AND MAIN DISHES

Assorted Vegetables in Cashew Gravy

Navratna korma

SERVES *4*   PHOTOGRAPH ON PAGE 81

One of the most famous and irresistible Indian curries. Robust and aromatic, yet mild, it can be found on restaurant menus all over the world. It is one of my children's all-time favorites, and I always make it when they have friends over for dinner.

1. Boil the vegetables in lightly salted water. Drain and put to one side.
2. For the cashew paste, dry roast the cashews, coriander seeds, cumin seeds, cloves, and peppercorns over low heat until fragrant. Using a food processor, blend to a smooth paste with the green chili, coriander leaves, and spearmint leaves, mixed with a little water.
3. In a large saucepan, heat the oil and sauté the onion over medium heat until soft and light brown. Mix in the Ginger Garlic Paste and sauté for about 1 minute.
4. Add the tomatoes, turmeric, and salt to taste. Cook covered for 2–3 minutes, until the tomatoes soften. Add the cashew paste and the 1 cup water. Bring to a simmer.
5. Add the sugar and lemon juice, then toss in the boiled vegetables. Bring to a boil, then turn down the heat and simmer for 4–5 minutes. Serve hot with paratha or rice. Saffron Rice with Almonds and Cashews (see page 27) goes particularly well with this dish.

1 medium cauliflower, cut into florets
1 medium carrot, diced
2 medium potatoes, peeled and diced
1 cup (100g) green beans, diced
⅔ cup (100g) green peas
1 tablespoon vegetable oil
1 medium onion, finely chopped
1 teaspoon Ginger Garlic Paste (see below)
4 medium tomatoes, chopped
½ teaspoon turmeric
Salt to taste
1 cup (240ml) water
1 teaspoon castor sugar
2 teaspoons lemon juice

FOR THE CASHEW PASTE
3 tablespoons cashew nuts
2 tablespoons coriander seeds
2 teaspoons cumin seeds
3–4 cloves
½ teaspoon black peppercorns
1 fresh green chili
1 cup fresh coriander leaves
¼ cup fresh spearmint leaves

Ginger Garlic Paste   *Pisa hua adrak lasun*   MAKES *1 tablespoon*

3 cloves garlic, peeled
1 piece of ginger, walnut sized, peeled

This is a delightfully pungent paste used in many North Indian recipes. This paste not only enhances the flavor of Indian dishes, but it can be used to good effect in your freestyle cooking efforts as well.

Blend the garlic and ginger to a smooth paste, using few drops of water. Keep in a sealed container in the refrigerator. Keeps for 1 week.

Cauliflower and Potato with Spices

Aloo gobi masala

SERVES *4*

SERVES *4*   PHOTOGRAPH ON PAGE 82

1 tablespoon vegetable oil
1 teaspoon mustard seeds
1 teaspoon fennel seeds
Pinch of asafetida
1 fresh hot green chili, cut in half lengthwise
1-inch (2.5-cm) cube fresh ginger, peeled and finely
   chopped
½ teaspoon turmeric
1 teaspoon coriander powder
1 small head of cauliflower, cut into florets
2 medium potatoes, peeled and cut into thick strips
Salt to taste
2 tablespoons water
½ teaspoon cayenne pepper
½ teaspoon garam masala (see page 16)
½ teaspoon mango powder
Ginger julienne, for garnish, optional
Coriander leaves, for garnish, optional

A classic north Indian curry, usually cooked as a dry dish. It is simple to make and impossible to resist, which is why most Indians serve it at their dinner parties and every restaurant has it on the menu. Leftovers can be used as a filling for samosas or a pita sandwich.

1. Heat the oil in a nonstick saucepan and add the mustard seeds and fennel seeds. When they splutter, add the asafetida and reduce the heat, then add the chili and ginger and stir-fry for 10 seconds before adding the turmeric and the coriander powder.
2. Add the cauliflower and potatoes and season with salt. Stir to coat the vegetables with the spices. Sprinkle 2 tablespoons of water over the vegetables and cook covered for 10–12 minutes over medium-low heat, until the potatoes are tender.
3. Uncover and gently toss the vegetables. Stir in the cayenne pepper, garam masala, and mango powder.
4. Garnish with ginger julienne and coriander leaves and serve hot.

Chickpea Curry

Chana masala

SERVES *4*   PHOTOGRAPH ON PAGE 82

1 cup (200g) dried chickpeas
4 cups (960ml) water
1 teaspoon salt
1 tablespoon vegetable oil
2 cardamom pods
1 small stick cinnamon
2 bay leaves
1 teaspoon cumin seeds
Pinch of asafetida
1 large onion, finely chopped
1 fresh hot green chili, halved lengthwise
½-inch (1-cm) cube fresh ginger, peeled and grated
11 ounces (310g) tomatoes, pureed
Salt to taste
½ teaspoon turmeric
½ teaspoon garam masala (see page 16)
½ teaspoon cayenne pepper
½ teaspoon mango powder
1 teaspoon coriander powder
Sliced onions and fresh coriander leaves, for garnish

FOR THE ROASTED SPICE MIXTURE
1 teaspoon coriander seeds
2–3 cloves
½ teaspoon cumin seeds
1 dried red chili

Chickpeas are popular among the Punjabis of north India who call them *chole* and often prepare them for breakfast with bhatura bread (see page 35). This recipe was handed down to me by my mother. The roasted coriander and cumin seeds that she uses, together with the generous amount of ginger, give it a distinctive flavor.

1. Dry roast all the roasted spice mixture ingredients and grind to a powder.
2. Soak the chickpeas overnight in 4 cups water. Then place the soaked chickpeas with the soaking water in a pressure cooker with 1 teaspoon salt. Cook for 18–20 minutes if using a pressure cooker, and about an hour if cooking in a pan. The chickpeas should be well cooked—until they are slightly broken. Drain, and reserve the cooking liquid.
3. In a large frying pan, heat the oil and add the cardamom, cinnamon, bay leaves, and cumin seeds. Stir over medium heat until fragrant. Add the asafetida and onion and sauté for 10–12 minutes until browned.
4. Add the fresh green chili, ginger, and the pureed tomatoes. Cover

19

the frying pan and simmer for 3–4 minutes. Add the salt, turmeric, garam masala, cayenne pepper, mango powder, and coriander powder. Stir thoroughly.

5. Add the cooked chickpeas and stir gently. Add some of the reserved drained cooking liquid to bring it to the desired consistency. Add the roasted spice mixture, bring to a simmer, then turn off the heat.

6. Serve garnished with sliced onions and coriander leaves.

* Two cans of chickpeas can be used in place of the dried. Mash them slightly before adding to the gravy.

Eggplant in Tomato Gravy   *Tamatar wale baingan*

SERVES *4*

Vegetable oil for deep-frying
5–6 small eggplants or 2 large ones, cut into bite-sized chunks
1 teaspoon coriander powder
½ teaspoon cayenne pepper
Salt to taste
1½ cups (360ml) Tomato Gravy (see below)
Finely chopped scallions, for garnish

All my friends love this dish. Quick and easy to prepare, it goes well with rice and makes a colorful addition to any party menu. The small, tender Japanese variety of eggplant is ideal for this dish, if you can get hold of any. Leftovers make a great pasta sauce, topped with chopped basil and parsley.

1. Heat the oil for deep-frying to 350°F (180°C) and deep-fry the eggplant until well browned. Remove from the oil with a slotted spoon, drain on kitchen paper, and sprinkle with the coriander powder, cayenne pepper, and salt. Set to one side.

2. In a saucepan, heat the Tomato Gravy. Stir in the eggplants until they are heated through. Remove from the heat and serve garnished with finely chopped scallions.

Tomato Gravy   *Tamatar ki gravy*   MAKES *3 cups (720ml)*

3 tablespoons vegetable oil	1 teaspoon coriander powder
1 teaspoon cumin seeds	1 teaspoon fenugreek powder
1 teaspoon Ginger Garlic Paste (see page 18)	1 teaspoon cayenne pepper
1¼ pounds (600g) tomatoes, coarsely pureed	1 teaspoon garam masala (see page 16)
4 tablespoons tomato paste	½ teaspoon ground black pepper
½ cup (120ml) water	½ teaspoon cardamom powder
2 teaspoons castor sugar	½ teaspoon salt

This versatile gravy with its tangy flavor can be used as a base or a finish for vegetable or lentil dishes. Create an exotic dish for family and friends by simply stir-frying some vegetables and tossing in some of this gravy.

1. Heat the oil in a wok, then sauté the cumin seeds and the Ginger Garlic Paste.
2. Stir in the pureed tomatoes, tomato paste, and the water. Add the sugar, coriander powder, fenugreek powder, cayenne pepper, garam masala, pepper, cardamom powder, and salt. Simmer for 5–7 minutes over medium heat, until the gravy thickens and the spices are thoroughly blended.
3. Allow to cool, then store in an airtight jar. Keeps for 1 week.

Mushroom and Green Pea Curry *Khumbi matar*

1 tablespoon vegetable oil
½ teaspoon cumin seeds
2 cups (480ml) Almond Gravy (see below)
11 ounces (310g) button mushrooms, thinly sliced
1 cup (160g) cooked green peas
½ cup (120ml) water
Salt to taste
1 cup fresh coriander leaves

The delicate almond sauce lends a mild yet rich flavor to this elegant curry, which is one of my children's favorites. I always include this in my dinner menu for friends who are not so familiar with Indian spices. The mushrooms absorb the flavor of this delicate sauce and the green peas add the perfect hint of color.

1. Heat the oil in a saucepan, then put in the cumin seeds. When they start to sizzle, add the Almond Gravy and stir for 2–3 minutes over medium heat until fragrant.
2. Put the mushrooms, peas, and water into the saucepan with the sauce. Season with salt and bring to a simmer. Cover and cook over medium heat for 8–10 minutes, until the mushrooms are tender.
3. Stir in the coriander leaves and remove from the heat. Transfer to a serving bowl and serve hot.

Almond Gravy *Badaam ki gravy* MAKES *2 cups (480ml)*

1 cup (145g) blanched almonds
2 tablespoons poppy seeds
1 cardamom pod
3 fresh hot green chilies, chopped
½-inch (1-cm) cube fresh ginger, peeled and finely chopped
1 cup (240ml) water

Pinch of nutmeg
½ teaspoon salt
½ teaspoon ground black pepper
3 tablespoons vegetable oil
2 medium onions, finely chopped
1 cup (240ml) coconut milk

This is a nutty gravy that imparts richness and delicacy to any dish. My children love it, as do most of my Japanese friends. They particularly enjoy the variety of vegetables than can be mixed in with it. Cauliflower, beans, and potatoes all work well. White mushrooms and green peas make a colorful combination. It can also be used as a delicious alternative to the cashew paste in Assorted Vegetables in Cashew Gravy (page 18)

1. Mix the almonds, poppy seeds, cardamom, green chilies, and ginger with the water and grind to a smooth paste. Add the nutmeg, salt, and pepper.
2. Heat the oil in a wok, and sauté the onions for 8–10 minutes over medium heat, until evenly browned. Add the almond paste, lower the heat, and gently stir for 6–8 minutes. Add the coconut milk and heat through.
3. The gravy is ready to be used. If serving with vegetables, heat the vegetables in the sauce first. The gravy will keep for 1 week in a sealed container in the refrigerator.

North Indian Potato Curry

Dum aloo

SERVES *4*

This classic Indian dish is also known as Kashmiri Dum Aloo. *Dum* means steamed slowly in a covered pot over low heat, but this recipe is a quick and easy variation on the traditional method. Usually the potatoes in this dish are deep-fried, but I prefer boiled potatoes.

1. Boil the potatoes in their skins for 5–7 minutes in salted water. Then peel each potato and pierce with a fork in several places so that they will absorb the gravy.
2. Heat the 2 tablespoons of oil in a large frying pan, then add the onion, garlic, and cardamom. Sauté for 5–6 minutes, until the onions are soft. Remove from heat with a slotted spoon and blend to a paste with the poppy seeds and ginger, using a food processor.
3. Heat the 1 tablespoon oil in a saucepan, then put in the cumin seeds. Add the paste from step 2, and sauté for 2–3 minutes over medium heat. Add the red chili, coriander, fennel, and cumin powder, and the turmeric. Stir to mix.
4. Add the tomatoes, sugar, and salt to taste. Add 1 cup of water and bring to a boil. Add the boiled potatoes and simmer over low heat for 8–10 minutes. Garnish with coriander leaves and serve hot.

12–15 baby potatoes
2 tablespoons vegetable oil
1 medium onion, finely chopped
2 cloves garlic, finely chopped
2 green cardamom pods
1 tablespoon poppy seeds
½-inch (1-cm) cube fresh ginger, peeled and finely chopped
1 tablespoon vegetable oil
½ teaspoon cumin seeds
½ teaspoon cayenne pepper
1 teaspoon coriander powder
2 teaspoons fennel powder
½ teaspoon cumin powder
½ teaspoon turmeric
3 medium tomatoes, pureed
1 teaspoon sugar
Salt to taste
1 cup (240ml) water
Fresh coriander leaves

Parsee Lentil and Vegetable Curry

Dhansak

SERVES *4*

This is a simplified version of a famous Parsee dish, usually served with Browned Rice (see page 26) and Onion Kachumber. Whether you are enjoying a cool night on the balcony or having some friends over, this wholesome puree of lentils and vegetables always fits the occasion.

1. Wash the pigeon peas and, if time allows, soak for 30 minutes. Drain and set aside.
2. Heat the oil in a pan, sauté the sliced onions until brown, add the Ginger Garlic Paste, sauté briefly, then add the Dhansak Masala. Sauté for 2–3 minutes until the spices are well blended and fragrant.
3. Put the pigeon peas and all the other ingredients into the pan with the spices. Bring to a boil, then simmer until the pigeon peas and vegetables are tender, making sure there is sufficient water at all times. Allow the pigeon pea and vegetable mixture and the cooking liquid to cool.
4. Blend the pigeon pea and vegetable mixture to a thick smooth paste, using an electric blender. You may add a little water if it seems too thick.
5. Heat through, and serve with rice and Onion Kachumber.

2 cups (90g) pigeon pea dal
3 tablespoons vegetable oil
3 medium onions, sliced
1 tablespoon Ginger Garlic Paste (see page 18)
2 tablespoons Dhansak Masala spice mix (see page 23)
½ cup (50g) pumpkin, chopped into bite-sized cubes
1 small eggplant, chopped
2 small tomatoes, chopped
1 large onion, chopped
2 tablespoons fresh or 1 teaspoon dried fenugreek leaves
4½ cups (1L) water
Salt to taste

Onion Kachumber *Kanda kachumber*

1 medium onion, finely chopped
1 fresh hot green chili, finely chopped
2 teaspoons lemon juice
1 tablespoon fresh coriander leaves
¼ teaspoon salt
½ teaspoon cumin seeds, roasted (see method for toasting sesame seeds on page 42), and coarsely ground

Combine all the ingredients in a bowl and toss well.

Sindhi Vegetable and Lentil Curry   *Sai bhaji*

SERVES *4*

1 cup (170g) split yellow lentils
2 tablespoons vegetable oil
½ teaspoon cumin seeds
2 cloves garlic, finely chopped
½-inch (1-cm) cube fresh ginger, peeled and finely chopped
2 fresh hot green chilies, finely chopped
1 medium onion, finely chopped
4 medium tomatoes, finely chopped
1 medium potato, peeled and diced
1 medium carrot, diced
1 small eggplant, diced
8 cups (400g) spinach, chopped
½ teaspoon turmeric
½ teaspoon cayenne pepper
1 teaspoon coriander powder
Salt to taste
3½ cups (840ml) water

This curry is originally from the Sind region, which is now part of Pakistan. A multitude of delectable flavors result from this combination of lentils and vegetables. A great one-dish meal, perfect for a Sunday evening.

1. Wash the lentils and soak for 30 minutes. Drain and set aside.
2. Heat the oil in a large saucepan and add the cumin seeds. Sauté the garlic, ginger, chilies, and onion for 2–3 minutes over medium heat, until the onions are soft.
3. Add the drained lentils, tomatoes, potato, carrot, eggplant, spinach, turmeric, cayenne pepper, coriander, and salt to taste. Stir to mix. Add the 3½ cups water and cook covered for 15–18 minutes, stirring occasionally until all the vegetables and the lentils are tender.
4. Mash to a coarse mixture with a wooden spoon. Serve with rice.

Spicy Roasted Eggplant Curry   *Baingan bhurta*

SERVES *4*

2 large eggplants
3 tablespoons vegetable oil
1 teaspoon cumin seeds
1 large onion, finely chopped
1 tablespoon Ginger Garlic Paste (see page 18)
2 fresh hot green chilies, finely chopped
4 medium tomatoes, coarsely puréed
½ cup (80g) green peas, cooked
½ teaspoon turmeric
1 teaspoon coriander powder
1 teaspoon cayenne pepper
1 teaspoon garam masala (see page 16)
Salt to taste
1 teaspoon lemon juice
1 tablespoon fresh coriander leaves

Another traditional and highly popular curry from the north Indian state of Punjab. The eggplants in this dish are roasted over an open flame, which imparts a distinctive smoky flavor that will take you by surprise. The green peas and tomato lend an attractive color. For a more authentic flavor, use mustard oil instead of vegetable oil.

1. Place the eggplants on a wire tray over a gas flame and cook over high heat, turning from time to time, until the outer skin has charred all over. An alternative, but slower, method is to roast them in an oven preheated to 350°F (180°C) for 20–30 minutes.
2. Pick up the eggplants with tongs and briefly dip them in cold water to cool. Peel off the skin and mash the flesh coarsely.
3. Heat the oil in a large saucepan and sauté the cumin seeds and onion over medium heat until golden. Add the Ginger Garlic Paste and green chilies and stir for 10 seconds.

4. Mix in the tomatoes and green peas, and add the turmeric, coriander powder, cayenne pepper, garam masala, and salt to taste. Cover and cook for 2–3 minutes, until the tomatoes and spices have blended to make a thick gravy.
5. Add the mashed eggplant and heat through, stirring all the time. Sprinkle with the lemon juice and garnish with coriander leaves. Serve hot with paratha (see page 36) or rice.

Stuffed Eggplant, Squash, and Potato Curry

Sambhariu shak

SERVES *4*

This is a traditional Gujarati dish, a typical Sunday afternoon indulgence for my family. You can enhance the color and taste of this dish by using purple yam, if locally available, in place of the 8 small potatoes.

1. Cut the eggplant, sweet potato and squash into 1½-inch (4-cm) cubes. Make a cross-shaped incision about ¾ inch (2 cm) deep on one side of each of the cubes and on each of the small potatoes.
2. Mix together all the spice mix ingredients.
3. Fill the slits in the vegetables with a generous amount of the spice mix. Keep any remaining spice mix aside.
4. Heat the oil in a large flat nonstick pan and add the asafetida. Place the stuffed vegetables into the pan. Add ½ cup water and cook covered over medium heat for 10–12 minutes, stirring occasionally to avoid sticking. Reduce the heat and sprinkle a little water over the vegetables.
5. Cook for another 7–8 minutes, until the vegetables are tender. Sprinkle any remaining spice mix over the vegetables and cook for 2 minutes. Serve hot with chapati (see page 35).

4 small eggplants
1 small sweet potato, about 7 ounces (200g)
3½ ounces (100g) zucchini or other green squash
8 small potatoes, peeled
3 tablespoons vegetable oil
¼ teaspoon asafetida
½ cup (120ml) water

FOR THE SPICE MIX
4 tablespoons fresh coriander leaves
1 tablespoon Ginger Chili Paste (see page 30)
4 tablespoons grated coconut, fresh or desiccated
2 tablespoons peanuts, ground
2 tablespoons chickpea flour
1 tablespoon sesame seeds
2 tablespoons coriander powder
1 teaspoon cayenne pepper
2 teaspoons castor sugar
2 teaspoons lemon juice
1 teaspoon salt

Vegetable Curry with Bread Rolls   *Pav bhaji*

SERVES *4*

2 tablespoons vegetable oil
1 cup (240ml) Basic Curry Sauce (see below)
2 teaspoons Pav Bhaji Masala *
1 medium head cauliflower, boiled and coarsely
   mashed
3 medium potatoes, boiled and coarsely mashed
½ cup (80g) cooked green peas
1 green bell pepper, finely chopped
½ cup (120ml) water
1 teaspoon salt
½ cup (10g) fresh coriander leaves and stalks, chopped
8 soft bread rolls
1 medium onion, sliced thinly, for garnish
Lemon wedges, for garnish

There is hardly any Indian whose eyes don't glitter in anticipation at the mention of this dish. From roadside vendors to five star hotels, everyone includes this on their menus. My sisters and I never miss a chance to eat Pav Bhaji every time we go to Juhu Beach in Mumbai, and my brother can be heard shouting instructions to the vendor to make it extra spicy and to give him extra onions.

1. Heat the oil in a saucepan and sauté the Basic Curry Sauce for 2–3 minutes over medium heat, until fragrant. Add the Pav Bhaji Masala and stir to mix.
2. In a bowl, combine the cauliflower, potatoes, green peas, and bell pepper, then put in the saucepan with the curry sauce. Add the water and stir to mix. Add the salt and coriander and cook for 6–7 minutes over medium heat until the vegetables are heated through. Transfer to a serving bowl.
3. Slice the bread rolls without cutting them completely in two. Heat a frying pan and warm the bread, gently pressing on it to make it slightly crisp.
4. Serve the rolls with the curry, and onion and lemon wedges on the side. To eat, place a spoonful of the curry in the roll, then top with some sliced onions and a sprinkling of lemon to make a scrumptious sandwich.

* Can be bought ready made at Indian stores.

Basic Curry Sauce   *Roz ka masala*   MAKES *2 cups (480ml)*

2 tablespoons vegetable oil
1 teaspoon cumin seeds
3 medium onions, finely chopped or coarsely
   ground
4–5 medium tomatoes, finely chopped
4 ounces (115g) tomato puree
1½ tablespoons fresh ginger, peeled and grated
2 cloves garlic, grated
2 fresh hot green chilles, finely chopped

1 cup (240ml) water
½ teaspoon turmeric
1 teaspoon salt or to taste
1 teaspoon coriander powder
½ teaspoon cayenne pepper
1 teaspoon garam masala (see page 16)
½ teaspoon ground black pepper
½ teaspoon cumin powder

This versatile sauce is great for dressing up cooked vegetables. It also makes a rich base for a lentil or vegetable curry. With a jar of this sauce in your fridge, it will only take a few minutes to put together an exotic curry. For a milder sauce, reduce the quantity of green chilies.

1. Heat the oil in a nonstick saucepan. Add the cumin seeds, let them sizzle, then stir in the onions and fry for 15–20 minutes over medium heat until golden brown. Sprinkle the mixture with water if it seems dry. Be careful not to scorch.
2. Add the chopped tomato, tomato puree, ginger, garlic, and chilies and stir to mix. Cook for 1 minute.
3. Add the water, turmeric, and salt. Turn up the heat and cook covered for 4–5 minutes, until the sauce thickens enough to coat a spoon.
4. Reduce the heat and add the coriander powder, cayenne pepper, garam masala, pepper, and cumin powder. Stir to mix.
5. Cool and store in a sterilized jar in the refrigerator. Keeps for 1 week, or can be frozen for later use.

RICE DISHES

Biryani
Biryani

SERVES *4*   PHOTOGRAPH ON PAGE 83

Biryani is the pride of Hyderabad, a region greatly influenced by Moghul rulers from the north of India. The basmati rice is cooked with whole spices and vegetables to create an aromatic dish.

1. Heat the oil in a nonstick saucepan and put in the cumin seeds. As soon as they start to sizzle, put in the onion and sauté for 4–5 minutes until soft. Add the bay leaves, cardamom, cinnamon stick, and the Ginger Garlic Paste and sauté for a few seconds over medium heat until fragrant. Add the tomatoes and cook covered for 2 minutes.
2. Add the turmeric, cayenne pepper, garam masala, potato, carrot, cauliflower, green beans, peas, salt, and ground almonds. Stir to mix, then put in the water and bring to a boil.
3. Stir in the rice and cover. Reduce the heat to medium and cook for 8–10 minutes until the vegetables are tender and the water is completely absorbed. Turn off the heat, cover, and leave to steam for another 5 minutes. Fluff up with a fork and serve hot.

1 tablespoon vegetable oil
1 teaspoon cumin seeds
1 medium onion, sliced
2 bay leaves
2 cardamom pods
1 small stick cinnamon
1 teaspoon Ginger Garlic Paste (see page 18)
2 medium tomatoes, chopped
½ teaspoon turmeric
½ teaspoon cayenne pepper
½ teaspoon garam masala (see page 16)
1 medium potato, peeled and diced
1 medium carrot, peeled and diced
8–10 cauliflower florets
6–8 green beans, cut into 1-inch (2.5-cm) pieces
2 tablespoons green peas
2 tablespoons ground almonds, mixed with a little water
3 cups (720ml) water
1½ cups (280g) basmati or long-grain rice
Salt to taste

Browned Rice
Dhansak chawal

SERVES *4*

This rice is the traditional accompaniment to the famous Parsee Lentil and Vegetable Curry (see page 22), but will complement any lentil or vegetable curry just as well.

1. Wash the rice and soak for 10 minutes. Drain and set aside.
2. Heat the oil in a saucepan and sauté the cumin seeds briefly. Put in the sugar and stir over medium heat for 15–20 seconds until it turns dark brown.
3. Put the cinnamon stick, salt, and drained rice in the saucepan and sauté for 1 minute. Add the water and bring to a boil. Cook for 8–10 minutes over medium heat. Lower the heat and cook for a further 8–10 minutes, until all the water has evaporated. Turn off the heat and gently fluff the rice with a fork.

1⅔ cups (300g) basmati rice
2 teaspoons vegetable oil
1 teaspoon cumin seeds
1 teaspoon castor sugar
1 small stick cinnamon
Salt to taste
3½ cups (840ml) water

* For an easy variation, slice 1 medium onion, sauté until brown, and mix into the sautéed rice before adding the water.

Saffron Rice with Almonds and Cashews

Zaffrani chawal

SERVES *4*

1½ cups (280g) basmati or long-grain rice
1 tablespoon vegetable oil
1 teaspoon cumin seeds
1 medium onion, finely sliced
1 small stick cinnamon
2 cardamom pods
2 bay leaves
½ teaspoon saffron strands
1 cup (160g) green peas, cooked
2 tablespoons almond slices, lightly roasted *
1½ cups (360ml) hot water
Salt to taste
Sliced almonds, for garnish
10–12 cashews, lightly roasted,* for garnish

This delicately spiced rice with its sprinkling of almonds and cashews is popular in the north of India and is inspired by Persian pilafs. Its exotic flavor and color is imparted by the queen of all spices—saffron.

1. Wash the rice and soak for 10–15 minutes. Drain and set to one side.
2. Heat the oil in a nonstick saucepan. Put in the cumin seeds and onion. Sauté for 5–6 minutes, until the onion is soft. Put in the cinnamon, cardamom, and bay leaves and stir-fry until fragrant. Add the saffron, green peas, and half of the almond slices (reserve the rest for the garnish). Stir to mix.
3. Put in the drained rice, hot water, and salt. Bring to a boil and cover. Turn the heat to medium-low and cook for 8–10 minutes, until the water is absorbed by the rice. Uncover and fluff up the rice with a fork. Garnish with sliced almonds and the cashews and serve hot.

* Roast in a dry frying pan for about 2 minutes over low to medium heat, shaking the pan so that they are evenly and lightly browned.

Spiced Rice with Mung Beans and Vegetables

Masala kichidi

SERVES *4*

1½ cups (280g) basmati rice
⅔ cup (140g) split mung beans
1 tablespoon vegetable oil
1 teaspoon cumin seeds
2–3 cloves
½ teaspoon cayenne pepper
½ teaspoon turmeric
1 cup (150g) mixed diced vegetables (potatoes, carrots, beans)
Salt to taste
4 cups (960ml) water
Kachumber, to serve

This could be called the spicy Indian version of creamy risotto, though definitely a lighter one. The rice, mung beans, and vegetables combine to make it a perfect one dish meal. As children, whenever we returned home after a day at the beach, my mother would quickly put together this dish while the rest of us set the table and prepared a kachumber.

1. Wash the rice and mung beans together, and soak for 30 minutes. Drain.
2. Heat the oil in a saucepan and add the cumin seeds and cloves, and briefly stir. Add the cayenne pepper, turmeric, and the vegetables. Add salt to taste and sauté for a minute.
3. Add the water and bring to a boil. Put in the drained rice and mung beans. Cook covered for 15–18 minutes over high heat. Lower the heat and cook for a further 2–3 minutes, until all the water has been absorbed.
4. Serve with Crunchy Red Cabbage Kachumber (see page 14) or Onion Kachumber (see page 22).

SIDE DISHES

Cabbage and Potato Dry Curry *Patta gobi aur aloo subzi*

SERVES *4*

Ready in minutes, this is an easy yet substantial addition to a lunch or dinner menu. Mustard seeds enhance the flavor and the potato lends volume to the *subzi*, which literally means "vegetable dish."

1. Rub the salt on the cabbage and let it stand for 2–3 minutes. Julienne the potatoes.
2. Heat the oil and add the mustard seeds. When they splutter, add the asafetida and curry leaves. Add the potatoes, 3 tablespoons water, salt, and turmeric. Cover and cook for 4–5 minutes over medium-low heat.
3. When the potatoes are almost cooked, add the cabbage and bell pepper. Stir to mix.
4. Cook for a further 3–4 minutes, until the potatoes are tender. Add the cayenne pepper and coriander powder. Toss gently to mix. Garnish with coriander leaves and serve.

4 cups (180g) white cabbage, shredded
Pinch of salt
3 medium potatoes, peeled
1 tablespoon vegetable oil
1 teaspoon mustard seeds
Pinch of asafetida
3–4 curry leaves
3 tablespoons water
Salt to taste
½ teaspoon turmeric
1 green bell pepper, sliced
½ teaspoon cayenne pepper
1 teaspoon coriander powder
Fresh coriander leaves, for garnish

Savory Sponge Cakes

Khaman dhokla

SERVES *4*   PHOTOGRAPH ON PAGE 86

These delicious steamed cakes, made from chickpea flour, are the pride and trademark of a Gujarati home. Healthy and tasty, they can be served at any time of day. Their spongy texture makes them suitable for breakfast food as well as an elegant teatime snack. During the height of the mango season in Mumbai, dhokla is made almost everyday with *aam ras*—fresh mango juice—as part of a meal.

1. In a large bowl, mix the chickpea flour with the semolina. Add the Ginger Chili Paste, salt, turmeric, sugar, oil, lemon juice, and baking powder. Gradually add the water, stirring all the time, until you have a thick smooth batter.
2. Dissolve the fruit salt in a little warm water and add to the batter. Mix thoroughly. Set aside for 15 minutes until the batter rises and becomes frothy.
3. Pour the mixture into a greased flat mold and place in a steamer. Cover and steam for 15 minutes over high heat.

1 cup (90g) chickpea flour
1 tablespoon semolina
2 teaspoons Ginger Chili Paste (see page 30)
Salt to taste
½ teaspoon turmeric powder
2 teaspoons brown sugar
1 tablespoon vegetable oil
1 teaspoon lemon juice
1 teaspoon baking powder
⅔ cup (160ml) water
1 teaspoon fruit salt

FOR THE TEMPERING

1 tablespoon oil
1 teaspoon mustard seeds
1 teaspoon white sesame seeds
2 fresh hot green chilies, finely chopped
Pinch of asafetida
3 tablespoons water
Fresh coriander leaves, for garnish

4. Remove the mold from the steamer and cool. Cut the cake into squares or diamonds and arrange on a serving dish.
5. Heat the oil for the tempering in a saucepan. Add the mustard seeds and let them splutter. Add the sesame seeds, chilies, and asafetida. Add 3 tablespoons water, mix, and spoon the tempering over the cakes. Garnish with coriander leaves.

Sesame Potatoes

Til wale aloo

SERVES *4*

5 medium potatoes, peeled
1 tablespoon vegetable oil
1 teaspoon mustard seeds
Pinch of asafetida
1 teaspoon black sesame seeds
1 teaspoon ginger julienne
2 fresh hot green chilies, chopped
3–4 curry leaves
¼ teaspoon turmeric
½ teaspoon cayenne pepper
1 teaspoon coriander powder
1 teaspoon brown sugar
1 tablespoon fresh coriander leaves
1 teaspoon lemon juice

This dry curry was the signature dish of my mother-in-law, a meticulous cook. Often included in our Sunday lunches and a popular feature at my dinner parties, it is enjoyed by adults and children alike. This dish goes well with Masala Poori (see page 37).

1. Cut the potatoes into ½-inch (1-cm) thick sticks. Boil in salted water for 8–10 minutes until almost cooked. The potatoes should still be firm.
2. Heat the oil in a broad saucepan and add the mustard seeds. Let them splutter. Add the asafetida and sesame seeds. Reduce the heat and add the ginger, green chilies, and the curry leaves. Stir to mix. Add the turmeric, cayenne pepper, coriander powder, and sugar.
3. Mix in the julienned potato and toss gently to coat with the seasonings. Cook for 3–4 minutes, stirring occasionally until crisp and lightly browned on all sides. Sprinkle with the coriander leaves and lemon juice before serving.

Spiced Zucchini and Potato

Masala aloo dur zucchini

SERVES *4*

PHOTOGRAPH ON PAGE 86

1 pound (450g) new potatoes, boiled
1 tablespoon vegetable oil
½ teaspoon mustard seeds
½ teaspoon cumin seeds
Pinch of asafetida
1 clove garlic, finely chopped
½ teaspoon turmeric
½ teaspoon cayenne pepper
1 teaspoon coriander powder
½ teaspoon mango powder
Salt to taste
2 medium zucchini, sliced into thin rounds

Traditionally this dish is made with a tiny squash called *tindi*, but zucchini is the perfect substitute, adding freshness as well as an earthy texture to this popular Gujarati dish.

1. Peel and thinly slice the potatoes.
2. Heat the oil in a flat frying pan, then add the mustard seeds and cumin seeds. When the mustard seeds start to splutter, add the asafetida and garlic and sauté for 4–5 seconds until fragrant.
3. Put the turmeric, cayenne pepper, coriander powder, mango powder, and salt in the pan, and stir. Put in the potatoes and zucchini and toss to mix. Cook covered over medium heat, shaking the pan occasionally to avoid sticking, until the vegetables are lightly browned. Serve hot.

Spicy Stuffed Chilies

Masale wali mirchi

SERVES **4**

PHOTOGRAPH ON PAGE 84

20–25 mild green chilies, whole
½ teaspoon cayenne pepper
3 teaspoons coriander powder
¼ teaspoon turmeric
¼ teaspoon salt
2 teaspoons vegetable oil
1 teaspoon mustard seeds
Pinch of asafetida
1 teaspoon lemon juice

Milder chilies work best with this dish. I like the Japanese *shishi-togarashi*, but any variety of mild chili is fine. They make a great accompaniment to rice.

1. Make a lengthwise slit down the side of each chili, leaving the top and bottom of the chili intact. Remove the seeds.
2. Mix together the cayenne pepper, coriander, turmeric, and salt. Fill each chili with a little of this mixture, until it is all used up.
3. Heat the oil in a flat saucepan and add the mustard seeds. When they splutter, add the asafetida, then add the chilies and stir-fry over medium heat for 2–3 minutes, tossing a few times.
4. Drizzle the lemon juice over the chilies and remove from heat. Transfer to a bowl and serve.

Stuffed Okra with Coriander

Sambharia bhinda

SERVES **4**

12 ounces (340g) okra
½ cup (45g) desiccated coconut
½ cup (10g) fresh coriander leaves
1 teaspoon Ginger Chili Paste (see below)
1 teaspoon castor sugar
½ teaspoon turmeric
2 teaspoons coriander powder
½ teaspoon cumin powder
1 teaspoon lemon juice
½ teaspoon garam masala (see page 16)
2 teaspoons vegetable oil
Salt to taste

FOR THE TEMPERING
2 tablespoons vegetable oil
½ teaspoon cumin seeds
¼ teaspoon asafetida

Even people who don't call themselves okra fans will relish this dish with its mild coconut flavor and aroma of fresh coriander.

1. Wash the okra and pat dry with a kitchen towel. Slice off the tops, and make a lengthwise slit from the top almost to the bottom, leaving the tip of the okra intact.
2. In a bowl, mix together the coconut, coriander leaves, Ginger Chili Paste, sugar, turmeric, coriander powder, cumin powder, lemon juice, garam masala, oil, and salt.
3. Fill the slit okra with a generous amount of the spice mixture. Keep any leftover spice mixture to one side.
4. For the tempering, heat the oil in a saucepan and add the cumin seeds and the asafetida. Add the stuffed okra and cook covered over medium heat for 6–8 minutes, shaking the pan a few times to avoid sticking. Sprinkle any leftover spice mixture over the okra and stir to mix. Cook for another 2–3 minutes, until the okra is tender.

Ginger Chili Paste

Pisi hui adrak mirchi   MAKES **1 tablespoon**

5 fresh hot green chilies
1 piece of fresh ginger, walnut sized, peeled

This refreshingly spicy paste can be used in most dishes that do not require the strong flavor of garlic. I always have some freshly prepared paste handy, to perk up any dish at the last minute.

Blend the chilies and ginger to a smooth paste, using a few drops of water. Keep in an airtight jar in the refrigerator. Keeps for 2–3 days.

SNACKS

Bengal Gram and Spinach Kebabs

Hara bhara kebab

SERVES *4*

2¼ cups (385g) split yellow lentils
2 cloves garlic
½-inch (1-cm) cube fresh ginger, peeled
2 fresh hot green chilies
Salt to taste
1 tablespoon vegetable oil
1 teaspoon vegetable oil
1 teaspoon cumin seeds
4½ cups (200g) spinach, cooked and pureed
Salt to taste
½ cup (50g) bread crumbs
1 teaspoon garam masala (see page 16)
½ teaspoon cayenne pepper
1 teaspoon fenugreek powder
½ teaspoon ground black pepper
Vegetable oil for frying
Tamarind and Date Chutney (see page 34), to serve

These kebabs are delicious served with mint chutney at a cocktail party. They can be made ahead of time and warmed in the oven just before serving. For a crispier texture, they can be deep-fried, but here I have shallow-fried them to save on calories, so don't feel too guilty about picking up that one extra piece.

1. Soak the lentils in water for 30 minutes, then drain. Using a food processor, blend the lentils, garlic, ginger, and chilies to a smooth paste. Add salt to taste.
2. Heat the 1 tablespoon oil in a saucepan, then stir in the lentil paste. Cover and cook for 2 minutes over medium heat, then set aside.
3. Heat the 1 teaspoon oil in another saucepan and add the cumin seeds. Let them sizzle briefly. Add the spinach puree and salt to taste. Stir for 2–3 minutes. Add the lentil paste and bread crumbs, and season with the garam masala, cayenne pepper, fenugreek powder, and black pepper. Mix well and remove from heat.
4. Divide the mixture into 20 equal parts and flatten into discs. Heat a little oil in a flat saucepan and fry the kebabs until crisp and golden brown. Serve with Tamarind and Date Chutney.

Crispy Pumpkin Turnovers

Samosas

MAKES *30*

PHOTOGRAPH ON PAGE 87

2 teaspoons vegetable oil
½ teaspoon fennel seeds
½ teaspoon nigella
½ teaspoon cayenne pepper
½ teaspoon garam masala (see page 16)
6 cups (300g) pumpkin, cut into small dice
½ cup (120ml) water
Salt to taste
10 large spring roll wrappers
1 tablespoon flour mixed with 2 tablespoons water to form a paste
Vegetable oil for deep-frying
Fresh coriander, for garnish

These tiny bite-sized turnovers are among the most famous Indian snacks, and are commonly served as appetizers with mint chutney. I prefer pumpkin to the typical potato filling for its refreshing color and taste. I always have samosas in my freezer because it is the one snack my children's friends always look for, no matter what part of the world they are from. The spring roll wrappers give an irresistible crispiness. Once the filling has been prepared, samosas can be made easily using ready made spring roll sheets. They freeze well too. Defrost for 2–3 hours before cooking

31

1. Heat the oil in a large saucepan, then add the fennel and nigella seeds. As soon as they start to sizzle, add the cayenne pepper and garam masala and briefly stir.
2. Put the pumpkin and the ½ cup water in the saucepan. Add salt to taste. Cover and cook for 6–8 minutes, until the pumpkin is tender. Allow the mixture to cool.
3. Cut the spring roll wrappers into long strips (approx 7 inches [17 cm] long and 2½ inches [6 cm] wide). With each strip, have the narrow end facing you, then fold the bottom left corner over to meet the right side. Take the bottom right corner and fold over to meet the left side. Take the bottom left corner again, and fold over to meet the right side. You should now have a triangular cone, below an oblong flap. Fill the cone with a spoonful of the filling. Use the flour paste to seal the flap over the cone.
4. Heat the oil to 350°F (180°C). Deep-fry the samosas until crisp and golden. Drain on paper towel, garnish with coriander, and serve hot or at room temperature, with chutney.

Stuffed Potato Cakes

Aloo tikki

MAKES **8**

PHOTOGRAPH ON PAGE 86

4 medium potatoes, boiled and peeled
2 teaspoons vegetable oil
½ teaspoon cumin seeds
½-inch (1-cm) cube fresh ginger, peeled and chopped
2 fresh hot green chilies, finely chopped
1 tablespoon fresh coriander, finely chopped
1½ cups (240g) cooked green peas
½ teaspoon garam masala (see page 16)
½ teaspoon cayenne pepper
½ teaspoon mango powder
Salt to taste
All-purpose flour for dredging
1 tablespoon vegetable oil
Tamarind and Date Chutney (see page 34), to serve
Mint and Coriander Chutney (see page 34), to serve

This is typical Mumbai roadside food, conspicuous by its inviting aroma. On the way home from our classes at Sydenham College, my friends and I would stop to eat these crisp potato cakes with their filling of spicy peas, served on a paper plate with a little Tamarind and Date Chutney on the side.

1. Grate the potatoes using a large-holed grater—an efficient way of removing lumps—and season with salt. Divide the mixture into 8 portions.
2. Heat the vegetable oil in a flat saucepan and add the cumin seeds, ginger, chilies, and coriander. Stir in the peas, garam masala, cayenne pepper, and mango powder. Add salt to taste. Mash a little and toss to mix. Remove from the heat and allow to cool.
3. With lightly greased hands, roll the 8 potato portions into balls. On a dry surface, flatten each ball to a disc about 2 inches in circumference and ½ inch thick.
4. Divide the peas and spices mixture into 8 portions and place one portion at the center of each of the 8 discs. Bring the edges of each disc to the center to cover the filling. Press gently to flatten the discs. Lightly dredge in flour.
5. Heat the 1 tablespoon oil in a flat nonstick pan. When the oil is hot, place the potato cakes in the pan and cook for 2–3 minutes on each side until crisp and brown. When both sides are evenly browned, remove from the pan and serve with chutney.

Tapioca and Potato Patties

Sabudana vada

SERVED *1*

½ cup (75g) tapioca pearls
4 medium potatoes, boiled and mashed
2 tablespoons peanuts, roasted and coarsely ground *
1 teaspoon cumin seeds, roasted and ground *
2 fresh hot green chilies, chopped
½-inch (1-cm) cube fresh ginger, peeled and finely
   chopped
1 tablespoon coriander leaves
½ teaspoon salt
Vegetable oil for deep-frying
Mint and Coriander Chutney, to serve (see page 34)

* Roast the peanuts and seeds using the toast
ing method for sesame seeds on page 42.

This famous Gujarati snack is loved by all. The tapioca seeds add a pearly look and a gluey texture to these crunchy patties. Serve piping hot with afternoon tea or as an appetizer with Mint and Coriander Chutney. Back home in India, we often serve them as a side dish with lunch or dinner.

1. Soak the tapioca seeds in cold water for 5 minutes. Drain and set aside for 30 minutes, until the seeds are soft.
2. In a mixing bowl, combine the potatoes with the tapioca seeds.
3. Add the peanuts, cumin, chilies, chilies, ginger, coriander leaves, and salt. Mix well.
4. Divide the mixture into 18–20 balls. Press each ball to make a flat disc.
5. In a wok, heat the oil for deep-frying to 350°F (180°C). Deep-fry the patties, a few at a time, until golden brown. Drain on kitchen paper and serve with Mint and Coriander Chutney.

Vegetable Fritters

Pakoras

SERVES *4*

Vegetable oil for deep-frying
1 medium onion, cut into thin rings
1 medium potato, cut into thin rounds
1 small eggplant, cut into thin rounds
4 cauliflower florets
Mint and Coriander Chutney (see page 34), to serve

FOR THE BATTER
1 cup (90g) chickpea flour
2 teaspoons vegetable oil
½ teaspoon ajwain seeds
½ teaspoon salt
Pinch of baking powder
1 fresh hot green chili, finely chopped
½ cup (10g) fresh coriander leaves and stems,
   finely chopped
1 cup (240ml) water

Mention the word pakora to Indians, and we immediately think about the monsoon rains in India. We make travel plans during the monsoon season to enjoy the misty air and the drizzle of the rain in exotic locations, and along the highways we stop to eat hot pakoras sold by roadside vendors. Minced onions, potato, and eggplant can be added to the batter for a quick variation.

1. To make the batter, put the flour in a bowl with the oil, ajwain seeds, baking powder, chili, and coriander. Gradually add the water, stirring all the while, to make a smooth batter
2. In a wok, heat the oil for deep-frying to 350°F (180°C). Dip the vegetable pieces in the batter then slide into the hot oil. Deep-fry in small batches until crisp and golden brown. Drain on kitchen paper and transfer to a serving dish. Serve hot with Mint and Coriander Chutney.

■ CHUTNEY

Mint and Coriander Chutney

Pudine ki chutney MAKES **1 cup (240ml)**

5½ cups (115g) fresh spearmint leaves
3½ cups (70g) fresh coriander leaves
2 cloves garlic, chopped
¼ medium onion
1 green bell pepper
1 small piece ginger, peeled
3–4 fresh hot green chilies
1 teaspoon cumin seeds, roasted and ground
3–4 teaspoons lemon juice
Salt to taste

This refreshing and aromatic chutney is served with snacks and as an accompaniment to meals. It will keep for two weeks in the fridge, and can be frozen for later use. The chilies are essential to its flavor, but you can adjust the quantity to suit your taste.

Puree all the ingredients in a food processor until smooth. Pour into a sterilized jar, seal, and refrigerate. Keeps for a week.

Tamarind and Date Chutney

Imli ki chutney MAKES **1½ cups (360ml)**

2-ounce (60-g) block tamarind
15–20 dates, pitted
1 cup (240ml) water
4 tablespoons palm sugar
½ teaspoon coarse salt
½ teaspoon cayenne pepper
¼ teaspoon coriander powder
1 teaspoon cumin seeds, roasted and ground

This sweet, fruity chutney is an exceptionally versatile sauce that enhances any snack or starter, and I always have some in my freezer. In the summer, keep only a small portion in the fridge and freeze the rest. Dates add a velvety texture, although in north India the chutney is made using only tamarind for a thinner consistency.

1. Place the tamarind, dates, and water in a saucepan and bring to a boil. Turn the heat to medium and cook for 8–10 minutes, until the tamarind has become soft and pulpy. Allow to cool, then blend the mixture to a paste. Pass through a sieve to remove any hard ends, seeds, or fibers.
2. Return the sieved tamarind mixture to the pan and place over low heat. Add the sugar, coarse salt, chili, and coriander powder. Simmer for 3–4 minutes until the sugar has dissolved. Stir in the roasted cumin. Add a little water if the mixture seems too thick. Adjust the seasonings to taste. Allow to cool. Pour in a sterilized jar and refrigerate. Keeps for a week.

Tomato Chutney *Tamatar ki chutney* MAKES **1 cup (240ml)**

1 tablespoon vegetable oil
½ teaspoon mustard seeds
1 clove garlic, finely chopped
2 bay leaves
Pinch of asafetida
½ teaspoon cayenne pepper
A few curry leaves, optional
1 onion, finely chopped
2 medium tomatoes, chopped *
Salt to taste
1 teaspoon raisins
1 tablespoon castor sugar
½ teaspoon cumin powder
¼ teaspoon garam masala (see page 16)

1. Heat the oil in a small saucepan and add the mustard seeds. When they start to splutter, put in the garlic, bay leaves, asafetida, cayenne pepper, and curry leaves and sauté briefly.
2. Add the onion and sauté for 3–4 minutes over medium heat until soft. Add the tomatoes and salt to taste. Cover and cook for 3–4 minutes until the tomatoes have the consistency of a thick chutney.
3. Add the raisins, sugar, cumin powder, and garam masala. Simmer for a minute until fragrant. Remove from the heat and allow to cool. Store in an airtight container in the refrigerator. It keeps well for a week.

* Canned tomatoes may be used. They give a deeper color to the chutney but have a tart taste, so you may need to add a little more sugar.

BREADS

Bhatura

MAKES *12*

2 cups (250g) all-purpose flour
3 teaspoons vegetable oil
½ teaspoon baking soda
½ teaspoon salt
½ cup (120ml) bottled soda water
1 teaspoon vegetable oil
Vegetable oil for deep-frying

Bhatura is a deep-fried bread made with all-purpose flour. It is traditionally eaten with Chickpea Curry (see page 20) and the combination is called Chana Bhatura, a dish sold everywhere along the beaches of Mumbai, from the most humble street stall to the most expensive restaurant.

1. Sift the flour into a large bowl. Add the 3 teaspoons oil, baking soda, and salt and mix by hand until the flour is crumbly. Add the bottled soda water gradually, mixing all the time, to make a soft but firm dough. Cover the dough with a damp cloth and set aside for 10 minutes.
2. Dribble the 1 teaspoon oil over the dough and knead again until pliable. Divide the dough into 12 balls. On a dry surface, roll out each ball of dough to a 2¼-inch (6-cm) diameter circle. Set to one side.
3. Heat the oil for deep-frying in a wok to 350°F (180°C), and fry the bhatura one at a time until puffed up to a golden brown on both sides—approximately 1 minute per bhatura. Drain on kitchen paper, and serve hot.

Chapati

MAKES *6–8*

1½ cups (180g) whole wheat flour
⅓ cup (80ml) lukewarm water
1 teaspoon vegetable oil, optional
Flour for rolling

Wheat is the main cereal in most of urban India. Even today, many Indians prefer to buy their grain whole and get it custom-ground to achieve the right texture and consistency of flour. Types of bread vary from region to region and according to the preferences of individual households, but most are made with the same basic dough recipe. A chapati is a flat, pancake-like bread, made on a griddle.

1. Mix the flour and water together and knead to a smooth dough. If you prefer a softer dough, add 1 teaspoon vegetable oil, and knead for longer.

2. Divide the dough into 6–8 equal portions, and form each portion into a ball. Dab a ball of dough in flour and place on a rolling board. Roll out gently, turning it around a few times, so that the dough is of an even thinness, about 4 inches (10 cm) in diameter. Sprinkle a little flour to facilitate the rolling, but note that too much flour will make the chapati hard.

3. Shake off the excess flour then place the round of dough on a hot griddle. Cook for 10–12 seconds on each side over medium heat. Remove from the heat and press both sides gently with a folded towel for 4–5 seconds.

4. Repeat this process for each chapati. Serve with Spicy White Lentil Soup (see page 16) or Seasoned Okra with Coriander (see page 30).

Lachedar Paratha

MAKES *12*

1½ cups (180g) whole wheat flour
½ cup (60g) all-purpose flour
2 tablespoons vegetable oil
½ teaspoon salt
½ cup (120ml) water
Flour for rolling
Vegetable oil for drizzling

The light coating of oil between the layers gives the bread its distinct flaky texture. Parathas can be eaten at any time of the day, but they are often served as breakfast food in north Indian homes.

1. Mix the whole wheat flour and all-purpose flour in a large bowl. Add the oil and the salt and mix by hand until the flour is crumbly. Gradually add the water, kneading to a soft dough. Make a smooth ball of dough and cover with a damp cloth for 10 minutes. Knead the dough again and divide into 12 balls.

2. Flatten the balls and roll in the flour. Roll out each ball of dough into a thin circle. Spread ½ teaspoon oil over each circle and fold the top and bottom of the circle to the center to make a rectangular shape. Then fold in the right and left sides to the center to make a square. Dab each square in the flour and roll out until it is about 4 inches (10 cm) square.

3. Heat a nonstick pan or griddle and grease the surface. Place the paratha on the surface and cook for 30–40 seconds over medium heat until the underside begins to turn brown. Flip over and cook the other side for 30 seconds. Drizzle a little oil on the surface of the paratha and spread it evenly with a spoon. Turn over and oil the other side. Press gently on the paratha with a slotted spoon, turning until both sides have a golden brown color.

4. Keep the cooked parathas covered with a towel or foil until ready to use. The parathas can be reheated in a preheated oven. Serve with Eggplant in Tomato Gravy (see page 20), or North Indian Potato Curry (see page 22).

Masala Poori

MAKES 20

2 cups (120g) whole wheat flour
2 teaspoons oil
½ teaspoon ajwain seeds
¼ teaspoon turmeric
¼ teaspoon cayenne pepper
Salt to taste
½ cup (120ml) water
Vegetable oil for deep-frying

Pooris are similar to bhaturas, but are made with whole wheat flour. They are served on all auspicious and special occasions along with elaborate meals. You can make pooris of various sizes to suit your meal.

1. Sift the flour and rub in the oil. Add the ajwain seeds, turmeric, cayenne pepper, and salt to taste. Add the water gradually and knead to a firm dough. Set aside for 10 minutes. Knead the dough again until smooth.

2. Divide the dough into 20 pieces and roll each piece into a smooth ball between your palms. Roll out the dough into thin 4-inch (10-cm) circles and set aside on a dry surface.

3. Heat the oil for deep-frying to about 375°F (190°C).* Drop in the poori one at a time and gently pat with the bottom of the frying spoon. This will help the poori to puff up. After 10–12 seconds, when the underside is lightly brown, flip it over and brown the other side. Remove from the oil and drain on a paper towel. Repeat with the rest of the poori and serve while hot. Serve with Cauliflower and Potato with Spices (see page 19).

* The oil must be hot for the poori to puff up completely.

Naan

MAKES 12

3 cups (380g) all-purpose flour
1½ teaspoons baking soda
2 tablespoons vegetable oil
½ teaspoon salt
1 teaspoon castor sugar
½ cup (120ml) bottled soda water
1 teaspoon vegetable oil
Flour for dusting

Naans originated in the northern region of India. As a child, I used to love watching the restaurant chefs throwing the naan dough into the hot clay oven and then, with a long iron hook, pulling out an irresistibly crisp browned bread. Naans can be difficult to make in a regular oven, so for home cooking, I recommend this easy method.

1. Sift the flour in a large bowl and add the baking soda, oil, salt, and sugar. Mix gently. Gradually add the soda water and knead to a soft but firm dough. Cover with Saran wrap and set aside for an hour. Roll out again with the 1 teaspoon oil, until smooth. Divide the dough into 12 balls.

2. Dust each ball of dough in flour, then roll into a circle about 6 inches in diameter. Pull one end to give it a teardrop shape.

3. Heat a griddle or a nonstick pan. Using a little water, wet one side of the naan and place the wet side on the hot surface. Cook for 1 minute over medium heat, until bubbles appear on the surface. Flip over and cook the other side for 1 minute, so that it is evenly browned on both sides. Using tongs, hold the naan over an open flame for a crispy finish. Serve hot.

4. Serve hot: goes well with Assorted Vegetables in Cashew Gravy (see page 18) and Mushroom and Green Pea Curry (see page 21).

DRINKS AND DESSERTS

Indian Spiced Tea
Chai masala

SERVES *2*

Although chai masala is easy to buy ready-made these days, I prefer to put it together at home using my mother's recipe. After my weekly cooking class when the students have dutifully washed the dishes and tidied the kitchen, their faces light up when I mention chai masala, and promptly one of them gets the milk ready, someone else grates the ginger, others get busy bringing out the cups, while I put together the tea. Once the tea is ready, we all sit down to share a few more laughs before we part for the week.

1. Put the water and soy milk in a saucepan and bring to a boil.
2. Put the sugar, ginger, and Chai Masala Spice Mix in the pan. Simmer for 1 minute. Add the spearmint and tea leaves and simmer for a further 3–4 minutes, until the tea has turned a golden color.
3. Turn off the heat and keep covered for a minute. Strain into 2 teacups and serve hot.

1½ cups (360ml) water
1 cup (240ml) soy milk
2 teaspoons castor sugar
A pea-sized piece of fresh ginger, peeled and crushed
Pinch of Chai Masala Spice Mix (see below)
Few sprigs of fresh spearmint, optional
2 teaspoons tea leaves or 2 tea bags

Chai Masala Spice Mix
MAKES *3 tablespoons*

10 cardamom pods, whole	15 black peppercorns
1 small cinnamon stick	1 teaspoon ginger powder
12 cloves	

Grind together in an electric grinder, store in an airtight container, and use as required. Keeps for several months.

Semolina Pudding
Sheera

SERVES *4*   PHOTOGRAPH ON PAGE 88

In India, auspicious occasions and celebrations would be incomplete without this rich dessert. The pudding is usually one of the first foods to be given to toddlers.

1. Place the water, sugar, saffron, and crushed cardamom in a saucepan and bring to a boil. Turn the heat to low and simmer for 4–5 minutes.
2. Heat the oil in a large saucepan and add the semolina. Fry, continuously stirring over low heat until evenly browned and fragrant, about 3–4 minutes.
3. Put the raisins and cardamon pods in the pan with the semolina, then gently add the sugar, saffron and cardamom mixture, stirring frequently to avoid lumps. Allow the liquid to be absorbed by the semolina to give a thick pudding.
4. Transfer to a serving bowl and decorate with almonds and pistachios. Serve warm.

2 cups (480ml) water
1 cup (220g) brown sugar
½ teaspoon saffron strands
1 green cardamom pod, crushed
2 tablespoons vegetable oil
1½ cups (250g) semolina
1 tablespoon raisins
2 green cardamom pods
10–12 almonds, chopped
8–10 pistachios, chopped

Japan

My first dining experience in the country that has become my second home was a huge success, except that I got the order of seating, serving, and eating all wrong! I struggled to hold the food with the slippery lacquer chopsticks and in doing so managed to drop the tempura into my miso soup, which I then poured over my sushi rice, to the utter horror of the hostess.

I've come a long way. The hostess and I became best of friends and the dishes that I sampled at her home that night have since become a part of our family's weekly dining routine.

Like all things Japanese, discipline, detailing, and aesthetics define the country's cuisine. This fine attention to detail and elegant presentation is as integral to its enjoyment as spice is to Indian food. There is no room for brash expression or overstatement. The subtle flavors of soy sauce, sugar, salt, sake, mirin, vinegar, and miso gently mingle to give a harmonious whole that is Japanese in its elegance and frugality.

Japan also has a long history of vegetarian cuisine that stems from the six-hundred-year old tradition of Zen temple cooking called *shojin ryori*, which emphasizes simplicity in living and harmony with nature.

All the recipes included in this section have been carefully selected to represent the most popular Japanese dishes and the personal favorites of my family, friends, and students.

■ DASHI AND RICE

The soup stocks known as *konbu dashi* and *shiitake dashi*, and Japanese rice, are at the heart of Japanese cuisine.

Dashi Soup Stock

Dashi stock is used as the base liquid for most dishes. There is a simple rule to ensure the delicate and optimum flavor of the dashi: never boil it. Leftover dashi can be kept for a day in the refrigerator or frozen in an ice cube tray. Either of the two dashi recipes below can be used for any of the Japanese recipes in this book. The Shiitake Mushroom Dashi is the richer of the two.

Konbu Dashi

MAKES *3 cups (720ml)*

This basic dashi, made from a variety of kelp known as konbu, is used widely in Japanese cooking. The finest konbu comes from Hokkaido, Japan's northernmost island.

3 pieces of konbu kelp, each approx 4 inches × 2 inches (10 cm × 5 cm)
3½ cups (840ml) water

1. Wipe the konbu with a damp cloth. Do not wash it, as it will lose its flavor.
2. Soak the konbu in the water for 1 hour, then remove the konbu, and use the water as dashi. (If short of time, place the water and konbu in a saucepan and bring to a simmer over low heat. As soon as the water starts to boil, remove the konbu.)

Shiitake Mushroom Dashi

MAKES *about 1¾ cups (420ml)*

This dashi forms the base for most vegetarian Japanese cooking. It is widely used by Buddhist priests in their temple cooking. Shiitake dashi may be combined with konbu dashi for a richer taste.

4 dried shiitake mushrooms
3 cups (720ml) water

1. Wash the shiitake briefly.
2. Soak the shiitake in the 3 cups water. Place a small lid or plate on top of the mushrooms to prevent them from floating. Leave for 4–5 hours, then remove the shiitake and use the water as stock. (If short of time, pour 3 cups of boiling water over the mushrooms and let them stand for 10 minutes.) A good shiitake stock will have an amber color and the fragrance of mushroom. The reconstituted shiitake can be used in many other dishes.

How to cook Japanese rice

Short-grain glutinous rice is the staple food of Japan and an integral part of most Japanese meals. The grains of the rice stick together when cooked, making it easy to eat with chopsticks. Rice is brought out piping hot from the rice cooker after all the other dishes have been served, and marks the end of the meal.

The key to shiny and fluffy rice is in the swift washing. Wash the rice in several changes of water until the water runs clear. Once the rice is washed, cover it with the correct quantity of water, using the table below as a guideline, and allow to soak (about half an hour in the summer and a little longer in the winter months). If using an electric rice cooker, transfer the rice with the soaking water to the rice cooker and cook in the usual way. To cook the rice on the stove, follow the steps below.

1. Place the rice and water in a saucepan. Cover and cook over medium heat for 5 minutes.
2. Turn the heat to high and cook for another 5 minutes. Do not remove the lid.
3. Lower the heat to medium again, and cook for a further 10 minutes.
4. Turn the heat as low as possible and cook for another 5 minutes.
5. Turn off the heat and let the rice stand covered for 10 minutes, so that it continues to cook in its own steam.

RICE AND WATER QUANTITIES

RICE		WATER		COOKED RICE	
1 cup	(200g)	1¼ cups	(300ml)	2½ cups	(465g)
2 cups	(400g)	2½ cups	(600ml)	5 cups	(930g)
3 cups	(600g)	3¾ cups	(900ml)	7½ cups	(1.4kg)
4 cups	(800g)	5 cups	(1.5L)	10 cups	(1.86kg)

Sushi Rice

MAKES *5 cups (930g)*

Good sushi rice needs to be dressed with the perfect combination of rice vinegar, mirin, and sugar. The rice should be firm when cooked, so less water is used than for regular rice.

2 cups (400g) short-grain white rice	2 tablespoons castor sugar
2 cups (480ml) water	1 tablespoon mirin
1 piece dried konbu, 1 inch (2.5 cm) square	1 tablespoon sake, optional
⅓ cup (80ml) rice vinegar	⅔ teaspoon salt

1. Cook the rice according to the instructions on this page, adding the konbu to the cooking water.
2. Combine the rice vinegar, sugar, mirin, sake, and salt in a small bowl. Stir until the sugar has dissolved.
3. Transfer the freshly cooked rice to a wooden tub, or a flat bottomed wide bowl. Pour the vinegar mixture all over the rice while the rice is still hot, and mix quickly, using slicing motions, with a spatula. This helps the flavors of the vinegar mixture to be absorbed by the rice.
4. For best results, use the rice immediately, although it will keep for an hour or two if covered with a damp dish towel at room temperature. Sushi rice is never kept in the refrigerator.

SOUPS AND SALADS

Broccoli with Tofu Dressing *Burokkori no shira-ae*

SERVES *4*   PHOTOGRAPH ON PAGE 90

Broccoli will never taste the same again. Tofu and sesame seeds combine to create a divine dressing with a mild flavor. Spinach, carrot, and shiitake mushrooms are often used in this dish, but I like broccoli for its color, texture, and nutritional content.

1. Wrap the tofu in a thick dish towel and place in the refrigerator for 30 minutes.
2. Bring the water to a boil in a saucepan. Put in the broccoli florets with the salt. Simmer for 3–4 minutes then drain, and allow to cool completely.
3. Grind the sesame seeds using a pestle and mortar or food processor.
4. Pass the tofu through a sieve, using a wooden spatula, to make a smooth paste.
5. Add the ground sesame seeds to the sieved tofu and mix with a wooden spatula until smooth. Add the sake, sugar, sesame paste, and soy sauce and mix well.
6. Combine the sesame and tofu dressing with the broccoli and mix gently. Serve chilled, garnished with sesame seeds.

7 ounces (200g) silken tofu, drained
2 cups (480ml) water
1 cup (100g) broccoli florets
Pinch of salt
4 tablespoons white sesame seeds, toasted *
1 tablespoon sake
1 tablespoon castor sugar
1 tablespoon sesame paste
2 teaspoons soy sauce
Sesame seeds, for garnish

* Raw sesame seeds should always be toasted before using. Toast in a dry frying pan over low heat until the seeds start to pop and release an aromatic smell.

Crunchy Vegetable Salad with Japanese-style Dressing *Shaki shaki wafu sarada*

SERVES *4*

This aromatic dressing is a national favorite and my family's too. I always include this colorful and crunchy salad on my menu when I am cooking a Japanese meal—it's a perfect complement to simmered and stir-fried dishes.

1. Cut the daikon, carrot, and cucumber into 1-inch long julienne strips. Shred the cabbage leaves and coarsely tear the lettuce. Soak all the vegetables in iced water for 15 minutes. Drain and set aside.

3½ ounces (100g) daikon radish, peeled
1 carrot, peeled
1 cucumber
1 cup (45g) red cabbage
A few lettuce leaves, for garnish

FOR THE DRESSING
½-inch (1-cm) cube fresh ginger, peeled and grated
1 teaspoon ginger juice (see opposite)
1 teaspoon white sesame seeds, toasted (see above)
2 teaspoons sesame oil
1 tablespoon rice vinegar
1 tablespoon soy sauce
½ teaspoon castor sugar
Pinch of salt

2. Mix all the dressing ingredients together. On a serving dish, make a bed of lettuce leaves. Combine the daikon, carrot, cucumber, and cabbage in a bowl, then arrange over the lettuce leaves. Pour the dressing around the sides of the dish first and then over the vegetables. Serve chilled.

Miso Soup with Tofu and Wakame   *Miso shiru*

SERVES *4*

3½ ounces (100g) silken tofu
⅓ cup (5g) dried wakame seaweed
3 cups (720ml) dashi (see page 40)
3 tablespoons white miso
Chopped chives, for garnish

Seaweeds such as wakame are in plentiful supply in the island nation of Japan. Rich in minerals and with a variety of tastes and textures, they are found in many different dishes. Here, wakame is used in a simple but tasty miso soup. Miso is always added to the soup at the end of preparation time. It is never boiled, as it will lose its flavor.

1. Wash and cut the tofu into medium dice. Wash the wakame and soak in water for 10 minutes. Trim the hard ends and cut into 1-inch (2.5-cm) pieces.
2. Bring the dashi to a boil in a saucepan over medium heat. Put the tofu and wakame in the saucepan with the dashi and simmer for 3 minutes.
3. Turn off the heat. Pour a little hot soup into a small bowl, and mix in the miso. Put the miso mixture in the saucepan and stir gently to mix. Serve garnished with chives.

Mizuna Salad with Fried Burdock and Garlic   *Age gobo to ninnniku no mizuna sarada*

SERVES *4*   PHOTOGRAPH ON PAGE 92

3½ ounces (100g) mizuna leaves
Vegetable oil for deep-frying
2 ounces (60g) burdock, cut into diagonal slices
2 cloves garlic, finely sliced

FOR THE SESAME LEMON DRESSING
  2 tablespoons lemon juice
  2 tablespoons soy sauce
  1 tablespoon sesame oil
  1 tablespoon rice vinegar
  1 tablespoon sesame seeds, toasted (see opposite)
  ½ teaspoon ground black pepper
  ¼ teaspoon salt

Mizuna is a highly versatile green from Kyoto that has a slightly tangy taste and a crunchy texture. It makes a delicious addition to any salad, one-pot dish, or miso soup.

1. Wash and cut the mizuna leaves into 1-inch (3-cm) lengths.
2. Heat the oil for deep-frying to 350°F (180°C). Deep-fry the burdock and garlic until golden brown. Drain on kitchen paper.
3. In a bowl, combine the dressing ingredients. Mix well and set aside.
4. Arrange the mizuna leaves in a serving bowl. Scatter the fried burdock and garlic over the leaves.
5. Pour the dressing over the salad and serve.

Persimmon
with Walnut Dressing

Kaki no kurumi-ae

SERVES *4*

Shojin ryori is Japanese Buddhist temple food, made and eaten by priests who follow strict vegetarian diets. Carefully prepared food is served in attractive dishes and bowls—truly a feast for the eyes and the soul. This is one of my favorite recipes from the shojin ryori cooking classes I attended. The crunchy walnuts are a good match for the soft, sweet persimmon.

1. Peel the persimmon and remove the seeds. Slice thinly and set aside. Coarsely grind the walnuts using a food processor.
2. In a deep bowl, combine the sesame paste, sugar, soy sauce, and sake and whisk until smooth.
3. Put the persimmon slices in the bowl with the dressing, and toss to coat evenly. Serve chilled.

3 firm ripe persimmons
10–12 walnuts
1 tablespoon sesame paste
2 teaspoons castor sugar
2 teaspoons soy sauce
1 tablespoon sake

Sesame Almond
Green Beans

Ingen no goma to amando-ae

SERVES *4*

The green beans are dressed with almond and sesame seeds, which lend a rich texture and aroma to this salad. They are cooked very briefly to retain their refreshing green color and their crispness.

1. Bring a pan of lightly salted water to the boil, then put in the green beans and cook for 2 minutes. Drain, and transfer to a flat dish. Sprinkle the beans with the 2 teaspoons soy sauce, and allow to cool.
2. For the dressing, use a food processor to grind the almonds and sesame seeds to a powder. Transfer the powder to a bowl, and add the sesame paste, sugar, sake, and soy sauce. Mix until you have a smooth dressing.
3. Put the beans in the bowl with the dressing and gently toss to coat evenly.

2 cups (200g) green beans, strings removed
2 teaspoons soy sauce

FOR THE DRESSING
20 almonds, blanched briefly and skinned
2 tablespoons white sesame seeds, toasted (see page 42)
1 tablespoon sesame paste
1½ tablespoons sugar
1 tablespoon sake
1 tablespoon soy sauce

Spinach with Sesame Dressing
Horenso no goma-ae

4 cups (200g) spinach
½ teaspoon soy sauce
½ medium carrot, grated
White sesame seeds, toasted, for garnish (see page 42)

FOR THE DRESSING
4 tablespoons white sesame seeds, toasted (see page 42)
1 tablespoon castor sugar
1 tablespoon sake
½ tablespoon soy sauce
1 teaspoon sesame paste

SERVES *4*   PHOTOGRAPH ON PAGE 90

*A*e means to mix, and here spinach is mixed with a nutty sesame dressing. Spinach has never tasted so good. My children could eat this entire amount between themselves.

1. Bring a pan of water to the boil, put in the spinach and cook for 2 minutes. Remove and immerse in cold water to stop further cooking and to retain a deep green color. Squeeze out the excess water and sprinkle with soy sauce. Cut into 3 cm lengths and squeeze out the water once again.
2. For the dressing, use a pestle and mortar or food processor to grind the sesame seeds to a coarse powder. In a bowl, combine the ground sesame seeds, sugar, sake, soy sauce, and sesame paste and mix until smooth.
3. Put the spinach and carrot in the bowl with the dressing and mix to coat evenly. Mixing with chopsticks is the best way to ensure that the spinach is evenly coated with the dressing, but a fork can also be used. Transfer to a serving bowl and sprinkle with the sesame seeds. Serve at room temperature.

Tofu and Vegetable Soup
Kenchin jiru

7 ounces (200g) firm tofu
3½ ounces (100g) daikon radish
1 ounce (30g) burdock
¼ medium carrot
1 leek
3 fresh shiitake mushrooms, stems discarded
2 teaspoons vegetable oil
4 cups (960ml) dashi stock (see page 40)
1 teaspoon soy sauce
3 tablespoons miso
Chopped chives, for garnish

SERVES *4*   PHOTOGRAPH ON PAGE 89

*J*apanese miso varies greatly in terms of ingredients, texture, and taste depending on the region it comes from. Hatcho miso comes from Nagoya and has a sharp, concentrated flavor. A combination of different kinds of miso can be used to suit your taste. Miso is a key ingredient in this wholesome root-vegetable soup, a warming dish for a cold day.

1. Wrap the tofu in a thick dish towel and place a weight, such as a dinner plate, on top of it. Allow to stand for 10 minutes. Cut into bite-sized pieces.
2. Cut the radish, burdock, carrot, and leek into bite-sized pieces. Slice the shiitake.
3. Heat the oil in a saucepan and sauté the daikon, burdock, carrot, and shiitake for 2 minutes, until glazed. Add the tofu and stir to mix.
4. Pour the dashi into the pan with the vegetables, and bring to a boil. Cook for 10–12 minutes, until the vegetables are tender. Add the soy sauce.
5. Turn the heat to low, stir the miso into the soup until it dissolves, then turn off the heat. Serve garnished with chives.

Tomato, Okra, and Tofu Salad with Yuzu Dressing

Tomato, okura, to tofu no yuzu sarada

SERVES *4*

Yuzu is a Japanese citrus fruit, with an aromatic, characteristically Japanese flavor, and a yellow rind that makes an attractive garnish. This dressing works beautifully with any salad greens. Use freshly squeezed lime juice if you can't get hold of yuzu.

1. Cut the tomatoes into bite-sized pieces. Top and tail the okra, cut into thin diagonal slices, then immerse in boiling water for 1 minute and drain. Cut the mizuna into 1½-inch (4-cm) lengths.
2. Wrap the tofu in a thick dish towel and place a weight, such as a dinner plate, over it. Allow to stand for 10 minutes. Gently cut into bite-sized pieces.
3. Combine the dressing ingredients and whisk until smooth.
4. Arrange the tomato, okra, and mizuna leaves on a serving dish. Gently place the tofu pieces over them. Pour the dressing first around the sides of the dish and then over the tofu and vegetables.

2 ripe medium tomatoes
3–4 okra
3½ ounces (100g) mizuna leaves
11 ounces (310g) silken tofu

DRESSING

2 tablespoons freshly squeezed yuzu juice
2 tablespoons soy sauce
2 tablespoons sesame oil
½ teaspoon ground black pepper
½-inch (1-cm) cube fresh ginger, peeled and grated
1 teaspoon ginger juice (see page 43)

Vinegared Cucumber and Wakame

Kyuri to wakame no sunomono

SERVES *4*

Vinegared dishes are served cold—often as palate cleansers—and are made with fresh or lightly cooked vegetables. Slightly sweet vinegared dishes such as this one make a great accompaniment to soft fluffy white rice.

1. Slice the cucumbers thinly. Place in a bowl and sprinkle with salt. Mix with the hands, then set aside for 5 minutes. Squeeze out the excess liquid by hand or with the back of a spoon, then drain.
2. Soak the wakame in hot water for 5 minutes. Drain and cut into ¾-inch (2-cm) pieces.
3. Slice the myoga thinly.
4. Combine all the vinegar dressing ingredients in a small bowl.
5. Arrange the cucumber, wakame, and myoga on a serving dish in small groups of color. Pour the vinegar dressing around the sides of the dish, and serve chilled.

2 Japanese cucumbers
½ teaspoon salt
⅓ cup (5g) dried wakame
2 myoga shoots

FOR THE DRESSING

1½ tablespoons rice vinegar
2 teaspoons castor sugar
1 tablespoon soy sauce
1 tablespoon dashi stock (see page 40)

MAIN DISHES

Bitter Gourd and Tofu Stir-fry   *Goya champuru*

SERVES *4*

2 bitter gourds, 3½ ounces (100g) each
Salt for sprinkling
1¼ pounds (600g) firm tofu
2 teaspoons vegetable oil
2 teaspoons sesame oil
½-inch (1-cm) cube fresh ginger, peeled and grated
2 tablespoons soy sauce
Pinch of salt
Dash of white pepper

This dish is from Okinawa, a semi-tropical island archipelago at the southern tip of Japan, whose inhabitants have one of the longest life spans in the world. One of the reasons for this is their healthy diet. Okinawa is abundant in exotic vegetables with health-giving properties, such as the bitter gourd, which is said to burn body fat.

1. Slice the bitter gourds in half lengthwise. Using a spoon, scrape out all the seeds and fibrous flesh from the center of the gourd. Cut into very thin slices and transfer to a flat dish. Sprinkle salt over the bitter gourd and rub to mix. Set aside for 10 minutes. The salt will release a lot of moisture and with it the bitterness will be reduced. Wash under running water and drain.

2. Wrap the tofu in a thick dish towel and place a weight, such as a dinner plate, on top of it. Allow to stand for 10 minutes. Slice the tofu into strips ½ inch (1 cm) wide.

3. In a frying pan, heat the 2 teaspoons vegetable oil and sauté the tofu over high heat for 2–3 minutes, until all excess moisture has been absorbed and the tofu strips are lightly browned.

4. In another frying pan, heat the sesame oil and sauté the ginger over medium heat for 10 seconds. Put in the bitter gourd, turn the heat to high, and sauté for 1 minute. Add the sautéed tofu strips, the soy sauce, salt, and pepper and gently toss to mix. Serve with steaming hot white rice.

* Fu (dried wheat gluten, available from Japanese supermarkets) can be used for an easy variation. Use 7 ounces (200g) fu instead of the bitter gourd. The fu needs to be soaked for 10 minutes in tepid water before use.

Fried Tofu Cutlets

Koyadofu tonkatsu

SERVES *4*

Tonkatsu is a breaded deep-fried cutlet, a robust and hearty dish in Japan. *Katsu* means victory, and this dish is often eaten before sports tournaments, exams, or elections to ensure success. Tonkatsu is always served with a heap of shredded cabbage on the side, and tonkatsu sauce, a thick Worcestershire sauce, available from Japanese supermarkets. This recipe uses freeze-dried tofu, called koyadofu, which adds a delicious and healthy touch to this popular dish.

1. Soak the koyadofu cakes in hot water for 10 minutes, then drain.
2. In a saucepan, combine the simmering sauce ingredients and bring to a boil. Put in the drained koyadofu and simmer for 8–10 minutes over medium heat, until all the liquid is absorbed.
3. Dab the koyadofu in the dusting flour. Mix the 1 cup flour and ½ cup water to make a thick paste. Dip the floured koyadofu in the flour-and-water paste, then roll each cake in the bread crumbs. Set aside.
4. Heat the oil for deep-frying to 350°F (180°C). Slide the breaded tofu pieces into the oil in batches and deep-fry until crisp and golden brown. Drain on kitchen paper and serve hot with shredded cabbage, lemon wedges, and tonkatsu sauce.

8 cakes koyadofu, about 6 ounces (170g) in total
All-purpose flour for dusting
1 cup (125g) all-purpose flour
½ cup (120ml) water
1 cup (100g) bread crumbs
Vegetable oil for deep-frying
Shredded white cabbage, for garnish
Lemon wedges, for garnish
Tonkatsu sauce

SIMMERING SAUCE

2 cups (480ml) dashi stock (see page 40)
2 tablespoons soy sauce
1 tablespoon mirin
½-inch (1-cm) cube fresh ginger, peeled and grated
½ teaspoon grated garlic

Mixed Vegetable Fritters

Kakiage

MAKES *4*

This is a combination of mixed vegetables fried together to make one large piece of tempura for each person. It is often served with soba or udon noodles. When served with hot noodles, the tempura is placed in the bowl on top of the noodles. When served with cold noodles, it is served on the side and eaten with a dipping sauce.

1. Wash the burdock and cut into 2-inch (5-cm) long julienne strips. Soak in water to which 1 teaspoon of rice vinegar has been added, until ready to use.
2. Peel and cut the carrot into 2-inch (5-cm) long julienne strips. Slice the onion thinly.
3. Make the batter following the instructions on the page opposite.
4. Lightly dust the burdock, carrot, and onion with flour, then add to the batter and mix gently.
5. Heat the oil for deep-frying to 350°F (180°C). Take a heaping ladleful of the battered vegetables and slide into the oil.

3½ ounces (100g) burdock
1 carrot
1 medium onion
Flour for dusting
Vegetable oil for deep-frying
1 tablespoon grated daikon radish, for garnish, optional
1 tablespoon fresh grated ginger, for garnish, optional

FOR THE BATTER

1½ cups (185g) all-purpose flour
⅔ cup (160ml) iced water
1 tablespoon potato starch
Pinch of baking soda
¼ teaspoon salt

6. Deep fry until golden brown and crisp. Remove from the oil and drain on kitchen paper.
7. Repeat the deep-frying process until all the batter has been used. Serve with Chilled Buckwheat Noodles (see page 53) or Wheat Noodles in Soup (see page 55), or on the side with cold noodles and individual bowls of dipping sauce (see below) to which a little grated daikon radish or fresh grated ginger can be added.

Tempura Dipping Sauce

Tentsuyu   MAKES *about 1½ cups (360ml)*

1½ cups (360ml) dashi stock (see page 40)
4 tablespoons mirin
5 tablespoons soy sauce
1 teaspoon sugar

Combine all the ingredients in a saucepan and bring to a boil over medium heat. Simmer for a minute, then turn off the heat.

Tempura Batter   *Koromo*   MAKES *2 cups (480ml)*

⅔ cup (160ml) iced water   Pinch of baking powder
1¼ cups (155g) all-purpose flour   ¼ teaspoon salt
1 tablespoon potato starch

Chilled batter is the key to making crisp tempura. For best results, keep a tray of ice under the bowl while making the batter. The batter should be lumpy, not smooth.

Place a deep bowl over a tray of ice. Pour the iced water into the bowl. Add the sifted flour, potato starch, baking powder, and salt and mix lightly, using chopsticks or a fork. Unmixed flour should still be visible around the sides of the bowl and the batter should be lumpy. Keep away from heat until ready to use.

1 pound (450g) firm tofu
5 ounces (140g) dried harusame noodles or
   9 ounces (250g) fresh shirataki noodles
4 pieces of fu (dried gluten chunks), each 1 inch
   (2.5 cm) square, optional
4 leeks
8 fresh shiitake mushrooms, stems discarded
3 cups (135g) Chinese cabbage
3½ ounces (100g) enoki mushrooms
1 cup (60g) spring chrysanthemum leaves, roughly torn
2 tablespoons chopped chives, for garnish
2 tablespoons grated daikon radish, for garnish
Cayenne pepper, for garnish
Sesame oil for drizzling

FOR THE SAUCE

2 cups (480ml) dashi stock (see page 40)
4 tablespoons soy sauce
3 tablespoons mirin
1 tablespoon sake
1 tablespoon sugar

Sukiyaki   *Sukiyaki*

SERVES *4*

In this vegetarian version of the classic one-pot dish, an array of delicious vegetables is cooked with tofu and noodles in a delicately seasoned sauce. In Japan, guests usually sit around a low table where the sukiyaki pan is placed on a hotplate, and serve themselves directly from the pan. If you don't have a hotplate, you can easily make it on the kitchen stove, bring the pan to the dining table, and have guests help themselves.

1. Wrap the tofu in a thick dish towel and place a weight, such as a dinner plate, on top of it. Allow to stand for 10 minutes.
2. Cook the harusame noodles in boiling water for 2 minutes. Drain and set aside. (If using fresh shirataki noodles, dip them in boiling water, drain, and set aside.) Soak the fu in hot water for 10 minutes. Drain and set aside.
3. Slice the leeks diagonally into bite sized pieces. With a knife, score a cross on each shiitake cap. Cut the cabbage and tofu into bite sized pieces. Slice the enoki mushrooms.
4. Arrange the leeks, shiitake, cabbage, tofu, enoki, and spring chrysanthemum leaves on a large plate, in separate groups.

5. Arrange the garnishes on communal serving dishes and set out.

6. Combine all the sauce ingredients in a small pan and bring to a boil. Remove from the heat and set aside.

7. Heat a heavy frying pan and drizzle some sesame oil over it. Turn the heat to high. Put in half the leeks and cook on high heat for 1 minute, until soft and lightly browned. Push to the side of the pan, then put in half of the remaining vegetables and fu and stir-fry over high heat for a few minutes. Pour a little sauce over the vegetables and fu and cook for 2–3 minutes. Mix in half the tofu and half the noodles and heat through.

8. Serve immediately, with guests helping themselves from the pan. The guests can add the garnish of their choice. Repeat the cooking process with the remaining ingredients when the guests are ready for some more. More seasonings may be added as needed.

Tofu Teriyaki Steak with Sautéed Asparagus and Mushrooms *Teriyakidofu*

MAKES *1 steak*   PHOTOGRAPH ON PAGE 93

This protein-rich tofu steak is especially good for people on a diet. The teak is glazed with a yuzu-flavored teriyaki sauce. Asparagus lends a touch of texture and color to this delicious dish.

1. Wrap the tofu in a thick dish towel and place a weight, such as a dinner plate, on top of it. Allow to stand for 10 minutes. Transfer to a flat plate. Sprinkle with the flour to coat evenly. Remove the woody ends of the asparagus and cut the spears in half. With a knife, score a cross on each shiitake cap.

2. For the sauce, combine the dashi, soy sauce, and mirin in a small saucepan. Bring to a simmer and turn off the heat. Put in the yuzu zest and mix.

3. In flat saucepan, heat the 2 tablespoons sesame oil, then put in the block of tofu and cook both sides over medium heat until crisp and golden brown. Pour 3 tablespoons of the yuzu sauce over it and cook for 1 minute, turning once.

4. In a small saucepan, heat the 1 teaspoon sesame oil and sauté the asparagus and shiitake for 2–3 minutes over high heat, until lightly browned. Turn the heat to medium, put the remaining yuzu sauce in the saucepan, and cook covered over medium heat for 2 minutes. Season with salt and pepper.

5. Arrange the tofu steak on a serving dish, removing any excess liquid. Top the steak with the sautéed asparagus and shiitake and serve with a green salad and fluffy hot white rice.

1 block firm tofu, about 11 ounces (310g)
2 tablespoons plain flour
2 asparagus spears
2 fresh shiitake mushrooms, stems discarded
2 tablespoons sesame oil
1 teaspoon sesame oil
Pinch of salt
Dash of white pepper

FOR THE SAUCE
½ cup (120ml) dashi stock (see page 40)
3 teaspoons soy sauce
2 teaspoons mirin
1 teaspoon grated yuzu zest

Vegetable Pancakes

Okonomiyaki

SERVES *4*

2 cups (250g) all-purpose flour
½ teaspoon baking powder
1 cup (240ml) dashi stock (see page 40)
2 teaspoons white miso
1 tablespoon mirin
1 tablespoon sake
2 cups (90g) Chinese cabbage, finely shredded
4 fresh shiitake mushroom caps, finely sliced
4 scallions, finely sliced
1 cup (120g) cooked sweet corn kernels, optional
2 tablespoons beni shoga pickled ginger
Salt to taste
¼ teaspoon ground white pepper
Vegetable oil for frying
Sesame oil for frying
1 sheet nori seaweed, toasted* and cut into fine strips
Tofu Mayonnaise (see page 52)

FOR THE SAUCE

½ cup (120ml) dashi stock (see page 40)
½ teaspoon potato starch
4 tablespoons tomato ketchup
¼ teaspoon karashi mustard
2 tablespoons soy sauce
½ teaspoon grated garlic
½ teaspoon grated ginger
2 tablespoons castor sugar
1 tablespoon rice vinegar
1 tablespoon mirin

* To toast nori, hold the sheet over the gas or electric burner (taking care not to touch the flame or element) until crisp.

This savory pancake is popular in Osaka and Hiroshima. A typical okonomiyaki restaurant has small wooden tables with a large iron griddle in the center where you can custom cook your own pancake. This was one of my first Japanese restaurant experiences. My husband took me to a quaint little place in a narrow Tokyo backstreet, where I was welcomed with enthusiastic shouts of *Irrasshaimase* from the staff into a place crowded with noisy customers drinking beer and sake. The ingredients and sauces were brought to the table, and under the expert guidance of my husband, I created my own original okonomiyaki. This dish is easy to make at home, so don't let the long list of ingredients scare you.

1. Sift the flour and baking powder into a deep bowl. In a separate bowl, combine the dashi, miso, mirin, and sake. Add the dashi mixture to the flour and mix to combine. Stir in the cabbage, shiitake, scallions, corn, and pickled ginger and season with salt and pepper. Mix thoroughly.

2. Heat a little vegetable oil in a large frying pan over medium heat. Put in a quarter of the vegetable batter. Spread out to make a thick pancake. Cook for 3–4 minutes, then drizzle a little sesame oil around the sides of the pan. Turn the pancake over and cook the other side for 3–4 minutes. Press down on the pancake while cooking to make it crispy and golden. Remove from the frying pan and place on a serving dish. Repeat this process until all the batter has been used.

3. Combine all the ingredients for the sauce in a small saucepan and bring to a boil. Simmer for 3–4 minutes, until the sauce has thickened.

4. Take a tablespoon of the sauce and brush over each pancake. Garnish with nori and serve with Tofu Mayonnaise. Keep the remaining sauce in a small communal bowl for guests to use as required.

Tofu Mayonnaise   MAKES *1½ cups (360ml)*

7 ounces (200g) silken tofu
4 tablespoons vegetable oil
4 tablespoons white miso
1 tablespoon white sesame seeds, toasted (see page 42)
2 tablespoons lemon juice
2 tablespoons rice vinegar
¼ teaspoon ground white pepper
1 teaspoon salt

This delicious protein-rich mayonnaise can be used as a dressing for salads and is a good complement for dishes such as Vegetable Pancakes (see above). It's delicious on a warm baguette or in a burger, and you can add it to mashed potato with slivers of carrot, cucumber and onions to make a quick potato salad. This recipe uses white miso, but you can use red miso for a stronger flavor.

Combine all the ingredients in a food processor and blend until smooth. Transfer to an airtight container, cover, and store in the refrigerator. Keeps for 3–4 days.

Vegetable Tempura

Yasai no tempura

SERVES *4*   PHOTOGRAPH ON PAGE 94

2 small eggplants
4 shishito peppers, or mild green chili peppers
4 fresh shiitake mushrooms, stems discarded
1 medium sweet potato
2 green bell peppers
Vegetable oil for deep-frying
4 shiso leaves
Lime wedges, to serve
Flour for dusting

FOR THE BATTER

1¼ cups (155g) all-purpose flour
⅔ cup (160ml) iced water
1 tablespoon potato starch
Pinch of baking powder
¼ teaspoon salt

Tempura, one of Japan's most famous culinary delights, consists of a rich variety of battered, deep-fried vegetables, typically served with a dipping sauce, or simply with salt. Tempura can also be served with hot or cold soba and udon noodles to make a substantial meal.

1. Cut the eggplants in half lengthwise and make incisions in a diagonal pattern on the skin. Pierce the shishito peppers at a few points to avoid oil splattering when fried. With a knife, score a cross on each shiitake cap. Slice the sweet potato diagonally into very thin slices. Halve the bell peppers and remove the seeds.
2. Make the batter, following the instructions on page 49.
3. Heat the oil for deep-frying to 350°F (180°C). The pan should ideally be 70 percent full. Drop a little batter in the oil. If it floats immediately, the oil is ready. Lightly dust the vegetables and shiso leaves with flour and dip in the batter. In batches of 2 or 3 gently slide into the oil. Deep-fry until the batter is crisp. Drain on a paper towel before serving.
4. Arrange on a serving plate, and serve piping hot. Tempura Dipping Sauce (see page 49), Green Tea Salt, or Curry Salt (see below) all enhance the flavors of the tempura. If serving with salt, drizzle the tempura with lime juice.

Green Tea Salt *Matcha shio*	Curry Salt *Kare shio*
1 teaspoon matcha powdered green tea 1 teaspoon salt	1 teaspoon curry powder 1 teaspoon salt
Mix and use.	Mix and use.

NOODLES

Chilled Buckwheat Noodles

Zaru soba

SERVES *4*

7 ounces (200g) soba noodles

1 sheet of nori seaweed, toasted (see page 51)

1 tablespoon fresh ginger, peeled and grated into fine strips, for garnish

3 tablespoons finely chopped chives, for garnish

Wasabi horseradish, for garnish

FOR THE DIPPING SAUCE

2 cups (480ml) dashi stock (see page 40)

½ cup (120ml) soy sauce

½ cup (120ml) mirin

1 teaspoon sugar

1 tablespoon sake

Soba noodles, made from buckwheat flour, can be eaten hot or cold. When eaten hot, they are served in broth, which one drinks from the bowl. Cold soba is dipped in a separate dipping sauce, which, once the soba has been eaten, is diluted with the water the soba has been cooked in to make a kind of soup. Japan's favorite summertime food—refreshing and cool.

1. Bring a large saucepan of water to a boil. Put in the noodles, and when the water returns to a boil, add a cup of cold water. Bring to a boil again. This process will take 2-3 minutes. The noodles should be tender, but not overcooked.

2. Drain the noodles in a colander, and rinse briefly under cold running water to keep the noodles firm. Drain and divide between 4 individual serving bowls.

3. With a pair of scissors, cut the nori into very fine strips.

4. Place the dipping sauce ingredients in a small saucepan and bring to a boil. Remove from heat, allow to cool, then divide between small individual bowls.

5. Serve each person one individual bowl of noodles and one individual bowl of dipping sauce. Sprinkle the nori over the noodles before serving. Small amounts of grated ginger, chives, or wasabi can be added to the dipping sauce according to individual taste. To eat, pick up the noodles with a chopstick or a fork, dip in the sauce, and slurp!

* A Mixed Vegetable Fritter (see page 48) may be served with the soba. The dish is then called Tempura Soba.

Fine Noodles

Somen

SERVES *4*

Chilled somen noodles are a welcome addition to the summertime menu during Japan's hot summer. Cucumber lends a refreshing touch, and the ginger perks up the appetite.

1. Place the dipping sauce ingredients in a saucepan and bring to a boil over high heat for 1 minute. Allow to cool, then chill.
2. Bring the water to a boil. Add the cooked noodles, and bring to a boil again. Transfer to a colander and drain. Wash the noodles under cold running water, squeezing and turning with the hands to get rid of any stickiness. Drain well.
3. Pour a little iced water into 4 individual serving bowls. Divide the noodles between the bowls, and garnish with cucumber and radish sprouts.
4. Take 4 more small bowls for the dipping sauce. Divide the dipping sauce between them. Place the grated ginger and sliced myoga on the side, and mix into the sauce as required.

8 cups (2 L) water
1¾ pounds (800g) cooked somen noodles
Iced water, to serve
2 cucumbers, thinly sliced
Kaiware radish sprouts, for garnish
2-inch (5-cm) cube fresh ginger, peeled and grated
4 myoga buds, thinly sliced

FOR THE DIPPING SAUCE
2½ cups (600ml) dashi stock (see page 40)
½ cup (120ml) mirin
½ cup (120ml) soy sauce
Pinch of salt
1 tablespoon sake

Fried Noodles

Yakisoba

SERVES *4*

Yakisoba originated from the Chinese chow mein, but it has become one of Japan's national dishes, found everywhere from school cafeterias, fast food restaurants, convenience stores, roadside vendors, and airlines. It is usually stir-fried with vegetables. In spite of the long list of ingredients, this is an easy dish to put together.

1. Pour boiling water over the shiitake and leave to stand for at least 10 minutes, or several hours if time permits, then drain, reserving the liquid, and thinly slice the caps. Cut the onion into thin slices, and the scallions and carrot into thin diagonal slices. Cut the cabbage into 1-inch (3-cm) pieces and the bamboo shoot and bell pepper into thin strips. Wash the bean sprouts and remove any brown ends.
2. Pour hot water over the yakisoba noodles to remove excess oil. Drain and separate.
3. Combine all the sauce ingredients in a small bowl. Add 4 tablespoons of the reserved shiitake liquid, and stir to mix.
4. Heat a large wok and put in the sesame oil. Sauté the garlic and ginger for a few seconds. Put in the onions, scallions, and carrots. Stir-fry over high heat for 2–3 minutes. Put in the shiitake, cabbage,

4 dried shiitake mushrooms
1 medium onion
2 scallions
1 carrot
4 cups (180g) Chinese cabbage
1¾ ounces (50g) bamboo shoot
1 green bell pepper
⅓ cup (30g) bean sprouts
1 pound (450g) yakisoba noodles
2 tablespoons sesame oil
1 clove garlic, grated
½-inch (1-cm) cube fresh ginger, peeled and grated
1 sheet nori seaweed, toasted (see page 51)
Beni shoga pickled ginger, to serve

FOR THE SAUCE
2 tablespoons tomato ketchup
2 tablespoons Worcestershire sauce
2 teaspoons sugar
2 teaspoons rice vinegar
2 teaspoons soy sauce
1 tablespoon mirin
¼ teaspoon pepper
Pinch of salt

bamboo shoot, and bell pepper and keep stirring continuously for 2–3 minutes until the vegetables are slightly browned. Put in the bean sprouts and reduce the heat to medium. Toss to mix.

5. Mix in the noodles and sprinkle a few tablespoons of the reserved shiitake liquid over them. Add the sauce and toss to mix evenly. Heat through.

6. Serve garnished with nori strips and pickled ginger.

Wheat Noodles in Soup
Nabeyaki udon

SERVES *4*

4 dried shiitake mushrooms
¼ cup (60ml) dashi stock (see page 40)
1 teaspoon castor sugar
1 tablespoon soy sauce
1 tablespoon mirin
14 ounces (400g) udon noodles
4 cups (960ml) Soup for Noodles (see below)
2 scallions, sliced diagonally into ¾-inch (2-cm)
  lengths, for garnish
4 Mixed Vegetable Fritters, optional (see page 48)
Shichimi pepper or cayenne pepper

Traditionally the noodles and vegetables are cooked in a large clay pot with the simmering broth. The combination of thick udon wheat noodles, hot soup, and vegetable fritters makes a hearty meal. On cold winter evenings, my children would often ask for this dish when they were too tired to sit through an elaborate meal.

1. Pour boiling water over the shiitake and leave to stand for at least 10 minutes. Drain and slice thinly.

2. In a small saucepan, combine the dashi with the sugar, soy sauce, and mirin and bring to a simmer. Put in the sliced shiitake and continue to simmer for 5–7 minutes, until the liquid has been absorbed. Set the shiitake aside.

3. Bring a large saucepan of water to a boil. Put in the noodles, and when the water returns to a boil, add a cup of cold water. Bring to a boil again and cook for 3–4 minutes, until the noodles are just tender, taking care not to overcook. Drain and rinse under cold running water.

4. Bring the Soup for Noodles to a boil in a saucepan. Divide the noodles between 4 serving bowls. Pour the soup over the noodles to cover them. Arrange the shiitake, scallions, and vegetable fritters, if serving, on top of the noodles.

5. Serve immediately, sprinkled with shichimi pepper or cayenne pepper to taste.

Soup for Noodles
Kakejiru   MAKES *about 4 cups (960ml)*

4 cups (960ml) dashi stock
4 tablespoons soy sauce
2 tablespoons sake
3 tablespoons mirin
Pinch of salt

This is a basic dashi, which can be served as a soup for all kinds of noodles

Combine all the ingredients in a saucepan and bring to a boil. Cover and simmer for 5 minutes. Adjust the seasonings as required.

RICE

Fried Rice with Pickled Mustard Greens
Takana gohan

SERVES *4*

2 tablespoons vegetable oil or sesame oil
1 teaspoon garlic, finely chopped
3 ½ ounces (100g) takana, finely chopped
3 cups (550g) cooked short-grain rice (see page 40)
2 tablespoons soy sauce
1 teaspoon white sesame seeds, toasted, for garnish (see page 42)

The pickled mustard greens known as *takana* in Japanese are simple but versatile, traditionally made in preparation for long winter months. These days, takana can be found ready-made in Japanese supermarkets, and most households keep a supply in their homes. This quick, tasty dish is a great way to use leftover rice.

1. Heat the oil in a flat saucepan and sauté the garlic for 10–12 seconds. Put in the takana and sauté for 2–3 minutes.
2. Put in the cooked rice and mix in quick strokes to break any lumps that may have formed and to evenly coat with the takana.
3. Season with the soy sauce and sprinkle with sesame seeds. Mix gently and serve immediately.

Mushroom Rice Balls
Kinoko no takikomi gohan

SERVES *4*   PHOTOGRAPH ON PAGE 94

3 cups (600g) short-grain rice
5 dried shiitake mushrooms
1¾ ounces (50g) burdock
1 carrot
3½ ounces (100g) assorted fresh mushrooms, such as shimeji, maitake, enoki
1 sheet abura-age deep-fried tofu
1 cup (240ml) Konbu Dashi (see page 40)
3 tablespoons sake
3 tablespoons soy sauce
½ teaspoon salt
Beni shoga pickled ginger, to serve
Radish, Ginger, and Cabbage Pickle (see opposite), to serve

In Japan, various combinations of vegetables are served as garnishes with rice, or cooked with the rice to allow their fragrance and flavor to blend in. This is a popular dish for fall, when rice and mushrooms are at their best. Mushrooms give off liquid when cooked so the rice needs less cooking water.

1. Wash the rice in several changes of water until the water runs clear. Soak in water for 30 minutes. Drain and set aside.
2. Pour 2 cups of boiling water over the shiitake and soak for at least 10 minutes. Drain, reserving the soaking water, and slice the shiitake thinly. Shave the burdock and carrot into thin slices. Cut the assorted mushrooms into bite-sized pieces. Place the abura-age pouch in a colander and pour boiling water over it to remove excess oil. Cut the abura-age into thin strips.
3. Put the shiitake, assorted mushrooms, burdock, carrot, and abura-age in a large saucepan or rice cooker. Add the rice, the reserved

shiitake soaking water, and the konbu dashi. Add the sake, soy sauce, and salt, then follow the instructions for cooking rice on page 40.
4. When the rice is cooked, use the hands to form into balls (see picture on page 94). Serve with beni shoga or Radish, Ginger, and Cabbage Pickle, and miso soup.

Scattered Sushi

Chirashi-zushi

SERVES *4*

PHOTOGRAPH ON PAGE 95

3½ ounces (100g) lotus root
½ cup (120ml) dashi stock (see page 40)
2 tablespoons rice vinegar
1 tablespoon castor sugar
Pinch of salt
1 medium carrot, julienned
4 tablespoons dashi stock (see page 40)
½ teaspoon rice vinegar
1 teaspoon sugar
Pinch of salt
10 dried shiitake mushrooms
⅔ cup (160ml) dashi stock
3 tablespoons castor sugar
2 tablespoons mirin
2 tablespoons soy sauce
½ cup (50g) snow peas, strings removed
Sushi rice, double the quantity on page 41
½ cup (70g) white sesame seeds, toasted (see page 42)
Beni shoga pickled ginger, for garnish
1 sheet toasted nori seaweed (see page 51), cut into small strips, for garnish, optional

This colorful sushi is exactly as its name implies—sushi rice scattered with seasoned vegetables. Chirashi-zushi adorns the dining table on auspicious occasions such as New Year and the Doll Festival.

1. Pare the lotus root, cut into thin slices, and leave to soak in vinegared water.
2. In a saucepan, combine the dashi stock with the vinegar, sugar, and salt. Put in the lotus root and cook for 3–4 minutes over medium heat until tender. Set aside to cool.
3. Place the carrot, 4 tablespoons dashi, ½ teaspoon vinegar, 1 teaspoon sugar, and the pinch of salt in a saucepan. Cook for 2–3 minutes over medium heat, until the liquid is almost absorbed. Set aside to cool.
4. Rinse the shiitake quickly and soak in water for 5 minutes. Remove the hard stems. Place in a saucepan with the ⅔ cup dashi stock, 3 tablespoons sugar, mirin, and soy sauce and cook over medium heat for 4–5 minutes, until the liquid is absorbed. Transfer to a dish and slice thinly.
5. Parboil the snow peas in salted boiling water. Drain and slice in half diagonally.
6. Transfer the cooked sushi rice to a wooden tub or a flat bowl and cool to room temperature.
7. Scatter the rice with the sesame seeds, lotus root, carrot, shiitake and snow peas. Sprinkle with pickled ginger and nori slivers and serve at room temperature.

* A delicious variation is to use 7 ounces (200g) of ready cooked bamboo shoots, shredded, instead of the assorted mushrooms.

Radish, Ginger, and Cabbage Pickle

Radisshu, myoga, to kyabbetsu no shio-momi SERVES *4*

6½ cups (300g) white cabbage
8 small red radishes
4 myoga buds
1½ teaspoons salt

A traditional Japanese meal ends with rice, miso soup, and pickles. This pickle is quick to make and easy to assemble. Myoga, a flavorful bud with a gingerlike taste adds a delicious aroma, while the radish provides a hint of color. And don't worry about being traditional: pickles can add zest to any meal.

1. Separate the cabbage leaves, remove the hard ends, and cut into bite-sized pieces. Slice the radishes and the myoga thinly.
2. Place the vegetables in a large bowl and sprinkle with salt. Rub the salt into the vegetables firmly with the hands, then let them stand for 15 minutes. Tip away the excess water.
3. Rub again to extract as much water as possible from the vegetables.
4. Transfer to a bowl and keep chilled until ready to serve.

* Chinese cabbage may be used instead of white cabbage.

SIDE DISHES

Braised Onions and Potatoes   *Negi jaga*

SERVES *4*

This was one of the first Japanese dishes I tasted when I arrived in Tokyo. My Japanese friend invited me to her home, where her mother cooked us a meal for that included this dish, along with Miso Soup (page 43), Stir-fried Lotus Root (page 63), and Mushroom Rice Balls (page 56). I nearly always put negi jaga on the menu when I'm making a Japanese meal for my family.

1. Peel and cut the potato and carrot into bite-sized pieces. Slice the onion thinly.
2. Heat the oil in a flat pan. Put in the chili and onion and sauté for 2–3 minutes, until soft. Add the potato and carrot and stir to mix. Put in just enough of the dashi to cover the vegetables. Cover and cook over high heat for 5–7 minutes.
3. Turn the heat to medium and put the remaining dashi, the sake, sugar, mirin, and soy sauce into the pan. Cook for 4–5 minutes, stirring occasionally until the vegetables are tender and slightly mashed.
4. Turn the heat back to high for 1–2 minutes, until excess liquid has been absorbed. Transfer to a serving dish and allow to cool.

4 potatoes, about 14 ounces (400g) in total
1 carrot
1 medium onion
1 tablespoon sesame oil
1 dried red chili
2 cups (480ml) dashi (see page 40)
2 tablespoons sake
2 tablespoons sugar
2 tablespoons mirin
2 tablespoons soy sauce

Burdock and Carrot Kimpira   *Gobo to ninjin no kimpira*

SERVES *4*   PHOTOGRAPH ON PAGE 91

Vegetables cooked "kimpira" style are stir-fried quickly over high heat to retain their crispiness. Burdock is the most common ingredient for this dish, which is a regular feature of Japanese home cooking and is also sold ready-made at convenience stores throughout Japan.

1. Heat oil in a broad pan and stir-fry the burdock and carrot over high heat using chopsticks. When the vegetables are coated with oil, add the chilies. Lower the heat to medium and add the seasoning ingredients. Continue to stir-fry until all the liquid is absorbed.
2. Sprinkle with sesame seeds and drizzle with sesame oil. Transfer to a dish and allow to cool before serving.

1 tablespoon vegetable oil
7 ounces (200g) burdock, julienned
1 medium carrot, julienned
2 dried red chilies, seeds removed, and sliced
White sesame seeds, toasted (see page 42), for garnish
Sesame oil for drizzling

FOR THE SEASONING
1 teaspoon dashi stock (see page 40)
1 tablespoon sake
1 teaspoon brown sugar
2 tablespoons mirin
1½ tablespoons soy sauce

Deep-fried Tofu

Age-dashidofu

SERVES *4*

2 blocks silken tofu, about 11 ounces (310g) each
½ cup (80g) potato starch
Vegetable oil for deep-frying

FOR THE SAUCE

½ cup (120ml) dashi (see page 40)
2 teaspoons sake
2 teaspoons mirin
2 tablespoons soy sauce

FOR THE GARNISHES

2 ounces (60g) daikon, peeled and grated
1-inch (2.5-cm) cube fresh ginger, peeled and grated
Toasted nori seaweed (see page 51), cut into strips
Scallions, thinly sliced
Chopped chives
White sesame seeds, toasted (see page 42)

This popular dish with its mild sauce and exotic array of garnishes is often served in an izakaya—the traditional Japanese bar that the salaryman frequents after work for a drink and a quick bite before making the long commute home.

1. Wrap each block of tofu in a thick dish towel and place in a flat dish. Let stand for 30 minutes.
2. Cut each block of tofu in half. Dab each piece in the potato starch, turning to coat evenly. Set aside on a dry dish.
3. Arrange all the garnishes in small bowls and set them on the table.
4. In a small saucepan, combine all the sauce ingredients, and bring to a boil. Turn the heat to medium and simmer for 2 minutes. Remove from heat.
5. Fill one third of the frying pan with the vegetable oil and heat to 350°F (180°C). Put one coated tofu piece in the hot oil and deep-fry until both sides are crisp and golden brown. Repeat with the remaining tofu pieces. Drain on a paper towel.
6. Transfer the tofu pieces to individual bowls. Pour a little sauce around the sides. Garnishes can be added according to individual preferences.

Green Asparagus with Black Sesame Dressing

Asupara no goma-ae

SERVES *4*

7 ounces (200g) fresh green asparagus
1 teaspoon soy sauce
4 tablespoons black sesame seeds
2 teaspoons soy sauce
1 tablespoon sake
1 tablespoon sugar

Green asparagus is smeared with a black sesame dressing to create an aromatic and attractive dish. Traditionally, green beans are used for this dish, but the first time I made it, I used asparagus. My guests loved it and it has since been a regular feature on my Japanese menus.

1. Remove any woody ends from the asparagus and cut into 1½-inch (4-cm) lengths. Immerse in a saucepan of lightly salted boiling water, starting with the harder ends, and cook for three to four minutes, so that the asparagus remains firm. Do not overcook. Drain and set aside, sprinkle with the 1 teaspoon soy sauce, and leave to cool.
2. Toast the sesame seeds (see page 42), and grind to a powder in a food processor. Transfer to a bowl, add the 2 teaspoons soy sauce, the sake, and the sugar and mix until smooth.
3. Add the asparagus to the sauce and gently toss to evenly coat with the dressing. Serve at room temperature.

Grilled Tofu with Mushroom Sauce *Yakidofu*

SERVES *4*

2 blocks firm tofu, about 11 ounces (310g) each
7 ounces (200g) enoki mushrooms
3½ ounces (100g) shimeji mushrooms
3 fresh shiitake mushrooms, stems discarded
4 tablespoons plain flour
1 tablespoon cornstarch
2 teaspoons garlic, grated
1 tablespoon sesame oil
2 teaspoons vegetable oil
1 cup (240ml) dashi stock (see page 40)
3 tablespoons mirin
2 tablespoons soy sauce
1 teaspoon cornstarch mixed with a little water
Finely sliced scallions, for garnish

The different mushrooms impart a distinctive, rich flavor to the sauce, transforming the simple tofu into an exotic and substantial dish that is also healthy and low in calories.

1. Wrap each block of tofu in a thick dish towel and place a weight, such as a dinner plate, on top of it. Allow to stand for 30 minutes. Cut each block of tofu into half to give 4 pieces in all.
2. Cut the enoki into bite-sized pieces. Separate the shimeji mushrooms into clusters. Slice the shiitake thinly. Set to one side.
3. In a small bowl, mix the plain flour and the cornstarch. Dab the tofu pieces in the flour mixture, turning to coat evenly. Smear each piece with a little grated garlic and set aside.
4. In a flat saucepan, heat the sesame oil. Put in the tofu pieces and cook, turning, over medium heat, until both sides are crisp and brown. Remove from the pan and drain on kitchen paper.
5. In a frying pan, heat 2 teaspoons of vegetable oil and briefly sauté the enoki, shimeji, and shiitake over high heat. Put in the dashi, mirin, and soy sauce. Bring the sauce to a boil. Add the cornstarch-and-water mixture and stir until the sauce thickens.
6. Arrange the tofu pieces on individual serving dishes and pour some sauce over each of them. Garnish with the scallions.

Marinated Eggplant and Bell Peppers

Nasu to piman no age-bitashi

SERVES *4*

4 small eggplants
3 green bell peppers
3 shallots
1 medium tomato
Vegetable oil for deep-frying

FOR THE MARINADE
2 teaspoons vegetable oil
1 clove garlic, finely chopped
2 tablespoons rice vinegar
¾ teaspoon salt
1 teaspoon black pepper, freshly ground

Eggplant and green peppers are deep-fried in hot oil and marinated in a vinegar-based sauce. The onions and freshly ground black pepper give a zesty flavor to this colorful dish.

1. Cut the eggplants into quarters and then cut into thin slices. Slice the peppers and shallots thinly. Peel the tomato and cut into bite-sized cubes.
2. In a bowl, mix all the marinade ingredients.
3. Heat the oil for deep-frying to 350°F (180°C) and slide in the eggplant and peppers. Cook for 3–4 minutes until browned. Remove with a slotted spoon and drain on kitchen paper.
4. Place the fried eggplant and peppers in a serving bowl. Scatter the shallots and tomato pieces over them. Pour the marinade sauce over the top and around the sides of the vegetables. Allow to stand for 10 minutes before serving. Can be served at room temperature or chilled.

Scrambled Tofu

Iridofu

SERVES *4*

PHOTOGRAPH ON PAGE 93

1¼ pounds (600g) firm tofu
1 tablespoon vegetable oil
½-inch (1-cm) cube fresh ginger, peeled and grated
1 scallion, sliced
4 fresh shiitake mushroom caps, diced
3 tablespoons bell pepper, any color, diced
3 teaspoons soy sauce
Pinch of chili flakes
Pinch of salt
Chopped chives, for garnish
Kaiware radish spouts, for garnish
Shichimi pepper, to serve

Crisp vegetables and velvety tofu give this low-calorie, high-protein dish an array of textures and flavors. Filling, yet light, this was my son's standard dinner choice during his wrestling season at school. Black pepper can be used instead of chili flakes for a milder flavor. Use silken tofu instead of firm tofu to make it even lighter.

1. Wrap the tofu in a thick dish towel and place a weight, such as a dinner plate, on top of it. Allow to stand for 10 minutes.
2. Heat the oil in a saucepan and sauté the ginger. Put in the scallions, shiitake, and bell pepper and sauté over high heat for 1 minute.
3. Put the tofu in the pan, and mix with a wooden spoon until crumbled. Keep stirring for 2–3 minutes, until excess liquid has been absorbed. Add the soy sauce, chili flakes, and salt.
4. Serve garnished with chives and radish sprouts. Sprinkle with shichimi pepper to taste.

Simmered Daikon with Miso

Furofuki daikon

SERVES *4*

1 pound (450g) daikon radish
2 cups (480ml) dashi stock (see page 40)
1 teaspoon short-grain rice, uncooked
Yuzu zest, slivered, for garnish, optional
White sesame seeds, toasted, for garnish (see page 42), optional

FOR THE MISO SAUCE

4 tablespoons white miso
3 tablespoons sake
2 teaspoons castor sugar
1 tablespoon water

Daikon is available throughout the year in Japan. The summer daikon has a sweet taste, while the winter daikon is spicier. As root vegetables are known to have warming properties, daikon dishes are often made during the winter months.

1. Peel the daikon and cut into 4 slices, each about 1 inch (2.5 cm) thick. Run a peeler around the edges to smoothen. With a knife, score a cross on the flat of each slice to allow the cooking liquid to be absorbed easily.
2. Place the daikon in a flat saucepan, with the scored side down. Pour the dashi over the daikon. Put in the rice grains and bring to a boil. (The rice grains help the daikon cook faster.) Reduce the heat to medium and simmer for 12–15 minutes. Turn the heat to low for another 2–3 minutes, until the daikon is soft. Drain and set aside.
3. In a saucepan, combine the sauce ingredients over low heat and stir until you have a smooth paste. Remove from heat.
4. Arrange the daikon on a serving dish. Spoon 1 tablespoon of miso sauce over the surface of each daikon piece, and spread evenly. Serve while warm, garnished with yuzu and sesame seeds.

Simmered Pumpkin

Kabocha no nimono

SERVES *4*   PHOTOGRAPH ON PAGE 91

14 ounces (400g) pumpkin
2 cups (480ml) dashi stock (see page 40)
2 tablespoons soy sauce
1 tablespoon mirin
1 tablespoon castor sugar
1 tablespoon sake

This cooking method can be used with any root vegetables, such as potato, carrot, burdock, or lotus root. The simmering sauce is oil free, making this dish a light and healthy addition to any meal.

1. Remove the seeds and stringy fibers from the pumpkin, peel, and cut into 1½-inch (4-cm) chunks.
2. Place the pumpkin and the dashi in a saucepan and add the soy sauce, mirin, sugar, and sake. Bring to a boil over medium heat, then turn the heat down and simmer for about 15 minutes, until the pumpkin is almost cooked. Turn the heat to high for 1–2 minutes, stirring gently until the liquid is absorbed. Transfer to a serving dish.

* Simmered vegetables can be kept for a few days in the refrigerator.

Simmered Mixed Vegetables

Onishime

SERVES *4*

7 ounces (200g) lotus root
1 medium carrot
7 ounces (200g) taro
3½ ounces (100g) burdock
7 ounces (200g) bamboo shoots
8 fresh shiitake mushrooms, stems discarded
A few snow peas, for garnish

FOR THE SIMMERING STOCK
4 cups (960ml) dashi stock (see page 40)
¼ cup (60ml) sake
2 tablespoons castor sugar
⅓ cup (80ml) soy sauce
Pinch of salt
1 tablespoon mirin

This is a traditional New Year's dish prepared in advance on New Year's Eve to share with visiting family members as the first meal of the New Year. Traditionally, enough simmered vegetables are made to last for a few days, so that those responsible for cooking can also relax and enjoy the holiday season. Simmered vegetables are festively presented in a square, layered lacquer box along with seasoned konbu seaweed, chestnuts, sweet black beans, scattered sushi, and pickled vegetables.

1. Peel the lotus root, carrot, and taro and slice into diagonal chunks. Cut the burdock and bamboo shoots into diagonal chunks. With a knife, score a cross on each shiitake cap. Trim the snow peas and lightly boil. Drain and set aside.
2. Put the simmering stock ingredients in a saucepan. Add the lotus root, carrot, taro, bamboo shoot, and shiitake and bring to a boil. Cover and cook over medium heat for 10–15 minutes. Then turn the heat to high and cook for 5 more minutes, until the liquid is almost absorbed. Transfer the vegetables to a serving dish and garnish with the snow peas.

Stir-fried Eggplant and Green Peppers

Nasu no nabe-shigi

SERVES *4*

3 small eggplants
3 green bell peppers
2 tablespoons sesame oil
½-inch (1-cm) cube fresh ginger, peeled and grated
1 clove garlic, grated
2 tablespoons hatcho miso
Shichimi pepper

FOR THE SIMMERING STOCK
¾ cup (180ml) dashi stock (see page 40)
2 teaspoons sake
1 tablespoon sugar
2 tablespoons mirin
2 teaspoons soy sauce

Nabe-shigi is a type of dish where vegetables are stir-fried and glazed with miso. The combination of sesame oil and miso is particularly tasty. In this recipe I use hatcho miso, the dark, strong miso that is a specialty of the central Japanese city of Nagoya.

1. Trim the ends of the eggplants, cut in half lengthwise, and then cut into 2-inch (5-cm) long julienne strips. Leave to soak in water until ready to cook. Slice the bell peppers thinly.
2. Heat the sesame oil in a saucepan and briefly sauté the ginger and garlic until fragrant. Put the eggplant in the pan and stir-fry over medium heat for 2–3 minutes. Put in the peppers and stir-fry briefly with the eggplant until they are glazed with oil.
3. In a bowl, combine the simmering stock ingredients, then pour into the pan with the vegetables. Cook over medium heat for 3–4 minutes until the liquid reduces. Tip the pan so that the liquid collects at the base. Add the miso to the liquid and stir to mix with the vegetables. Turn off the heat, transfer the mixture to a serving bowl and sprinkle with shichimi pepper.

Stir-fried Lotus Root

Renkon kimpira

SERVES *4*

PHOTOGRAPH ON PAGE 91

11 ounces (310g) lotus root
1 tablespoon vegetable oil
1 dried red chili, finely sliced
2 tablespoons mirin
1 tablespoon sake
1 teaspoon castor sugar
2 tablespoons soy sauce
2 tablespoons dashi stock (see page 40)
1 teaspoon sesame oil
1 teaspoon white sesame seeds, toasted (see page 42)

Root vegetables cooked "kimpira" style are stir-fried in hot oil to which chili has been added. Kimpira style vegetables can be made in large quantities as they will keep for a couple of days. Lotus root is my favorite for this dish, because of its crunchy texture and flower-like appearance.

1. Scrape off the outer skin of the lotus root and slice into thin rounds. Lotus root discolors quickly, so immediately place in water to which 1 teaspoon of rice vinegar has been added until ready to use.
2. Heat the vegetable oil in a broad saucepan and stir-fry the lotus root quickly over high heat for 1 minute until glazed with oil. Put in the chili and mix.
3. Lower the heat and gradually add the mirin, sake, sugar, soy sauce, and dashi. Cover and cook over medium heat for 2 minutes. Turn the heat to low, remove the lid, and stir-fry until most of the liquid is absorbed. Drizzle the lotus root with the sesame oil and sprinkle with the sesame seeds. Remove from the heat, and transfer to a serving dish. Allow to cool before serving.

DESSERTS

Green Tea Ice Cream

Matcha aisukurimu

SERVES *4*

2 cups (480ml) soy milk
3 teaspoons matcha powdered green tea
1 cup (240ml) maple syrup
¼ cup (50g) castor sugar
A few drops vanilla essence
11 ounces (310g) silken tofu
2 teaspoons vegetable oil

This ice cream is made with matcha, the powdered form of green tea used in the tea ceremony. The blend of this traditional ingredient with ice cream—a Western import—makes this a perfect example of Japanese fusion cooking.

1. Put the soy milk in a saucepan and bring to a boil. Lower the heat to medium and put in the green tea powder, maple syrup, castor sugar, and vanilla essence. Stir to mix, then simmer for 3–4 minutes. Add the vanilla essence and turn off the heat.
2. Bring a pan of water to the boil. Immerse the tofu in the boiling water, turn the heat to medium, and simmer for 2 minutes. Drain and cool completely. Using a food processor, blend the tofu with the vegetable oil and the soy milk mixture until smooth.
3. Transfer the mixture to a bowl, cover, and refrigerate until cold. Blend once again in a food processor and place in a freezer tray. Freeze for two hours, then mix again. Repeat this process once more to ensure the finished ice cream has a smooth texture.

Tofu Shake with Blueberries and Banana

Buruberi to banana no tofu sheku

SERVES *4*

11 ounces (310g) silken tofu
1 banana
½ cup (75g) fresh blueberries
1 cup (240ml) soy milk
2 tablespoons castor sugar or maple syrup
A few drops of vanilla essence, optional
1 cup crushed ice

A protein-packed drink that will sustain you for several hours. When I know I have a busy day ahead, I like to have this nutritious and healthy shake for breakfast. Fresh strawberries and peaches make a colorful variation.

1. Wash the tofu under running water and drain. Peel and cut the banana into thick slices. Wash and drain the blueberries.
2. Blend all the ingredients in a food processor until smooth. Transfer to individual glasses and serve chilled.

China

When I was a child growing up in India, Chinese cuisine was the only popular foreign cuisine, and we would look forward with great anticipation to our occasional Sunday outings to the local Chinese restaurant. It was our only chance to "visit" a foreign land. Everything from the noodles to the revolving table and the tiny, handle-less tea cups was an object of curiosity and wonder. Today, I find myself wondering what the world would be like without Chinese food. What would we do without the wok, for example, or the endless ways to cook noodles?

My own children's love of Chinese noodles knows no limits. I often made stir fried noodles or soupy noodles with vegetables for them as an afternoon snack when they were young, and though both would have the exact same amount in their bowl, their eyes would always check to make sure they hadn't been short-changed.

A Chinese dinner at home was never complete without at least a few of our usual favorites. Spring rolls and sweet corn soup, perhaps, for a perfect start. Ma Po Dou Fu, silky tofu cubes swimming in the hot sauce, might follow, adding a touch of spice. Quickly tossed fried rice always makes the Chinese experience complete.

With my children around, leftovers were never an issue. They made their way into school lunch boxes the next day, which were often shared with friends. In fact, on some occasions, the teachers passing them in the school cafeteria at lunch time even offered to trade lunch boxes!

SOUPS AND SALADS

Crispy Noodle Salad

Zha mian qing cai sha la

SERVES *4*

PHOTOGRAPH ON PAGE 98

This refreshing, crunchy salad is my top choice when I have lunch at the Tokyo American Club. The vibrant colors of the vegetables make it a great addition to any buffet, and I often include it on my dinner party menu.

1. In a serving dish, combine the lettuce, cabbage, tomatoes, cucumber, bell pepper, and coriander.
2. In a separate bowl, combine the dressing ingredients.
3. Sprinkle the cashews over the vegetables. Break up the fried noodles and add to the vegetables. Pour the dressing over the salad and toss to mix. Serve immediately.

3 cups (60g) lettuce leaves, shredded
1 cup (45g) red cabbage, shredded
Handful cherry tomatoes, halved
1 cucumber, thinly sliced diagonally
A few slivers of red, orange, and green bell pepper
2 tablespoons fresh coriander leaves, chopped
10 dry-roasted cashews, broken
5 ounces (140g) thin wheat flour noodles, deep-fried

FOR THE SESAME DRESSING

2 tablespoons sesame oil
2 teaspoons vegetable oil
1 tablespoon white sesame seeds, ground
1 teaspoon white sesame seeds, toasted (see page 42)
1 tablespoon soy sauce
1 teaspoon castor sugar
1 teaspoon rice vinegar
1/4 teaspoon ground black pepper
1/4 teaspoon salt

Fried Vegetable Salad

Zha cai sa lui

Serves *4*

In Chinese cooking, I find it particularly exciting to combine cooking styles and seasonings to create exotic dishes. This spicy salad is sure to be one of your favorites.

1. Peel and thinly slice the lotus root. Soak in water with 1 teaspoon vinegar added to it. Drain and dry before use.
2. In a serving bowl, mix the arugula and lettuce and set aside.
3. In a small bowl, combine all the dressing ingredients.
4. In a deep bowl, combine the flour with the water, salt, and baking powder. Put in the lotus root, carrot, and shiitake and mix.
5. In a wok, heat the oil for deep-frying to 350°F (180°C). Slide in the battered vegetables, a few at a time, and deep-fry until crisp. Drain on kitchen paper and allow to cool.
6. Make a bed of arugula and lettuce on a serving plate, arrange the vegetables on top, pour over the dressing, and serve.

2 ounces (60g) lotus root
2 cups (40g) arugula
2 cups (40g) lettuce, shredded
1 cup (125g) all-purpose flour
3/4 cup (180ml) water
1/4 teaspoon salt
Pinch of baking powder
1 carrot, julienned
4 fresh shiitake mushroom caps, thinly sliced
Vegetable oil for deep-frying

FOR THE DRESSING

2 tablespoons sesame oil
1 teaspoon Chili Oil (see opposite)
2 tablespoons wine vinegar
2 tablespoons balsamic vinegar
1/2 teaspoon salt
1/2 teaspoon ground black pepper

Chili Oil
Gan shao zhi

MAKES ¾ *cup (180ml)*

¾ cup (180ml) peanut oil
7 dried red chilies
1 tablespoon Szechuan peppercorns

Heat the oil in a saucepan and add the chilies and peppercorns. Simmer over low heat for 3–4 minutes. Remove from the heat, allow to cool, then strain. Discard the chilies and peppercorns and store the chili oil in an airtight jar. Keeps for 1 month.

Sour and Spicy Soup

Shuan la tang

SERVES *4*

1 tablespoon sesame oil
1 teaspoon fresh minced ginger
3½ ounces (100g) atsuage deep-fried tofu, thinly sliced
3 fresh shiitake mushroom caps, thinly sliced
2 ounces (60g) bamboo shoots, sliced
½ carrot, cut into 4 diagonal slices
1 medium tomato, cut into wedges
2 wood ear mushrooms, reconstituted and chopped
1 tablespoon Chinese red chili paste
3 tablespoons rice vinegar
3 tablespoons soy sauce
½ teaspoon salt
¼ teaspoon ground black pepper
4 cups (960ml) Clear Vegetable Stock (see below)
1 teaspoon cornstarch mixed with 2 tablespoons water
Fresh coriander leaves, for garnish

A Chinese version of the famous Thai tom yum soup, using vinegar instead of tamarind. This quick and satisfying soup includes tofu and vegetables, making it hearty enough for a light meal.

1. Heat the oil in a saucepan and sauté the ginger for 10 seconds over medium heat.
2. Add the tofu, shiitake, bamboo shoots, carrot, tomato, and wood ear mushrooms. Turn the heat to high and stir-fry for 2–3 minutes.
3. Add the chili paste, vinegar, soy sauce, salt, and pepper. Stir to mix.
4. Add the vegetable stock and bring to a boil. Simmer for 3–4 minutes over medium heat.
5. Add the cornstarch-and-water mixture and stir continuously until well blended into the soup. Simmer for another 2–3 minutes.
6. Remove from the heat and divide between individual bowls. Garnish with fresh coriander and serve hot.

Clear Vegetable Stock
Su cai zhi

MAKES *6 cups (1.5 L)*

7 cups (1.8 L) water
2 cups (90g) white cabbage, roughly chopped
2 carrots, roughly chopped
1 cup scallions, with green part
8–10 black peppercorns, crushed
2 coriander roots
2 stalks celery
3–4 cauliflower florets

Place all the ingredients in a large saucepan and boil over medium heat for 15–20 minutes until the vegetables are completely cooked. Strain the stock and use as required. Will keep for about a week in an airtight container in the refrigerator.

Sweet and Sour Cucumber

Jian huang gua

SERVES *4*

This delightfully sweet and sour pickled cucumber was often on the menu in restaurants in Beijing when my family was there on holiday, and it quickly became a favorite of ours. The hint of chili and the aroma of sesame oil make it an instant hit.

1. Peel a few strips of skin lengthwise from the cucumber. This gives a pretty striped effect.
2. Quarter the cucumber lengthwise, then slice into 1-inch (2.5-cm) long pieces. Place the pieces in a bowl, sprinkle with salt, and let sit for 30 minutes.
3. Wash the cucumber well to remove the salt. Drain and pat dry with paper towels. Place the cucumber in a serving bowl.
4. Mix the sugar syrup with the vinegar and pour over the cucumber. Leave to marinate for 15 minutes, then stir in the coriander leaves and sesame oil.
5. Sprinkle with the red chili and garnish with strips of red and yellow pepper.

2 cucumbers
1 teaspoon salt
2 teaspoons sugar syrup *
2 tablespoons rice vinegar
3 tablespoons fresh coriander leaves, chopped
2 teaspoons sesame oil
1 dried red chili, chopped
Slices of red and yellow bell pepper, for garnish

* For a simple sugar syrup, dissolve ¼ cup (50g) sugar in ½ cup (120ml) water and bring to a boil. Cool before using.

Vegetable Sweet Corn Soup

Li mi tang

SERVES *4*

This soup brings back memories of my childhood in India, when eating out at the local Chinese restaurant was a great treat. This dish is always part of the menu when I make Chinese food for my family.

1. Heat the oil and sauté the garlic for 3 seconds, taking care not to let the garlic burn. Put in the green beans, mushrooms, carrot, and cauliflower and stir-fry over high heat for 1 minute, until all the vegetables are glazed.
2. Put in the creamed corn and sweet corn kernels and stir to mix, then add the vegetable stock and bring to a boil. Add the vinegar, soy sauce, salt, sugar, and pepper.
3. Put in the cornstarch-and-stock mixture and keep stirring continuously to avoid lumps.
4. Simmer for 4–5 minutes. Garnish with coriander leaves. Serve hot with Green Chilies in Vinegar.

2 teaspoons sesame oil
2 cloves garlic, chopped
10–12 green beans, finely chopped
3 button mushrooms, thinly sliced
¼ carrot finely chopped
2 cauliflower florets, finely chopped
1½ cups (350ml) creamed corn
2 tablespoons sweet corn kernels
4 cups (960ml) Clear Vegetable Stock (see page 67)
1½ tablespoons rice vinegar
3 teaspoons soy sauce
Salt to taste
½ teaspoon castor sugar
½ teaspoon ground white pepper,
2 tablespoons cornstarch, mixed with ¼ cup (60ml) Clear Vegetable Stock
Fresh coriander leaves, for garnish
Green Chilies in Vinegar, to serve (see below)

Green Chilies in Vinegar   *La cu*   Makes *¾ cup (180ml)*

6–7 fresh hot green chilies, chopped   ¾ cup (180ml) rice vinegar

In a bowl, combine the chilies with the vinegar. Allow to stand for at least 10 minutes before using. Store in an airtight jar in the refrigerator. Will keep for about a month.

MAIN DISHES

Eggplant in Chili Garlic Sauce

Ma po qie zi

SERVES *4*

6 small eggplants
Vegetable oil for deep-frying
1 tablespoon vegetable oil
1 teaspoon Chinese red chili paste
2 cloves garlic, finely chopped
½ cup (225g) minced soybean gluten
½ small scallion, finely chopped
1 medium tomato, chopped
1 tablespoon white miso
1 tablespoon sake
2 tablespoons soy sauce
½ teaspoon salt
1 teaspoon castor sugar
4 tablespoons water
2 teaspoons cornstarch mixed with 4 teaspoons water
Fresh coriander leaves, for garnish

This is one of the most popular eggplant preparations in Chinese restaurants in Tokyo. Plain white rice is the ideal complement for this dish, as it immediately absorbs the spicy miso sauce.

1. Cut the eggplants into bite-sized pieces. In a wok, heat the oil for deep frying to 350°F (180°C). Deep-fry the eggplant until golden brown and drain on kitchen paper.

2. In a saucepan, heat the 1 tablespoon vegetable oil and sauté the chili paste, garlic, soybean gluten, and scallions for 1–2 minutes until fragrant. Add the deep-fried eggplant and the tomato and mix.

3. In a small bowl, combine the miso, sake, soy sauce, salt, sugar, and water, and put in the saucepan with the eggplant mixture. Bring to a simmer over medium heat.

4. Add the cornstarch and water mixture and stir until the sauce thickens. Transfer to a serving dish and garnish with coriander leaves.

Eggplant with Ginger and Garlic

Wi xiang qie zi

SERVES *4*

Vegetable oil for deep-frying
5 small eggplants, cut into bite-sized pieces
½ teaspoon salt
½ teaspoon ground black pepper
2 tablespoons sesame oil
3-inch (8-cm) cube fresh ginger, peeled and finely chopped
4 cloves garlic, finely chopped
1 onion, finely chopped
1 scallion, thinly sliced
1 fresh red chili, finely chopped
1 fresh hot green chili, finely chopped
1 tablespoon sake
3 tablespoons soy sauce
1 teaspoon castor sugar
4 tablespoons Konbu Dashi (see page 40)
2 teaspoons sesame oil

This dish was created by the chef of the Grand Hyatt in Tokyo. The eggplant beautifully absorbs the flavors of the garlic sauce.

1. Heat the oil for deep-frying to 350°F (180°C). Deep-fry the eggplant, in small batches, until crisp and golden brown. Drain on kitchen paper. Transfer to a dish and sprinkle with the salt and pepper.

2. Heat 2 tablespoons sesame oil in a saucepan, sauté the ginger and garlic for 30 seconds, then add the onion and scallions. Stir for 2–3 minutes, then mix in the chilies. Add the deep-fried eggplant, sake, soy sauce, sugar, and dashi. Mix until the eggplant is heated through, drizzle with the 2 teaspoons sesame oil, and remove from the heat. Serve hot.

Gyoza

Guo the jiao zi

PHOTOGRAPH ON PAGE 96

1 tablespoon sesame oil
1 tablespoon vegetable oil
2 cloves garlic, finely chopped
½-inch (1-cm) cube fresh ginger, peeled and grated
3 fresh shiitake mushroom caps, finely chopped
1 cup (45g) Chinese cabbage, shredded
3 tablespoons chives, finely chopped
1 scallion, finely chopped
3½ ounces (100g) firm tofu, crumbled
1 tablespoon soy sauce
½ teaspoon salt
1 teaspoon cornstarch
30 round wonton wrappers
2 teaspoons sesame oil
¼ cup (60ml) water
Chives, for garnish
Spicy Soy Vinegar Sauce (see below), to serve

Gyoza are little rounds or squares of noodle dough encasing a savory filling. They may be deep-fried, steamed, or braised. Serve with a bowl of steamed rice for a satisfying meal.

1. In a saucepan, heat the 1 tablespoon sesame oil and 1 tablespoon vegetable oil and sauté the garlic and ginger for 1 minute over medium heat.
2. Add the shiitake, cabbage, chives, scallions, and tofu. Turn the heat to high and stir-fry for 2–3 minutes. Add the soy sauce and the salt and continue to stir over high heat for a further 2–3 minutes until the excess liquid has been absorbed. Sprinkle in the cornstarch and mix quickly. Transfer to a dish to cool.
3. Put a teaspoon of the vegetable mixture in the center of each wonton wrapper and moisten the edges of the wrapper with water. Fold to make a moon shape, making a few pleats to seal. (See photograph on page 96.)
4. Heat the 2 teaspoons sesame oil in a saucepan, then put in 10–12 gyoza. Cook both sides for 2–3 minutes over medium heat until well browned. Pour ¼ cup water over the wontons and cook covered for 2–3 minutes until the liquid has been absorbed. If necessary, remove the lid and shake the pan until all excess liquid has been absorbed. Transfer to a dish, garnish with chives, and serve with Spicy Soy Vinegar Sauce.

Spicy Soy Vinegar Sauce

Shuan la jiang you zhi   MAKES *½ cup (120ml)*

1 tablespoon chili oil (see page 67)
4 tablespoons soy sauce
4 tablespoons rice vinegar
3 tablespoons water
½ teaspoon karashi mustard paste

Combine all the ingredients in a small bowl. This is a great dipping sauce for Gyoza (see above) and other appetizers. Keeps for about a week refrigerated in an airtight jar.

Kung Pao Tofu

Gong bao dou fu

SERVES *4*

4 tablespoons vegetable oil
8 whole dried red chilies, soaked in water for 10
  minutes
7 ounces (200g) atsuage deep-fried tofu, diced
1 yellow bell pepper, diced
1 red bell pepper, diced
1 green bell pepper, diced
1 zucchini, sliced into thin rounds
2 wood ear mushrooms, reconstituted and chopped
2 scallions, cut into 1-inch (3-cm) pieces
½-inch (1-cm) cube fresh ginger, peeled and minced
3 tablespoons sweet soy sauce
3 tablespoons soy sauce
2 tablespoons Chinese red chili paste
2 tablespoons white miso
2 tablespoons sake
¾ cup (115g) cashew nuts, roasted
1 teaspoon sesame oil for drizzling
Fresh coriander leaves, for garnish

This attractive and tasty dish, with its Szechuan style flavoring and colorful vegetables, is one of our family favorites at the Tokyo American Club.

1. In a wok, heat the oil and stir-fry the chilies and tofu for 1–2 minutes over medium heat, until the color of the chilies deepens. Remove with a slotted spoon and set aside.
2. Put the bell peppers, zucchini, mushrooms, scallions, and ginger into the same oil. Stir-fry over high heat for 2–3 minutes.
3. In a bowl, combine the sweet soy sauce, soy sauce, chili paste, miso, and sake and pour into the wok over the vegetables. Stir in the tofu and chilies and cook for 2–3 minutes over medium heat.
4. Sprinkle the cashew nuts and drizzle the sesame oil into the wok. Remove from heat, garnish with coriander leaves, and serve.

Lettuce Wrap with Spicy Lotus Root

Zha lian gen

SERVES *4*

PHOTOGRAPH ON PAGE 99

8–10 lettuce leaves
9 ounces (255g) lotus root
1 tablespoon sesame oil
1 inch (3-cm) cube fresh ginger, peeled and finely
  chopped
1 carrot, julienned
1 tablespoon Chinese red chili paste
1 tablespoon soy sauce
2 tablespoons fresh coriander leaves, chopped
Plum sauce, to serve

I first tasted this delectable dish at the Chinese restaurant Good Earth in London. My friend confidently told me that I would love it, well aware of the Indian fondness for crunchy and spicy food. Ever since, this has been a dish that I have loved to make at home in Tokyo.

1. Halve the lettuce leaves and soak in iced water for 15–20 minutes. Drain and set aside. Peel and thinly slice the lotus root. Soak in water to which 2 teaspoons vinegar has been added. Drain and dry when ready to use.
2. In a saucepan, heat the oil and sauté the ginger briefly over medium heat. Add the lotus root and carrot and stir-fry for 2–3 minutes.
3. Add the chili paste and soy sauce and stir to mix. Cover and cook for 1 minute.
4. Remove from the heat and allow to cool. Place the lotus root mixture in the center of a large serving dish and garnish with coriander. Arrange the lettuce leaves around the edge of the dish. To eat, place a spoonful of the lotus root mixture into a lettuce leaf and fold to make a wrap. Dip into the plum sauce and enjoy!

Spicy Fried Vegetables

Chin jao ro su

SERVES *4*

Vegetables used in Chinese cuisine are always selected with harmony of color and texture in mind. Julienned vegetables are an attractive feature of this dish.

1. Heat the oil in a saucepan and sauté the garlic, ginger, and leek for 2–3 minutes over medium heat. Stir in the chili paste.
2. Add the carrot, peppers, celery, bamboo shoots, and the soybean gluten. Add 1 tablespoon water and cook covered for 2 minutes. Stir to mix. Turn the heat to low.
3. In a bowl, combine the soy sauce, miso, sake, sugar, and salt. Pour over the vegetables in the pan, turn the heat to medium and stir quickly. Add the cornstarch-and-water mixture, turn the heat to high, and stir briefly. Remove from the heat, and serve immediately.

3 tablespoons peanut oil
2 cloves garlic, finely chopped
1-inch (3-cm) cube fresh ginger, peeled and finely chopped
1 leek, finely chopped
1 tablespoon Chinese red chili paste
1 carrot, julienned
1 green bell pepper, julienned
1 red pepper, julienned
1 stick celery, julienned
3½ ounces (100g) bamboo shoots, julienned
7 ounces (200g) soybean gluten, cut into strips
1 tablespoon water
2 tablespoons soy sauce
1 tablespoon black Chinese miso
2 tablespoons sake
2 teaspoons castor sugar
½ teaspoon salt
1 teaspoon cornstarch mixed with 2 tablespoons water

Spicy Tofu

Ma po dou fu

SERVES *4*   PHOTOGRAPH ON PAGE 99

Spicy tofu is one of my children's all-time favorites. Their friends are always shocked that a vegetarian dish can taste so good!

1. Wrap the tofu in a dish towel to remove excess moisture, then dice.
2. Heat the oil in a saucepan and sauté the garlic and ginger for 2–3 minutes until fragrant. Stir in the chili paste.
3. Add the shiitake, scallions, and eggplant and sauté briefly over high heat. Add the soybean gluten and stir until it is heated through.
4. In a bowl, combine the miso, sake, soy sauce, and sugar and put into the saucepan with the eggplant mixture. Stir briefly, then put in the tofu and the water.
5. Stir in the cornstarch-and-water mixture and simmer for 2–3 minutes over high heat until the sauce thickens.
6. Transfer to a dish and garnish with the chives. Serve with steamed white rice.

7 ounces (200g) firm tofu
2 tablespoons sesame oil
2 cloves garlic, minced
½-inch (1-cm) cube fresh ginger, peeled and minced
2 teaspoons Chinese red chili paste
2 fresh shiitake mushroom caps, finely chopped
½ scallion, finely chopped
1 small eggplant, minced
2 tablespoons soybean gluten, minced
1 tablespoon white miso
1 tablespoon sake
2 tablespoons soy sauce
1 teaspoon castor sugar
¼ cup (60ml) water
1 teaspoon cornstarch mixed with 3 teaspoons water
2 tablespoons chopped chives, for garnish

Sweet and Sour Vegetables

Tang tsu tiao

SERVES 4

1 tablespoon Chinese red chili paste

4 tablespoons soy sauce

½ cup (120ml) tomato ketchup

2 teaspoons castor sugar

½ teaspoon salt

1 tablespoon rice vinegar

1 cup (240ml) water

2 teaspoons cornstarch mixed with 4 tablespoons water

2 tablespoons sesame oil

½-inch (1-cm) cube fresh ginger, peeled and finely chopped

5 baby corn ears, cut into ¾-in (2-cm) pieces

1 red bell pepper, diced

1 green bell pepper, diced

2 ounces (60g) cooked bamboo shoots, sliced

4 water chestnuts, sliced

½ carrot, sliced

2 slices canned pineapple, cut into chunks

7 ounces (200g) atsuage deep fried tofu, diced

This dish, with its alluring colors and contrasting textures, has been a favorite of mine ever since I was a child. It was often on the menu when my family and I visited our local Chinese restaurant.

1. In a saucepan, combine the chili paste, soy sauce, ketchup, sugar, salt, and vinegar with the water. Bring to a boil, then turn the heat to medium and simmer for 3–4 minutes. Add the cornstarch-and-water mixture, stirring until the sauce thickens. Remove from the heat and set aside.
2. Heat the sesame oil in a saucepan and sauté the ginger for 1 minute over medium heat. Add the baby corn, peppers, bamboo shoots, chestnuts, carrot, and pineapple and sauté over high heat for 2–3 minutes. Add the tofu and stir to mix.
3. Reheat the sauce and pour over the vegetable and tofu mixture. Serve with steamed rice.

Szechuan Asparagus, Baby Corn, Water Chestnuts, and Eggplant

Si chun lu shun

SERVES 4

Vegetable oil for deep-frying

7 ounces (200g) fresh green asparagus, cut into 1-inch (3-cm) pieces, hard ends discarded

4 baby corn ears, cut into 1-inch (3-cm) pieces

8 water chestnuts, quartered

4 small eggplants, cut into 1-inch (3-cm) pieces

1 tablespoon vegetable oil

1-inch (3-cm) cube fresh ginger, peeled and finely chopped

1 fresh hot green chili, finely chopped

½ scallion, finely chopped

1 tablespoon Chinese red chili paste

1 tablespoon Chili Oil (see page 67)

½ teaspoon konbu powder or 3 tablespoons Konbu Dashi (see page 40)

½ teaspoon ground black pepper

½ teaspoon castor sugar

2 teaspoons rice vinegar

2 tablespoons soy sauce

1 teaspoon cornstarch mixed with 3 tablespoons water

Fresh coriander leaves, for garnish

Ever wonder why Chinese food is always so shiny and glistening? I learned the secret when I was invited into the kitchen of a vegetarian Chinese restaurant in a bustling shopping mall in Tachikawa, in western Tokyo, where Chef Chin revealed the secret to me — oil blanching. He threw the vegetables into a wok of hot oil, deep-fried them quickly until crisp, then lifted the entire wok and poured the oil down the strainer. In the same wok he proceeded to stir-fry the oil-blanched vegetables with all the seasoning ingredients. The entire process took less than ten minutes.

1. In a wok, heat the oil for deep-frying to 350°F (180°C). Deep-fry the asparagus, corn, chestnuts, and eggplant for 3–4 minutes until crisp. Drain and set aside.
2. Heat the 1 tablespoon vegetable oil in a saucepan and sauté the ginger, chili, and scallions.
3. Add the chili paste, Chili Oil, konbu powder, pepper, sugar, vinegar, and soy sauce, turn the heat to high, and stir briskly for 1–2 minutes.
4. Add the cornstarch-and-water mixture and heat through. Transfer to a serving dish, and garnish with coriander.

73

Vegetable Manchurian

Su cai chu

SERVES *4*

This recipe reminds me of my parents' dinner parties years ago, when my mother would cook exotic dishes with help from a chef. Even though the main cuisine was Indian, it was considered trendy to include a Western-style dish, such as pasta, and a Chinese dish. The Manchurian was part of all such dinner parties. The Manchurian balls can be served on their own as a tasty starter or transformed into a main dish with a rich sauce such as this one.

1. In a deep bowl, combine all the Manchurian ball ingredients, except the oil. Shape into walnut-sized balls and set aside.
2. Heat the oil for deep-frying to 350°F (180°C). Deep-fry the balls, a few at a time, until golden brown. Drain on kitchen paper and set aside.
3. To make the sauce, heat the oil in a saucepan, add the garlic, chilies, ginger, and scallions, and sauté for 10 seconds over medium heat.
4. Add the stock, soy sauce, sugar, salt, and the cornstarch-and-water mixture. Simmer for 3–4 minutes over medium heat until the sauce thickens. Remove from the heat and set aside until ready to serve.
5. Before serving, put the Manchurian balls in the pan with the sauce and bring to a boil. Remove from the heat, transfer to a serving bowl, and serve garnished with coriander leaves.

FOR THE MANCHURIAN BALLS

- 1 cup (100g) grated cauliflower
- 2 cups (90g) white cabbage, shredded
- 2 medium carrots, grated
- 1 scallion, finely chopped
- 1 cup (125g) all-purpose flour
- 1 tablespoon Ginger Garlic Paste (see page 18)
- 2 fresh green chilies, finely chopped
- 1 cup (20g) fresh coriander with stems, chopped
- ½ teaspoon black pepper
- ½ teaspoon salt
- Vegetable oil for deep-frying

FOR THE SAUCE

- 1 teaspoon sesame oil
- 1 tablespoon garlic, finely chopped
- 3 fresh hot green chilies, finely chopped
- 1½-inch (4-cm) cube fresh ginger, peeled and finely chopped
- 1 scallion, white part only, sliced
- 1 cup (240ml) Clear Vegetable Stock (see page 67)
- 2 tablespoons soy sauce
- ½ teaspoon castor sugar
- ½ teaspoon salt
- 1 tablespoon cornstarch mixed with 3 tablespoons water
- Fresh coriander leaves, for garnish

RICE AND NOODLES

Aromatic Vegetable Fried Rice *Su cai chao fan*

SERVES *4*

1 tablespoon peanut oil
1 clove garlic, finely chopped
3 cups (470g) cooked long-grain rice
½ teaspoon salt
2 tablespoons sesame oil
1 tablespoon peanut oil
2 cloves garlic, grated
½-inch (1-cm) cube fresh ginger, peeled and grated
2 stalks celery, cut into thin diagonal slices
3½ ounces (100g) green beans, cut into thin diagonal slices
1 carrot, grated
1 cup (100g) bean sprouts
5 ounces (140g) bamboo shoots, sliced
2 scallions, white part only, finely chopped
1 green bell pepper, sliced
¼ cup (60ml) Clear Vegetable Stock (see page 67)
2 tablespoons soy sauce
½ teaspoon salt
1 tablespoon fresh coriander leaves, for garnish

The secret of great fried rice, explained Chef Chin at the Kenpuku Chinese restaurant in Tachikawa, near Tokyo, is to first toss the cooked rice in peanut oil, and then mix in the seasoned vegetables.

1. Heat 1 tablespoon peanut oil in a saucepan and sauté the garlic for 10 seconds. Add the cooked rice and salt and toss to mix. Heat through, remove from the heat, and set aside.
2. In a separate saucepan, heat the 2 tablespoons sesame oil and 1 tablespoon peanut oil and sauté the garlic and ginger for 15 seconds over medium heat.
3. Add the celery, green beans, and carrot and stir-fry over high heat for 2–3 minutes. Add the bean sprouts and bamboo shoots and stir for 1 minute.
4. Stir in the rice, scallions, and green pepper and toss to mix. Stir-fry for 1 minute.
5. Add the vegetable stock, soy sauce, and salt. Continue to stir over high heat for 1–2 minutes, until the stock is absorbed. Garnish with coriander leaves and serve.

Noodles in Sesame Sauce *Dan dan mian*

SERVES *4*

14 ounces (400g) udon noodles, cooked
2 cucumbers, julienned

FOR THE SAUCE
8 tablespoons white sesame paste
2 tablespoons soy sauce
1 teaspoon salt
2 tablespoons rice vinegar
4 tablespoons sake
4 tablespoons water
½ teaspoon ground black pepper
1 tablespoon sesame oil

One of Beijing's most popular noodle dishes. The mild flavor of sesame makes this a favorite across all age groups.

1. In a bowl, combine all the sauce ingredients. Mix until smooth and set aside.
2. Immerse the udon noodles in 6 cups boiling water for 2–3 minutes to refresh. Drain and divide between individual bowls.
3. Dress each bowl of noodles with cucumber and a heaping tablespoon of sesame sauce. Mix well before eating.

Shanghai-style Chow Mein

Shanghai chao mian

SERVES *4*   PHOTOGRAPH ON PAGE 97

Known as hakka noodles in India, where Chinese cuisine is relished. As a child I remember sometimes going to the chop suey restaurant with my family on Sunday afternoons. Sweet corn soup, spring rolls, fried rice, hakka noodles, Manchurian Balls, and sweet and sour vegetables were always a part of our order. Amid laughter and chatter, everything was washed down with chilled Gold Coin apple juice.

1. Heat the oil in a saucepan and sauté the garlic, chilies, and onion over high heat for 1 minute.
2. Add the carrot, shiitake, cabbage, green pepper, and bean sprouts and stir-fry, with the heat still on high, for 2–3 minutes.
3. Add the soy sauce, vinegar, sugar, pepper, and salt.
4. Stir in the noodles and heat through. Serve garnished with chives.

2 tablespoons sesame oil
2 cloves garlic, finely chopped
2 dried red chilies
1 onion, finely sliced
1 carrot, sliced diagonally
2 fresh shiitake mushroom caps, sliced
2 cups (90g) white cabbage, cut into 1-inch (3-cm) pieces
1 green bell pepper, sliced
1 cup (100g) bean sprouts
1 tablespoon soy sauce
½ teaspoon rice vinegar
½ teaspoon castor sugar
¼ teaspoon black pepper
½ teaspoon salt
14 ounces (400g) wheat flour noodles, cooked
Chopped chives, for garnish

Spicy Noodles

Shuan la tang mian

SERVES *4*

This style of dish was traditionally sold by hawkers who went around the narrow streets of Szechuan villages on foot, carrying with them everything required to put together these spicy noodles.

1. Heat the oil in a saucepan and sauté the ginger for 10 seconds over medium heat. Add the soybean gluten and stir briefly. Add the 1½ tablespoons soy sauce and the sake.
2. In a bowl, mix the Chili Oil, ground sesame seeds, and 3 tablespoons soy sauce to make a sauce.
3. Immerse the udon noodles in 6 cups boiling water for 2–3 minutes to refresh. Drain and divide into individual bowls.
4. Spoon a heaping tablespoon of the sautéed soybean gluten mixture into each bowl of noodles, and sprinkle with a tablespoon of scallions and a heaping tablespoon of the chili sauce mixture. Mix thoroughly before eating.

1 tablespoon vegetable oil
½-inch (1-cm) cube fresh ginger, peeled and finely chopped
3½ ounces (100g) soybean gluten, minced
1½ tablespoons soy sauce
1 tablespoon sake
3 tablespoons Chili Oil (see page 67)
2 tablespoons white sesame seeds, toasted (see page 42) and coarsely ground
3 tablespoons soy sauce
14 ounces (400g) udon noodles, cooked
2 scallions, chopped

Stir-fried Bean Thread Noodles with Bok Choy

Xiang cai chao mian

SERVES *4*

2 tablespoons peanut oil

2 cloves garlic, minced

½-inch (1-cm) cube fresh ginger, peeled and grated

½ carrot, thinly sliced

2 ounces (60g) bamboo shoots, sliced

4 fresh shiitake mushroom caps, thinly sliced

½ cup (20g) sliced Chinese cabbage

2 scallions, sliced

½ cup (50g) bean sprouts

2 cups (90g) bok choy, sliced

¼ cup (60ml) Clear Vegetable Stock (see page 67)

2 tablespoons soy sauce

½ teaspoon salt

¼ teaspoon ground black pepper

1 tablespoon sesame oil

14 ounces (400g) bean thread noodles, soaked in water for 30 minutes

1 tablespoon soy sauce

Traditionally these noodles are made with black bean sauce, but this delicious version is one of my favorites. For a crispy variation, try deep-frying the noodles.

1. Heat the peanut oil in a saucepan and sauté the garlic and ginger for 10 seconds over medium heat.
2. Add the carrot, bamboo shoots, shiitake, cabbage, and scallions. Turn the heat to high and stir-fry for 3–4 minutes. Add the bean sprouts and bok choy and stir-fry for another minute until heated through. Add the stock, soy sauce, salt, and pepper.
3. Heat the sesame oil in a wok and sauté the noodles over high heat for 1 minute. Sprinkle with 1 tablespoon soy sauce and toss to mix.
4. Put the vegetables in the wok with the noodles and toss once again. Transfer to a serving dish.

Stir-fried Rice Noodles with Vegetables

Caho mi fen

SERVES *4*

2 tablespoons sesame oil

½-inch (1-cm) cube fresh ginger, peeled and finely chopped

1 carrot, sliced thinly on the diagonal

2 ounces (60g) bamboo shoots, sliced diagonally

½ red bell pepper, sliced

½ green bell pepper, sliced

4 button mushrooms, sliced

1 cup (45g) Chinese cabbage, cut into 1-inch (3-cm) pieces

½ cup (50g) snow peas, strings removed and sliced diagonally

4 tablespoons Clear Vegetable Stock (see page 67)

½ teaspoon salt

½ teaspoon castor sugar

1 tablespoon sake

2 tablespoons soy sauce

2 scallions, finely sliced

1 tablespoon vegetable oil

14 ounces (400g) rice vermicelli, soaked in water for 1 hour and drained

1 tablespoon soy sauce

1 teaspoon sesame oil

2 tablespoons chopped chives, for garnish

Rice vermicelli cooks very quickly, making this an easy addition to a meal. The vegetables are sliced diagonally to allow maximum cooking surface, thus reducing the cooking time.

1. Heat the sesame oil in a saucepan and sauté the ginger over medium heat for 10 seconds.
2. Add the carrot, bamboo shoots, red and green pepper, mushrooms, cabbage, and snow peas, turn the heat to high, and stir-fry for 2–3 minutes.
3. Add the stock, salt, sugar, sake, soy sauce, and scallions. Stir briskly for another 2–3 minutes.
4. In another saucepan, heat the vegetable oil and sauté the drained vermicelli with 1 tablespoon soy sauce for 2 minutes over high heat. Remove from heat and transfer to a large serving dish. Spoon the vegetables on top, and sprinkle with the sesame oil and chives.

Szechuan Noodles
with Vegetables

Si chuan chao mian

SERVES *4*

These tasty and spicy noodles are always a huge hit at my parties. The Szechuan Sauce transforms an ordinary noodle and vegetable dish into an exotic preparation.

1. Heat oil in a wok, and add the garlic and red chili. Stir-fry over high heat for a few seconds.
2. Add the scallions, carrot, and mushrooms. Stir to mix.
3. Add the peppers, bean sprouts, and cabbage and cook over high heat for 2 minutes.
4. Add the Szechuan Sauce, vinegar, soy sauce, pepper, and salt to taste. Toss to mix and cook for a further minute.
5. Put in the noodles and toss to mix. Sprinkle with coriander leaves and transfer to a serving platter.

1 tablespoon sesame oil
2 teaspoons garlic, chopped
1 dried red chili
2 scallions, chopped
¼ medium carrot, sliced
2 fresh shiitake mushroom caps, sliced
2 green bell peppers, sliced
1 cup (100g) bean sprouts
1 cup (45g) shredded white cabbage
1 tablespoon Szechuan Sauce (see below)
1 teaspoon rice vinegar
1 tablespoon soy sauce
¼ teaspoon black pepper
Salt to taste
14 ounces (400g) yakisoba noodles, cooked
Fresh coriander leaves, for garnish

Szechuan Sauce *Sichuan jyan*

MAKES *1½ cups (360ml)*

3 cups (720ml) water
15 dried red chilies
5 cloves garlic
3 tablespoons vegetable oil
1 tablespoon garlic, finely chopped
3 fresh hot green chilies, finely chopped
1-inch (2.5-cm) cube fresh ginger, peeled and grated

½ onion, finely chopped
1 stick celery, including leaves, finely chopped
1 tablespoon rice vinegar
¾ cup (180ml) Clear Vegetable Stock (see page 67)
2 teaspoons castor sugar
½ teaspoon salt
1 teaspoon cornstarch mixed with 2 tablespoons water

1. Bring the 3 cups water to a boil in a saucepan and put in the 15 dried red chilies and 5 cloves garlic for 4–5 minutes. Drain, and blend the chilies and garlic to a paste using a food processor.
2. Heat the oil in a saucepan and sauté the 1 tablespoon chopped garlic, green chilies, and ginger for 15 seconds. Add the onion and celery and stir-fry for 30 seconds over medium heat. Add the blended chilies and garlic and stir briefly. Add the vinegar, vegetable stock, sugar, and salt and bring to a boil.
3. Gradually add the cornstarch-and-water mixture and continue stirring until the sauce thickens. Remove from heat, allow to cool, and store in an airtight jar. Keeps for about a week, refrigerated.

SNACKS

Chinese Savory Crepes

Su cai jian bin

SERVES *4*

1½ cups (185g) all-purpose flour
1 teaspoon baking powder
¾ cup (180ml) warm water
1 teaspoon salt
¼ teaspoon ground black pepper
4 scallions, chopped
1 tablespoon vegetable oil

A popular breakfast food in Beijing, and convenient too, because unlike many other Chinese breads, it does not require any rising time.

1. In a mixing bowl, combine the flour, baking powder, water, salt, and pepper to make a smooth batter. Add the scallions and mix.
2. Heat a greased frying pan. Pour in a quarter of the batter and spread evenly to make a thin crepe. Drizzle a little of the vegetable oil around the sides of the crepe.
3. Cover and cook for 3–4 minutes over medium heat. Flip over and cook the other side, covered, for 1 minute. When both sides are lightly browned, slide onto a dish and serve.

Chinese Spring Rolls

Chun juen

MAKES *12*

1 tablespoon sesame oil
1-inch (2.5-cm) cube fresh ginger, peeled and finely chopped
1 leek, finely chopped
½ medium carrot, julienned
5 fresh shiitake mushroom caps, chopped
1 cup (45g) shredded white cabbage
1 cup (100g) bean sprouts
2 teaspoons soy sauce
1 tablespoon sake
½ teaspoon salt
1 teaspoon cornstarch mixed with 1 tablespoon water
12 sheets spring roll wrappers
2 teaspoons all-purpose flour mixed with 4 teaspoons water
Vegetable oil for deep-frying
Spicy Soy Vinegar Sauce (see page 70), to serve

In Beijing, spring rolls filled with fresh new vegetables are a symbol of the approach of spring after a long winter. It is a time to celebrate.

1. Heat the oil in a saucepan and sauté the ginger and leek for 2–3 minutes over medium heat. Add the carrot, shiitake, cabbage, and bean sprouts, turn the heat to high, and sauté for 1–2 minutes.
2. Put the soy sauce, sake, salt, and the cornstarch-and-water mixture into the pan with the vegetables and stir to mix. Remove from the heat and transfer to a dish to cool. Divide the mixture into 12 equal portions.
3. Place one spring roll wrapper on a dry surface. Place a portion of the vegetable mixture at the edge of the wrapper and fold in the sides. Roll up towards the top of the wrapper. Seal the edges with the flour-and-water mixture. Repeat with the remaining wrappers and filling.
4. Heat the oil for deep-frying to 350°F (180°C) and deep-fry the spring rolls, a few at a time, until crisp and golden brown. Serve with Spicy Soy Vinegar Sauce.

Chinese Yam Cakes

Shu tiao

MAKES **12**

These light and fluffy savory cakes are often part of a meal, but also make a great snack. My Chinese friend serves them with tea. Long white yam is a popular vegetable in China and Japan, where its viscous texture is relished.

1. Wash the yam and grate into a deep bowl. Add the flour, coriander, mushrooms, sesame seeds, and salt. Mix thoroughly, divide into 12 portions, and flatten each portion into a cake.
2. Heat the oil in a frying pan, and fry the yam cakes for about 3 minutes on each side. Slide them onto a serving dish, brush with soy sauce, sprinkle with lemon juice and coriander, and serve with Green Garlic Sauce.

14 ounces (400g) Chinese yam
1 cup (125g) all-purpose flour
1 large bunch coriander with stems, chopped
2 wood ear mushrooms, reconstituted and chopped
2 tablespoons white sesame seeds, toasted (see page 42)
½ teaspoon salt
3 tablespoons vegetable oil
2 tablespoons soy sauce
2 teaspoons lemon juice
Fresh coriander leaves, for garnish
Green Garlic Sauce, to serve (see below)

Green Garlic Sauce

Xiang cai shuan zhi   MAKES *½ cup (120ml)*

1 tablespoon finely chopped fresh coriander
3 fresh hot green chilies, finely chopped
5 cloves garlic, minced
1 teaspoon castor sugar
4 tablespoons rice vinegar
¼ cup (60ml) water
½ teaspoon salt

Mix all the ingredients together in a bowl. Allow to stand for at least 10 minutes before using. Keep for 1 week, refrigerated.

Deep-fried Mushroom Balls

Shi jing zha chu

SERVES **4**

These crunchy mushroom balls were served to us as a savory snack between dim sum courses in a Chinese restaurant in the trendy St. John's Wood neighborhood of London. My nieces, nephews, and children were all surprised to see me go through so many of them!

1. In a deep bowl, combine all the ingredients except the oil and mix well. Roll the mixture into small balls and set aside.
2. In a wok, heat the oil for deep-frying to 350°F (180°C) and slide in the balls a few at a time. Deep-fry until golden brown. Drain on kitchen paper and serve hot with Chili Garlic Sauce.

10 dried shiitake mushrooms, soaked in hot water for 10 minutes, drained, and finely chopped
5 fresh shiitake mushroom caps, minced
3½ ounces (100g) water chestnuts, minced
2 scallions, finely chopped
2 fresh hot green chilies, finely chopped
2 tablespoons fresh coriander leaves, finely chopped
⅔ teaspoon salt
½ teaspoon pepper
1 teaspoon castor sugar
2 teaspoons sesame oil
3 tablespoons cornstarch
Vegetable oil for deep-frying
Chili Garlic Sauce, to serve (see below)

Chili Garlic Sauce   *La suan zhi*   MAKES *¼ cup (60ml)*

5 fresh red chilies   3 teaspoons rice vinegar
4 cloves garlic   ½ teaspoon salt
1 teaspoon castor sugar   1 tablespoon finely chopped onion

Using a food processor, blend the chilies, garlic, sugar, vinegar, and salt to a smooth paste. Add the onion and mix. Store in an airtight jar. Keeps for 1 week, refrigerated.

Assorted Vegetables in Cashew Gravy (page 18)

LEFT: Cauliflower and Potato with Spices (page 19); RIGHT: Chickpea Curry (page 20); Assorted Breads (pages 35–37)

Biryani (page 26)

Sprouted Mung Bean and Avocado Salad (page 16)

Spicy Stuffed Chilies (page 30)

Crunchy Red Cabbage Kachumber (page 14)

Spiced Zucchini and Potato (page 29)

Savory Sponge Cakes (page 28)

Stuffed Potato Cakes (page 32)

Crispy Pumpkin Turnovers (page 31)

Semolina Pudding (page 38)

Tofu and Vegetable Soup (page 45)

FRONT: **Spinach with Sesame Dressing** (page 45); BACK: **Broccoli with Tofu Dressing** (page 42)

Simmered Pumpkin (page 62)

FRONT: Burdock and Carrot Kimpira (page 58); BACK: Stir-fried Lotus Root (page 63)

Mizuna Salad with Fried Burdock and Garlic (page 43)

Tofu Teriyaki Steak (page 50)

Scrambled Tofu (page 61)

CHINA

Gyoza (page 70)

Shanghai-style Chow Mein (page 76)

Crispy Noodle Salad
(page 66)

Lettuce Wrap with Spicy Lotus Root (page 71)

Spicy Tofu (page 72)

Asparagus, Baby Corn, Pepper, and
Tofu Satay (page 118)

Cucumber Salad with Roasted
Cashews (page 114)

Gold Bags (page 125)

Thai Stir-fried Noodles with Tofu (page 124)

Pumpkin in Coconut Cream (page 128)

VIETNAM

Vietnamese Transparent Spring Rolls (page 137).
SAUCES, LEFT: Spicy Peanut Sauce (page 137); RIGHT: Vietnamese Dipping Sauce (page 134)

Tamarind Soup with Pineapple and Okra (page 132)

Vietnamese Fried Rice (page 135)

Stir-fried Eggplant and Tofu in Spicy Sauce (page 135)

BURMA

Cauliflower Coconut Curry with Noodles (page 142)

Split Pea Fritters (page 148)

Stir-fried Spinach with Mushrooms (page 143)

INDONESIA

Mixed Vegetable Salad with Peanut Sauce (page 150)

Spicy Fried Tempeh (page 153)

Mixed Vegetable Coconut Curry (page 152)

Vegetable Soup (page 151)

MALAYSIA

Fragrant Lemongrass Rice (page 162)

Stir-fried Noodles with Vegetables (page 164)

Noodles in Spicy Coconut Soup (page 163)

KOREA

BACK: Korean Wok-seared Spicy Rice with Vegetables (page 179);
FRONT: Cabbage Radish Kimchi (page 171).

Vegetable Pancakes (page 176). SAUCES, FROM LEFT TO RIGHT: Multipurpose Sauce
(page 178), Soy and Sesame Dipping Sauce (page 174). Chili Sesame Oil (page 178).

Mushroom and Zucchini Fritters
(page 175)

Korean Noodles (page 178)

Thailand

Just the mention of Thailand brings startlingly clear images of food to my mind: fiery red curry, sweet and sour pad thai noodles, vibrant papaya salad. The aromas are there as well: of fresh coriander, and whole peppercorns ground with garlic. I can even imagine the flavors, especially the tangy lemongrass and the unique galangal.

I've always been fascinated watching master Thai chefs at work, tasting frequently and adding seasonings as they go: a few drops of soy sauce here or some thin strands of chili there. While basic guidelines exist, the cuisine eludes any rigid procedures, giving cooks the flexibility of an artist dabbling with his colors.

During one enjoyable stay in Bangkok, my friend Anju packed us all off to Rajdamnoen Avenue to a restaurant across from the temple Wat Rajchannadda, where we were greeted with a long queue of people all waiting patiently to be called. Anju assured me that the wait would be worth it. We were close to starving when we entered the restaurant through a small garden and were seated at an orchid-adorned table. Gentle music played in the background, as we worked our way through dish after dish, including the wok-seared Pad Thai Tao Hu and the aromatic Tom Yum Het soup found on the following pages. The ultimate indulgence was the dessert—Mango with Sticky Rice. As an Indian addicted to mangoes, this was simply heavenly! You'll find the recipe on page 128.

SOUPS AND SALADS

Cucumber Salad with Roasted Cashews
Yam tang kwa sai med mamoang himmapan

SERVES *4* PHOTOGRAPH ON PAGE 100

Thai salads are a kaleidoscope of strong flavors—hot chili, pungent garlic, sour lime juice, salty soy sauce, and sweet sugar—all used in generous proportions. This an ideal summer salad.

1. Julienne the cucumbers into 1½-inch (4-cm) long strips. In a bowl, combine the cucumber and coriander leaves and set aside.
2. In a frying pan, dry roast the cashews over medium heat, stirring so that they brown evenly. Allow the cashews to cool, then grind coarsely.
3. Using a food processor or a mortar and pestle, grind the garlic and chili. Mix in the lime juice, soy sauce, sugar, and red chili flakes.
4. Spoon the garlic-and-chili mixture over the cucumber and toss gently to mix. Sprinkle the cashews over the salad, toss briefly, and serve immediately.

2 cucumbers
Handful of fresh coriander leaves
½ cup (70g) cashews
1 clove garlic
1 small fresh hot green or red chili
2 tablespoons lime juice
1 tablespoon soy sauce
1 teaspoon castor sugar
½ teaspoon red chili flakes

Green Mango Salad
Yam mamunag

SERVES *4*

This elegant and tangy salad is as refreshing and cooling as it is spicy. Raw green mangoes are sold in markets across Thailand and they are also sold ready grated for busy city dwellers.

1. Using a food processor or a mortar and pestle, grind the garlic, chilies, and shallots until smooth. Place the mixture in a bowl, and add the soy sauce, lime juice, sugar, salt, and cashews. Stir thoroughly to mix.
2. Add the grated mango to the mixture and combine. Place in a serving bowl and garnish with coriander leaves.

2 cloves garlic, chopped
5 small fresh hot green or red chilies
3 shallots, finely chopped
1 tablespoon soy sauce
1 tablespoon lime juice
1 tablespoon palm sugar
½ teaspoon salt
2 tablespoons roasted cashews, coarsely ground
1 large raw green mango, peeled and grated
Fresh coriander leaves, to garnish

Hot and Sour Mushroom Soup   *Tom yum het*

SERVES *4*

1 tablespoon vegetable oil
3 tablespoons Thai Soup Paste (see below)
7 ounces (200g) atsuage deep-fried tofu, thinly sliced
6 fresh shiitake mushroom caps, sliced
1¾ ounces (50g) button mushrooms, sliced
3 tablespoons soy sauce
1 teaspoon castor sugar
2 tablespoons lemon juice
½ cup (10g) fresh coriander, chopped
½ cup (10g) fresh basil leaves, torn
Chilies in Oil (see below), to serve

FOR THE STOCK
4 cups (960ml) water
1 medium onion, quartered
2 stalks lemongrass, chopped
3–4 kaffir lime leaves, torn in half
1½-inch (4-cm) cube galangal, chopped
¾-inch (2-cm) cube fresh ginger, peeled and
   chopped
1 tablespoon tamarind pulp
3 dried red chilies, chopped
2 fresh hot green or red chilies

Tom Yum, one of the most famous Asian soups, is the pride of Thailand. It is made with mushrooms—shiitake and button mushrooms work well. Thai soups are fairly light and are served as one of several dishes in a meal alongside salad, curries, and rice, all neatly arranged at the center of the table.

1. Put all the stock ingredients in a saucepan and bring to a boil. Simmer for 15–20 minutes over low-medium heat. Remove from the heat and strain. Reserve the stock and discard the rest.
2. Heat the oil in a large saucepan and sauté the Thai Soup Paste for a minute until fragrant. Add the tofu, shiitake, and button mushrooms and stir-fry over high heat for 1 minute.
3. Bring the prepared stock to a boil. Turn the heat to medium and add the sautéed tofu and mushrooms, the soy sauce, sugar, and lemon juice. Simmer for 5–6 minutes over medium heat until the mushrooms are tender.
4. Sprinkle with the coriander and basil and remove from heat. Pour into individual bowls and serve hot, with Chilies in Oil.

Thai Soup Paste   *Tom yum*   MAKES *¼ cup (60ml)*

7 fresh red chilies
1 stalk lemongrass
6 kaffir lime leaves
1 inch (3-cm) cube galangal
3 cloves garlic
1 tablespoon vegetable oil

This spicy, tangy soup paste is extremely handy, as it is used not only as a base for Thai soups, but also for certain Burmese soups and curries, such as Cauliflower Coconut Curry (see page 142).

Using a food processor, grind all the ingredients to a smooth paste. Store in an airtight jar in the refrigerator. Keeps for about a week.

Chilies in Oil   *Nam prik pow*   MAKES *½ cup (120ml)*

4 tablespoons vegetable oil
3 dried red chilies
4 cloves of garlic, finely chopped
3 fresh red chilies, coarsely chopped
4 shallots, finely chopped
3 tablespoons castor sugar
1 teaspoon salt

These chilies are always served as an accompaniment to Tom Yum Soup

1. Heat the oil in a small saucepan and sauté the dried red chilies until crisp. Remove the chilies and put to one side. Put the garlic, fresh red chilies, and shallots into the same oil and sauté for 2–3 minutes.
2. Transfer the garlic, dried chilies, fresh chilies, and shallots from the saucepan to a food processor and grind until smooth. Stir in the sugar and salt. Store in an airtight jar in the refrigerator.

Roasted Eggplant Salad

Yam makeu pow

SERVES *4*

5 eggplants, about 14 ounces (400g) in total
2 tablespoons vegetable oil
2 cloves garlic, finely chopped
4 fresh shiitake mushroom caps, sliced
3 shallots, sliced
2 fresh hot green chilies, chopped roughly
2 tablespoons fresh coriander leaves
2 tablespoons tamarind juice
2 teaspoons soy sauce
½ teaspoon castor sugar
2 tablespoons peanuts, coarsely ground

Walking through a Thai vegetable market, with spectacular piles of colorful vegetables and fruits piled high, reminded me of the markets at home in Mumbai. I was astonished by the wide variety of vegetables. Eggplants, for example, are available in many different shapes, sizes, and colors—from purple to green to gold.

1. Heat the oven to 350°F (180°C) and dry roast the eggplants for about 20–25 minutes until the outer skin has blackened and the eggplant is soft. Alternatively, place them over the gas flame, turning until the outer skin is flaky and charred. Dip in water to cool. Remove the blackened outer skin and cut the flesh into small pieces.
2. In a frying pan, heat the oil and sauté the garlic and mushrooms over medium heat for 2 minutes. Add the chopped eggplant and shallots. Sauté briefly and remove from the heat.
3. Transfer the contents of the frying pan to a bowl. Add the chilies, fresh coriander, tamarind juice, soy sauce, and sugar. Toss gently to mix. Sprinkle with peanuts and serve.

Spicy Green Papaya Salad

Som tam

SERVES *4*

2 cloves garlic, halved
6 small fresh hot green chilies, chopped
1 cup (100g) green beans, cut into 1¼-inch (3-cm) lengths
2 tablespoons roasted peanuts
3 tablespoons soy sauce
3 tablespoons tamarind juice or lemon juice
1 tablespoon palm sugar
2 medium tomatoes, quartered
7 ounces (200g) raw green papaya, peeled and shredded
Peanuts, coarsely ground, for garnish

Som Tam is sold at stalls all over Thailand in crowded city areas such as shopping streets, bus stops, and railway stations. This healthy mix of shredded vegetables, flavored with lime juice, garlic, and chili, is tastiest when prepared by street vendors. Very often rice is thrown in with an order of som tam to make an inexpensive meal for the hurried traveler. The Thai way is to include a lot of chilies, but you can adjust the quantity of chilies to suit your taste.

1. Using a food processor or a mortar and pestle, grind the garlic and chilies coarsely. Add the green beans and grind again until well broken down. Add the peanuts, soy sauce, tamarind juice, and palm sugar and grind again. Turn the mixture with a spoon and grind again. Finally add the tomatoes, grind, then stir gently.
2. Place the shredded papaya in a deep bowl. Pour the tomato mixture over the shredded papaya and toss to mix. Arrange on a serving dish and serve immediately, garnished with the coarsely ground peanuts.

* Carrot may be used instead of papaya for an easy variation.

Spicy Vegetable Soup with Coconut

Tom kha phak

SERVES *4*

1 tablespoon vegetable oil
3 shallots, sliced
2 cloves garlic, halved
2 dried red chilies
1 cup (30g) coriander stems, chopped
2 cups (480ml) coconut milk
2 cups (480ml) Thai Vegetable Stock (see below)
1 cup (100g) cauliflower florets, thinly sliced
4 button mushrooms, thinly sliced
2 stalks lemongrass, cut into small pieces
¾-inch (2-cm) cube galangal, sliced
2–3 kaffir lime leaves
1 tablespoon soy sauce
½ teaspoon castor sugar
1 teaspoon lemon juice
Coriander leaves, for garnish

* Chinese cabbage and lotus root may also be used for this soup.

Thai soups are generally light, and meant to balance the stronger flavors of the hot curries and other dishes. The spices here blend with the coconut milk to create a delicious flavor.

1. Heat the oil in a small saucepan and sauté the shallots, garlic, and chilies over medium heat until fragrant. Remove from the oil.
2. Using a food processor or mortar and pestle, blend the sautéed shallots, garlic, and chilies with the coriander stems to a coarse paste.
3. In a large pan, heat the coconut milk with the vegetable stock. Add the cauliflower, mushrooms, lemongrass, galangal, kaffir lime leaves, soy sauce, and sugar. Bring to a boil, then turn the heat to medium and simmer until the cauliflower florets are tender.
4. Mix in the shallot paste and heat through. Turn off the heat, and stir in the lemon juice. Serve hot, garnished with coriander leaves.

Thai Vegetable Stock   *Nam tom phak*   MAKES *4 cups*

6 cups (1.5 L) water
¼ small white cabbage, roughly chopped
1 medium onion, sliced
2 carrots, cut into chunks
2 stalks celery, roughly chopped

5 ounces (140g) white radish
3 coriander roots with stems
Handful fresh basil leaves
1 teaspoon whole black peppercorns

1. Put all the ingredients in a large saucepan and bring to a boil. Cover and simmer over medium heat for 15–20 minutes, until all the vegetables are cooked and the liquid is reduced to two-thirds of its original quantity.
2. Remove the lid and turn off the heat. Allow to cool. Strain and use as required. Left-over broth may be frozen in an ice cube tray for later use.

MAIN DISHES

Asparagus, Baby Corn, Pepper, and Tofu Satay

Satay phak kab tao-hu

SERVES *4*   PHOTOGRAPH ON PAGE 100

Across from the Temple of the Emerald Buddha in Bangkok there is a small restaurant, where, thanks to our tour guide, there was a special meal ready for us to eat before heading out to see the Temple of Dawn. This delicious satay, served with peanut sauce, had my children licking their fingers, asking for more.

1. For the marinade, use a food processor or a mortar and pestle to blend the lime leaves, coriander roots, and garlic to a coarse paste. Place the paste in a flat bowl and add the coconut milk, vegetable oil, curry powder, sugar, soy sauce, and salt. Stir to mix.
2. Place the vegetables and tofu in the marinade and set aside for 25–30 minutes.
3. Remove the vegetables and tofu from the marinade and carefully thread them onto skewers. Grill until browned evenly.
4. Place the Sweet Peanut Sauce and Cucumber Relish in separate bowls in the middle of a large serving dish, and arrange the skewers of vegetables around the the bowls.

2 green asparagus spears, cut into 1½-inch (4-cm) lengths
1 medium onion, cut into bite-sized chunks
3 baby corn ears, cut into bite-sized pieces
1 red bell pepper, cut into bite-sized pieces
1 green bell pepper, cut into bite-sized pieces
5 button mushrooms, quartered
7 ounces (200g) atsuage deep-fried tofu, cut into bite-sized pieces
Sweet Peanut Sauce (see below), to serve
Cucumber Relish (see page 126), to serve

FOR THE MARINADE
3 kaffir lime leaves, chopped
3 coriander roots, with stems
4 cloves garlic, chopped
1 cup (240ml) coconut milk
2 tablespoons vegetable oil
2 tablespoons curry powder
2 tablespoons castor sugar
3 tablespoons soy sauce
1 teaspoon salt

Sweet Peanut Sauce   *Nam jim moo sate*   MAKES *1½ cups (360ml)*

2 teaspoons vegetable oil
2 tablespoons Red Curry Paste (see page 120)
1 cup (240ml) coconut milk
2 tablespoons palm sugar
2 tablespoons rice vinegar

2 tablespoons soy sauce
½ teaspoon salt
1 teaspoon lemon juice
4 tablespoons roasted peanuts, ground

Heat the oil in a small saucepan and sauté the curry paste until fragrant. Add the coconut milk, palm sugar, rice vinegar, soy sauce, salt, and lemon juice. Stir in the peanuts and transfer to a serving bowl.

Green Curry with Eggplant and Bamboo Shoot

Kaeng makhoe gap noumai

SERVES *4*

2 tablespoons vegetable oil

4 tablespoons Green Curry Paste (see below)

3 cups (720ml) coconut milk

3 kaffir lime leaves, torn

3½ ounces (100g) green or purple eggplant, chopped

3½ ounces (100g) bamboo shoots, sliced

1 red or yellow bell pepper, sliced

1¾ ounces (50g) button mushrooms, quartered

1 tablespoon soy sauce

½ teaspoon salt

2 tablespoons palm sugar

15–20 fresh basil leaves, torn

Aromatic Thai curries are a delicious contrast of strong flavors. Thinner than Indian curries, they have a coconut milk base, which adds natural sweetness. Lemongrass and lime leaves impart a distinctly tangy flavor. Thai curries are never served as stand-alone dishes and are always one part of a meal, their spices balanced by other milder and sweeter dishes, such as a salad, a stir-fried dish, or a dessert.

1. Heat the oil in a large saucepan, sauté the green curry paste briefly, and add the coconut milk. Bring to a simmer and add the lime leaves, eggplant, bamboo shoots, bell pepper, and mushrooms. Stir to mix. Cook over medium heat for 5 minutes.
2. Add the soy sauce, salt, and sugar, and cook for a further 5–7 minutes until all the vegetables are tender.
3. Mix in the basil leaves and turn off the heat.

Green Curry Paste

Nam prik gaeng khiao wan

MAKES *about 1 cup (240ml)*

10 small fresh hot green chilies

3 shallots, sliced

3 cloves garlic, halved

1¼-inch (3-cm) cube galangal, peeled and chopped

2 stalks lemongrass, finely chopped

1 teaspoon freshly grated lemon rind

1 ounce (30g) fresh coriander with stems and root

10 black peppercorns

1 tablespoon coriander seeds

1 teaspoon cumin seeds

½ teaspoon salt

1 teaspoon vegetable oil

1. Put all the ingredients, except the oil, in a food processor and grind to a smooth thick paste, or use a mortar and pestle to grind the ingredients, a few at a time.
2. Mix in the oil and store in an airtight container in the refrigerator for up to two weeks.

* For a richer flavor, dry roast the peppercorns, coriander seeds, and cumin seeds over low heat until fragrant. Grind to a powder and set aside. Blend the remaining ingredients, except the oil, in a food processor and combine with the ground spices.

Massaman Curry

Kaeng massaman

SERVES *4*

2 tablespoons vegetable oil

2 tablespoons Massaman Curry Paste (see page 120)

1 medium onion, finely chopped

2 medium potatoes, boiled and diced

3½ ounces (100g) atsuage deep-fried tofu, sliced into strips

1 cup (100g) green beans, sliced into 1¼-inch (3-cm) lengths

2 button mushrooms, sliced

3 cups (720ml) coconut milk

3 tablespoons roasted peanuts, coarsely ground

3 tablespoons tamarind juice

1 tablespoon palm sugar

1 teaspoon salt

1 tablespoon Crispy Fried Shallots (see page 131), for garnish

1 tablespoon roasted peanuts, crushed, for garnish

Chives, chopped, for garnish

The peanuts give this curry a distinctive nutty flavor and crunchy texture. Best served with piping hot jasmine rice.

1. In a saucepan, heat the oil and sauté the curry paste briefly over medium heat.
2. Add the onion, potato, tofu, green beans, and mushrooms. Stir to mix.
3. Add the coconut milk and cook over medium heat for 5–6 minutes. Add the 3 tablespoons coarsely ground peanuts, the tamarind juice, palm sugar, and salt and stir until the sugar is dissolved.
4. Transfer to a serving bowl and sprinkle with fried shallots, crushed peanuts, and chives.

Massaman Curry Paste

Massaman   MAKES ½ *cup (120ml)*

3 cardamom pods
1 teaspoon coriander seeds
1 teaspoon cumin seeds
⅔ teaspoon ground white
   pepper
½ teaspoon ground cinnamon
4–5 cloves

6 fresh red chilies, seeded
3 cloves garlic, halved
1 stalk lemongrass, chopped
4 shallots, chopped
1 tablespoon freshly grated
   lemon rind
½ teaspoon salt

Massaman curry paste is the mildest of the Thai curry pastes. The spices impart a distinctive flavor to the curry, which has its origins in the rich Indian curry of the Moghul era.

Put all the ingredients in a food processor and grind to a smooth paste. Or, use a mortar and pestle to grind the ingredients, a few at a time, then combine. Store in an airtight jar in the refrigerator. Keeps for about a week, refrigerated.

* For a richer flavor, dry roast the cardamom, coriander seeds, cumin seeds, and cloves until fragrant. Grind to a powder and set aside. Blend the remaining ingredients in a food processor and combine with the powdered spices.

Red Curry with Vegetables

Kaeng phet pak

SERVES *4*

The deep red color of this curry leads people to think that it is hotter than green curry, but this is not true. A tasty main dish served over rice or noodles.

1. Heat the oil in a large saucepan and sauté the red curry paste over low heat for 2–3 minutes. Add the peppers and keep stirring for 3 minutes until well blended.
2. Add the bamboo shoots and half of the coconut milk. Bring to a simmer. Add the remaining coconut milk, all the other vegetables, lime leaves, soy sauce, and sugar. Cook over medium heat for 8–10 minutes, until the vegetables are tender.
3. Transfer to a serving bowl and garnish with the red chilies, basil, and coriander.

3 tablespoons vegetable oil
3 tablespoons Red Curry Paste (see below)
2 red bell peppers, finely chopped
1¾ ounces (50g) bamboo shoots, sliced
3 cups (720ml) coconut milk
3 baby corn ears, sliced diagonally
½ cup (50g) green beans, cut into 1¼-inch (3-cm)
   lengths
½ cup (50g) eggplant, cut into 1¼-inch (3-cm) pieces
½ cup (50g) cauliflower florets
3 kaffir lime leaves
2 tablespoons soy sauce
2 teaspoons palm sugar
2 fresh long red chilies, sliced in half lengthwise
10–12 fresh basil leaves, torn
1 tablespoon fresh coriander leaves

Red Curry Paste

Nam prik gaeng daeng   MAKES *1 cup (240ml)*

15 fresh red chilies
3 shallots, chopped
4 cloves garlic, chopped
1¼-inch (3-cm) piece of galangal, peeled and chopped
1 red bell pepper, halved
2 stalks lemongrass, chopped
½ cup (30g) fresh coriander leaves with stems and root
2 kaffir lime leaves, mid-rib removed
1 teaspoon freshly grated lemon rind
10 black peppercorns
1 tablespoon coriander seeds
2 teaspoons cumin seeds
1 teaspoon salt
1 tablespoon vegetable oil

The famed red and green curry pastes are readily available in supermarkets, but it can be both enjoyable and rewarding to make them yourself. They act as a base not only for the curries but for many other stir-fried dishes. Do not let the long list of ingredients deter you. Once you have the herbs and condiments ready, all you need to do is put them in a food processor.

1. Put all the ingredients, except the oil, in a food processor and grind to a smooth thick paste, or use a mortar and pestle to pound the ingredients, a few at a time and then all together.
2. Mix in the oil and store in an airtight container in the refrigerator for about a week.

* For a richer flavor, dry roast the peppercorns, coriander seeds, and cumin seeds over low heat until fragrant. Grind to a powder and set aside. Blend the remaining ingredients, except the oil, in a food processor and combine with the ground spices.

RICE AND NOODLES

■ NOODLES

Noodles are one of Thailand's staple foods, and there are four main varieties used in Thai cooking.

When using dried noodles, you should soak them in cold water for about 10–15 minutes before cooking. It is not always necessary to boil the noodles before adding them to a dish, as soaked noodles cook quickly when stir-fried with the vegetables over high heat. That said, they can be immersed in boiling water for a couple of minutes to soften. This will reduce the time required for the actual cooking of the dish. The dry weight usually doubles after soaking: i.e., 2 ounces (60g) of dried noodles will become 4 ounces (115g) after being soaked.

Sen yai

Also called river noodles. Thick, flat rice sticks that can be bought fresh or dried. The fresh noodles need to be immersed in cold water to separate, as they are quite sticky.

Sen mee

Also called rice vermicelli. Thin, wiry looking rice noodles usually sold dried in a bundle.

Sen lek

This thin flat noodle, usually sold dried, is the most widely used in Thai dishes.

Wun sen

Also called cellophane noodles. Very thin, transparent noodles made from mung beans.

Toppings and Dressings for Noodles

Thai noodle dishes are carefully flavored during cooking, yet it is common practice in Thai homes and restaurants to have a set of these toppings and dressings at the table. The guests can then proceed to adjust the flavor of the noodles to their taste. Castor sugar and cayenne pepper are also served as condiments for noodles.

Chilies in Soy Sauce   *Ew khow kap prik*

15–20 small fresh hot green and red chilies, finely chopped
½ cup (120ml) soy sauce

Mix the chilies with the soy sauce and allow to stand for 10 minutes. Keeps refrigerated for about a month.

Sliced Chilies in Vinegar   *Prik nam som han*

8 fresh hot green and red chilies, thinly sliced
½ cup (120ml) rice vinegar

Mix the chilies with the vinegar and allow to stand for 10 minutes. Keeps refrigerated for about a month.

Minced Chilies in Vinegar   *Prik nam som bot*

8 fresh hot green and red chilies, thinly minced
½ cup (120ml) rice vinegar

Mix the chilies with the vinegar and allow to stand for 10 minutes. Keeps refrigerated for about a month.

Chili Fried Rice

Khao phat prik

SERVES **4**

4 cups (630g) cooked jasmine rice
3 tablespoons peanut oil
1 medium onion, finely chopped
1 fresh red chili, sliced
7 ounces (200g) firm tofu, diced
1 scallion, chopped
3 button mushrooms, sliced
1 tablespoon Red Curry Paste (see page 120)
2 tablespoons soy sauce
Dash of pepper
Pinch of salt
½ cup (10g) fresh coriander leaves, finely chopped

I was given this recipe by a Thai chef I met on a trip to Thailand. It is an easy dish to put together, especially with leftover rice, and it makes a great one-dish meal. I often pack this for my husband's lunch with Cucumber Salad with Roasted Cashews (see page 114).

1. Set the cooked jasmine rice aside and allow to cool so that the grains separate.
2. Heat the oil in a saucepan and sauté the onion over medium heat for 2–3 minutes. Add the red chili, tofu, scallions, and mushrooms. Stir-fry quickly over high heat for 1 minute.
3. Add the red curry paste, soy sauce, pepper, and salt. Stir to mix.
4. Mix in the cooked rice and heat through. Finally, sprinkle with coriander leaves, remove from the heat, and transfer to a serving dish.

Crispy Noodles

Mee krob

SERVES **4**

Vegetable oil for deep frying
11 ounces (310g) sen mee rice vermicelli (see page 121)
2 tablespoons peanut oil
2 cloves garlic, finely chopped
2 fresh red chilies, seeded and sliced
11 ounces (310g) firm tofu, diced
1 scallion, finely chopped
1 red bell pepper, thinly sliced
1 green bell pepper, thinly sliced
4 tablespoons rice vinegar
4 tablespoons castor sugar
4 tablespoons soy sauce
¼ teaspoon ground black pepper
1 cup (20g) garlic chives, chopped
1 cup (20g) coriander leaves, chopped

Delightfully crunchy and surprisingly sweet, these noodles make a perfect accompaniment to a Thai curry and rice. The first time I tried this noodle dish was at Erawan, a trendy Thai restaurant in Tokyo. The contrasting textures of the crisp noodles and the soft tofu was immediately appealing.

1. In a wok, heat the oil for deep-frying to 350°F (180°C). Deep-fry the vermicelli in small handfuls until it puffs up and turns golden, which will happen almost immediately. Quickly remove, and drain on kitchen paper.
2. Heat the peanut oil in a large saucepan and sauté the garlic and chilies briefly. Add the tofu, scallions, and red and green pepper and stir-fry over high heat for 2–3 minutes.
3. Stir in the vinegar, sugar, soy sauce, and black pepper.
4. When ready to serve, put the fried noodles, garlic chives, and coriander leaves in the saucepan with the other ingredients. Mix well and remove from the heat. Transfer to a serving platter and serve immediately.

Drunkard's Noodles

Kuy tiao pad kee mao

SERVES *4*

5 ounces (140g) sen yai noodles (see page 121)

3 tablespoons vegetable oil

2 cloves garlic, crushed

3 small fresh hot green chilies, finely chopped

½-inch (1-cm) cube fresh ginger, peeled and grated

1 medium onion, sliced

3 baby corn ears, sliced diagonally

½ green bell pepper, sliced

½ red bell pepper, sliced

1 cup (70g) Chinese kale, cut into 1¼-inch (3-cm) pieces

6–8 cherry tomatoes, halved

Handful of fresh basil leaves, torn

2½ tablespoons soy sauce

½ teaspoon castor sugar

½ teaspoon black pepper

A spicy noodle dish that is also a great hangover remedy! The strong flavors of the chilies and ginger will certainly wake you up. The broad, flat rice noodles, sen yai, are ideal for this dish.

1. Soak the noodles in water for 15 minutes. Drain and set aside.
2. Heat the oil in a wok and sauté the garlic, chilies, ginger, and onion for 2–3 minutes over medium heat, until fragrant.
3. Add the baby corn, bell pepper, and Chinese kale and stir-fry over high heat for 3–4 minutes. Stir in the cherry tomatoes and basil leaves and reduce the heat to medium.
4. Add the soy sauce, sugar, and black pepper, then put in the noodles and mix gently. Cover for 3–4 minutes until the noodles are cooked. Remove from the heat and arrange on a serving dish.

Fried Rice with Basil

Khao phat krapao

SERVES *4*

2 tablespoons vegetable oil

1 clove garlic, finely chopped

3 small fresh hot green or red chilies, finely chopped

1 medium onion, finely chopped

15 button mushrooms, quartered

1 red bell pepper, thinly sliced

3 tablespoons soy sauce

½ teaspoon castor sugar

30–40 fresh basil leaves, chopped

½ cup (10g) coriander leaves

4 cups (630g) cooked jasmine rice

A few lettuce leaves

Red bell pepper slices, for garnish

This aromatic jasmine rice dish, flavored with fresh basil and perked up with hot chilies, can be found in restaurants all across Thailand. The seasoned basil is usually served on the side of the jasmine rice.

1. Heat the oil in a wok or a frying pan and add the garlic and chilies. Stir-fry over medium heat until the garlic has browned.
2. Add the onion and mushrooms, turn the heat to high, and stir-fry for 3–4 minutes. Add the bell pepper, soy sauce, sugar, and basil leaves. Reduce the heat for 1–2 minutes to allow the flavors of the basil to infuse. Remove from heat and sprinkle with the coriander leaves.
3. Divide the rice into individual bowls, garnished with lettuce and slices of red pepper, with a portion of the seasoned basil on the side. Alternatively, toss the rice in the frying pan with the basil mixture, then serve.

Pineapple Fried Rice

Khao ob supparot

SERVES *4*

This majestic preparation of rice makes an attractive party dish when served in a scooped-out pineapple.

1. Cut the pineapple into half vertically and scoop out the flesh. Dice the flesh and set aside. Heat the oil in a saucepan and shallow-fry the cashews until golden. Remove from the oil with a slotted spoon.
2. Using the same pan, sauté the garlic and ginger until fragrant. Stir in the mushrooms, onion, and tomato. Cook over high heat for 1 minute, stirring all the time.
3. Add the bell pepper, tofu strips, ⅔ cup diced pineapple, the cooked rice, soy sauce, white pepper, and sugar. Mix thoroughly. Transfer to the pineapple shell and garnish with the scallions and coriander leaves.

1 large pineapple
2 tablespoons vegetable oil
20–25 cashew nuts
1 clove garlic, finely chopped
½-inch (1-cm) cube fresh ginger, peeled and grated
2 wood ear mushrooms, reconstituted and chopped
1 small onion, diced
1 medium tomato, chopped
1 small red or green bell pepper, diced
2 sheets abura-age deep-fried tofu, thinly sliced
⅔ cup (100g) fresh pineapple, diced
3 cups (470g) cooked jasmine rice
3 tablespoons soy sauce
½ teaspoon ground white pepper
½ teaspoon palm sugar
1 scallion, diagonally sliced, for garnish
Coriander leaves, for garnish

Thai Stir-fried Noodles with Tofu

Pad thai tao hu

SERVES *4*

PHOTOGRAPH ON PAGE 101

This one-dish meal is one of the most popular noodle dishes in Thailand. My friend and I once queued for half an hour outside the Jae Gee restaurant in Bangkok to sample this dish.

1. Soak the noodles in water for 15 minutes. Drain and set aside.
2. Place the palm sugar, castor sugar, tamarind-and-water mixture, cayenne pepper, and soy sauce in a small saucepan. Bring to a boil over low heat, then simmer for 2–3 minutes until thick and syrupy. Set the tamarind sauce aside.
3. Heat the oil in a large wok and sauté the garlic and shallot until golden brown. Add the tofu and stir-fry briefly. Add the drained noodles and tamarind sauce and mix well. Cook for a few minutes until the noodles are soft.
4. Add the radish, scallions, half the chives, half the peanuts, and half the bean sprouts. Stir well, then remove from heat. Transfer to a serving dish and garnish with the remaining peanuts and the coriander leaves. Arrange the remaining chives and bean sprouts and the lemon wedges on the side, so that guests can help themselves.

7 ounces (200g) sen lek noodles (see page 121)
1 tablespoon palm sugar
1 tablespoon castor sugar
1 tablespoon tamarind pulp dissolved in ½ cup (120ml) water
1 teaspoon cayenne pepper
2 tablespoons soy sauce
3 tablespoons vegetable oil
2 cloves garlic, finely chopped
1 shallot, sliced
3½ ounces (100g) atsuage deep-fried tofu, diced
1 small white radish, chopped
2 scallions, sliced
1 bunch chives, cut into 1¼-inch (3-cm) lengths
2 tablespoons roasted peanuts, coarsely ground
1½ cups (150g) bean sprouts
Fresh coriander leaves, for garnish
Lemon wedges, for garnish

SIDE DISHES AND SNACKS

1 tablespoon vegetable oil
1 tablespoon Red Curry Paste (see page 120)
4 fresh shiitake mushroom caps, finely chopped
7 ounces (200g) firm tofu, drained and crumbled
½ carrot, grated
2 tablespoons roasted peanuts, ground
1 tablespoon soy sauce
½ teaspoon castor sugar
½ teaspoon salt
20 sheets of wonton wrappers, or 5 large spring roll
　wrappers, quartered
1 tablespoon cornstarch mixed with a little water to
　make a paste
Vegetable oil for deep-frying
Sweet Chili Sauce (see below), to serve
Hot and Sour Dip (see below), to serve

Gold Bags

Thung ngun yuang

MAKES *20*

PHOTOGRAPH ON PAGE 101

Serving afternoon snacks is an old Thai tradition, and the range of tempting dishes is so vast that it is possible to make a meal out of them. These crispy treats also make a great party dish.

1. Heat the 1 tablespoon vegetable oil in a saucepan and sauté the red curry paste briefly. Add the mushrooms, tofu, and carrot and stir over high heat for 2–3 minutes.
2. Add the peanuts, soy sauce, sugar, and salt and stir to mix. Remove from the heat and transfer to a bowl. Set aside to cool.
3. Place the wonton wrappers on a dry surface. Place a spoonful of the vegetable mixture in the center of each wrapper. Wet the edges with the cornstarch-and-water paste. Press the edges together to seal.
4. Heat the oil for deep-frying to 350°F (180°C) and slide in the pouches, a few at a time. Deep-fry until crisp and golden brown. Drain on kitchen paper and serve hot with Sweet Chili Sauce or Hot and Sour Dip.

Sweet Chili Sauce *Nam jim* MAKES *about ¾ cup (180ml)*

5 large fresh red chilies, seeded
3 cloves garlic, chopped
½ cup (120ml) plum sauce
3 tablespoons castor sugar

4 tablespoons water
2 tablespoons rice vinegar
½ teaspoon salt

This sauce is best with fried snacks such as Gold Bags (see above), Mushroom Balls (see page 126), or Sweet Corn Cakes (see page 127).

1. Using a food processor or mortar and pestle, grind the chilies and garlic to a smooth paste.
2. Put the plum sauce, sugar, water, vinegar, and salt in a saucepan. Add the ground chilies and garlic and stir to mix. Simmer over low heat for 2 minutes, until the sauce thickens. Transfer to a bowl and cool. Keeps refrigerated for about a week.

*Orange marmalade may be used instead of the plum sauce.

Hot and Sour Dip

Nam jim tod man

MAKES *½ cup (120ml)*

6 tablespoons rice vinegar
4 tablespoons castor sugar
3 fresh hot green chilies, thinly sliced
1½-inch (4-cm) long piece cucumber, sliced into thin quarters
1 shallot, thinly sliced
2 tablespoons chopped chives

Most Thai dishes are served with a selection of dips and sauces. This dip goes well with dishes such as Sweet Corn Cakes (see page 127).

1. In a small bowl, combine the vinegar with the sugar. Stir until the sugar has dissolved.
2. Add the chilies, cucumber, shallot, and chives and mix. Keeps refrigerated for about a week.

Mushroom Balls

Luk chin het

SERVES *4*

A delicious starter made with some of the large variety of mushrooms available in Thailand. Sweet Chili Sauce (see page 125) is the perfect dipping sauce for this dish.

1. In a deep bowl, mix together all the mushrooms and set aside.
2. To prepare the batter, combine the corn flour with the chilies, Ginger Garlic Paste, pepper, and salt. Add the water gradually to make a thick batter. Add the mushrooms to the batter and toss gently to mix evenly.
3. Heat the oil for deep-frying to 350°F (180°C). Take a heaping tablespoon of the mushroom mix and slide into the hot oil. Deep-fry in small batches, until golden brown. Drain on kitchen paper. Serve hot with Sweet Chili Sauce.

5 dried shiitake mushrooms, soaked in hot water for 10 minutes, drained, and sliced
3½ ounces (100g) fresh straw mushrooms, chopped
3½ ounces (100g) fresh angel mushrooms, finely chopped
3½ ounces (100g) fresh wood ear mushrooms, chopped
1 cup (20g) corn flour
1 fresh hot green chili, chopped
1 teaspoon Ginger Garlic Paste (see page 18)
½ teaspoon ground black pepper
Salt to taste
½ cup (120ml) water
Vegetable oil for deep-frying
Sweet Chili Sauce (see page 125), to serve

Stir-fried Water Spinach

Phat phakbung fai daeng

SERVES *4*

In this recipe, water spinach is stir-fried quickly over a big red flame—*fai daeng*. The leaves of the water spinach remain firm, even after cooking. If you can't find water spinach, regular spinach is a good substitute.

1. Coarsely chop the water spinach into 2-inch (5-cm) lengths. Discard the white part of the scallions and diagonally slice the green part. Drain the tofu and cut into long thin strips. Drain the water chestnuts and slice thinly. Cut the lemongrass into 1¼-inch (3-cm) lengths and crush lightly.
2. Using a food processor or a mortar and pestle, coarsely blend the ginger, shallots, chilies, garlic, lime leaves, and salt.
3. Bring a pan of water to a boil and blanch the water spinach for 1 minute, then drain.
4. In a frying pan, heat the oil and stir-fry the tofu over medium heat until golden. Add the water chestnuts and give a quick stir. Remove the tofu and water chestnuts from the pan and set aside.
5. In the same oil, sauté the blended spice mixture for 2–3 minutes over medium heat, until fragrant. Add the lemongrass, scallions, tofu, water chestnuts, and water spinach and sprinkle with soy sauce. Cook for 1 minute over high heat, stirring constantly. Transfer to a serving dish and sprinkle with the chopped tomato.

4½ cups (250g) water spinach
2 scallions
5 ounces (150g) firm tofu
7-ounce (200-g) can water chestnuts
1 stalk lemongrass
¾-inch (2-cm) cube fresh ginger, peeled
3 shallots
3 fresh red or green chilies
2 cloves garlic
7–8 kaffir lime leaves, torn
Salt to taste
2 tablespoons vegetable oil
1 tablespoon soy sauce
1 large tomato, chopped

Sweet Corn Cakes

Tod man khao pohd

SERVES *4*

3 cups (360g) cooked sweet corn kernels
1 medium onion, finely chopped
2 scallions, finely chopped
1 tablespoon curry powder
1 clove garlic, finely chopped
1 teaspoon ginger, grated
3 tablespoons corn flour
1 tablespoon rice flour
3 tablespoons fresh coriander, chopped
2 tablespoons soy sauce
½ teaspoon salt
Vegetable oil for deep-frying
Sweet Chili Sauce (see page 125), to serve
Cucumber Relish (see below), to serve

Thai snacks are mild, but they are served with strongly flavored sauces. These make a delicious and attractive addition to any buffet. Serve on banana leaves, with a selection of dips and relishes on the side.

1. Place all the ingredients, except the oil, in a bowl and mix gently to make a coarse dough.
2. Heat the oil for deep-frying to 350°F (180°C). Form the dough into small cakes, about 1½ inches (4 cm) in diameter, and slide into the oil in small batches.
3. Deep-fry until golden brown. Drain on kitchen paper. Serve with Sweet Chili Sauce and Cucumber Relish.

Cucumber Relish

Tangkwa dong

MAKES *1½ cups (360ml)*

2 cucumbers
1 medium carrot
3 fresh hot green or red chilies
4 shallots

4 tablespoons castor sugar
½ teaspoon salt
4 tablespoons rice vinegar

This relish is quick and easy to make and goes well with any satay, rice, dish or snack.

1. Slice or dice the cucumber, carrot, chilies, and shallots finely, and mix
2. In a small bowl, combine the sugar, salt, and vinegar, and stir until the sugar has dissolved. Pour this mixture over the vegetables and serve. Keeps for about a week, refrigerated.

DESSERTS

Mango with Sticky Rice   *Khao niew mamoang*

SERVES *4*

2 cups (400g) glutinous rice
¾ cup (150g) castor sugar
½ cup (120ml) coconut cream
½ cup (120ml) coconut milk
3 ripe mangoes
2 tablespoons coconut cream for drizzling, optional

This is a seasonal dessert in Thailand, since mango is a summer fruit. Glutinous rice is essential to the flavor and texture of this famous and popular dish.

1. Drain and rinse the rice well. Cook following the instructions for Japanese rice (see page 41).
2. In a large saucepan, combine the sugar, coconut cream, and coconut milk and bring to a boil. Remove from the heat and allow to cool completely.
3. Put the cooked rice and the coconut cream mixture into a serving bowl, and mix thoroughly. Cover and allow to stand for 30 minutes.
4. Peel the mangoes, slice into long strips, and arrange on top of the rice. Drizzle with coconut cream and serve.

Pumpkin in Coconut Cream   *Sang ka ya fak tong*

SERVES *4*   PHOTOGRAPH ON PAGE 101

9 ounces (250g) pumpkin, seeds and stringy fibers removed
2½ cups (600ml) coconut milk
½ cup (100g) palm sugar
Pinch of salt
2 tablespoons thick coconut cream for drizzling

Liquid desserts, such as fruit and vegetables served in coconut milk, are common in Thailand. This delicately flavored dish will add an elegant touch to your Thai meal.

1. Peel the pumpkin and dice finely.
2. Put the coconut milk, sugar, salt, and pumpkin in a saucepan and cook covered for 5–7 minutes over medium-low heat, stirring occasionally to prevent sticking, until you have a thick, well-blended mixture.
3. Cool and pour into serving dish. Drizzle with the coconut cream and serve hot or chilled.

Vietnam

I can assure you that in the bustling streets of Hanoi and the floating markets of the Mekong Delta, chaos and vibrancy come in equal measure. Everywhere are beautiful crafts—embroidery, painting, lacquer, ceramics . . . And everywhere, the food reflects the same intriguing blend of energy and creativity.

Vietnamese cuisine defies easy definition. It retains many influences from neighboring Asian countries and even from Europe—a reflection of the country's eventful history— yet maintains its own unique identity. The northern region, with its proximity to the Chinese border, uses black pepper and ginger, while central Vietnamese cuisine tends to be hotter and spicier. South Vietnamese food incorporates a lot of fruit and vegetables. And France's long presence in the country is evident from the Vietnamese love of potatoes, asparagus, and French bread.

Vietnamese vegetarian cuisine embraces all the qualities of a healthy diet—low in carbohydrates, fat, and cholesterol; high in protein and fiber. Very little oil is used even while stir frying; yet the flavors are still potent and satisfying.

The diversity of Vietnamese cuisine only adds to its mystery. Balancing the sweet, salty, sour, and spicy flavors to strike a harmonious note is the essence of Vietnamese cooking. Feel free to adjust the soy sauce, lime juice, sugar, and chilies to suit your palette. The final taste is yours to create.

SOUPS AND SALADS

Asparagus Soup   *Sup mang tay*

SERVES *4*

I n Ho Chi Minh City, where there is a strong French influence, this is one of the most popular soups. It is often included on party menus, especially at weddings.

1. In a saucepan, bring 2 cups (480ml) of the vegetable stock to a boil. Add the asparagus and cook for 5–6 minutes over medium heat until tender. Season with salt and pepper.
2. In a mixing bowl, combine the cornstarch-and-water mixture with the remaining 1 cup (240ml) of vegetable stock. Gradually add to the soup, stirring constantly until it thickens.
3. Add the sesame oil and coriander stem to the soup. Remove from the heat and serve hot in individual bowls, garnished with coriander leaves.

3 cups (720ml) Vietnamese Vegetable Stock (see below)
15 ounces (425g) fresh green asparagus, cut into ½-inch (1-cm) pieces
½ teaspoon salt
Dash of pepper
½ tablespoon cornstarch mixed with 3 tablespoons water
1 teaspoon sesame oil
1 tablespoon coriander stem, chopped
Fresh coriander leaves, for garnish

Vietnamese Vegetable Stock   *Nuoc leo*   MAKES *6 cups (1.5 L)*

7 cups (1.8 L) water
2 carrots, sliced
3½ ounces (100g) daikon radish, sliced
1 stick celery, cut into 2-inch (5-cm) lengths
1 onion, sliced

2 leeks, chopped
1 cup (50g) coriander stem and root
1-inch (3-cm) piece fresh ginger, sliced
1 tablespoon salt

Bring the water to a boil in a large saucepan and put in all the vegetables, the coriander, and the ginger. Simmer over medium heat for 30–40 minutes. Add the salt and simmer for another 5 minutes. Strain the liquid and reserve the stock to use as required. Discard the vegetables.

Bamboo Shoot Salad   *Goi mang chay*

SERVES *4*

T his simple salad has been made in the countryside, where bamboo shoot is widely available, for hundred of years. Now it is popular in the cities too, and is widely sold in busy city marketplaces.

7 ounces (200g) bamboo shoots, cooked
1 cucumber
1¾ ounces (50g) daikon radish
1 carrot
1 cup (20g) fresh mint leaves, shredded
1 tablespoon Crispy Fried Shallots (see opposite)
1 tablespoon Crispy Fried Garlic (see opposite)

4 tablespoons soy sauce
1 teaspoon cayenne pepper
3 tablespoons lemon juice
1 tablespoon castor sugar
1 teaspoon sesame oil
1 teaspoon white sesame seeds, toasted (see page 42)
2 tablespoons roasted peanuts, coarsely ground
Fresh coriander leaves, for garnish

1. Slice the bamboo shoots, cucumber, daikon, and carrot into 2-inch (5-cm) long julienne strips. Place in a bowl and toss with the mint leaves, fried shallots, and fried garlic.
2. In a separate small bowl, combine the soy sauce, cayenne pepper, lemon juice, sugar, sesame oil, and sesame seeds. Stir to mix.
3. Pour the soy sauce mixture over the vegetables and mix in the peanuts. Garnish with coriander leaves and serve.

Crispy Fried Garlic and Garlic Oil

Toi phi　　　　　　　　　　　　MAKES *½ cup (120ml)*

½ cup (120ml) corn oil or vegetable oil
15 cloves garlic, thinly sliced
Pinch of turmeric

1. Heat the oil in a saucepan and sauté the garlic slices and turmeric over medium heat for 3–4 minutes, stirring continuously, until the slices turn golden brown and crisp.
2. Remove the garlic from the oil with a slotted spoon and drain on kitchen paper. Allow to cool, and store in an airtight jar. Keeps for a week, refrigerated.
3. Reserve the flavored garlic oil in a separate airtight jar for use in noodle dishes and salads. Store in the refrigerator. Keeps for two weeks, refrigerated.

Crispy Fried Shallots and Shallot Oil

Hanh tim phi　　　　　　　　MAKES *about 1 cup (240ml)*

1 cup (240ml) corn oil or vegetable oil
1 pound (450g) shallots, or red onion, thinly sliced
¼ teaspoon turmeric
½ teaspoon castor sugar

1. Heat the oil in a saucepan and sauté the shallots over medium heat for 10–15 minutes, stirring occasionally until lightly browned.
2. Add the turmeric and sugar and stir continuously for 2–3 minutes over medium-high heat until the shallots are well browned, taking care not to scorch them.
3. Remove the shallots from the oil with a slotted spoon and drain on kitchen paper. Allow to cool, and store in an airtight jar. Keeps for a week, refrigerated.
4. Reserve the flavored shallot oil in a separate airtight jar for use in salad dressings and other dishes. Store in the refrigerator. Keeps for two weeks, refrigerated.

3 cucumbers, finely chopped
1 carrot, shredded
½ teaspoon salt
1 fresh hot green chili, finely chopped
1 tablespoon soy sauce
1 teaspoon castor sugar
1 teaspoon ginger juice (see page 43)
2 teaspoons lime juice
2 tablespoons roasted peanuts, ground
1 tablespoon white sesame seeds, toasted (see page 42)
½ cup (10g) fresh coriander leaves, for garnish

Cucumber Salad with Sesame Seeds

Dua leo tron dau dam

SERVES *4*

Fresh, crunchy, seasonal vegetables are used beautifully in Vietnamese salads, gently flavored with simple dressings and fresh herbs such as coriander and mint. This delicious salad is perfect for a hot summer day.

1. Mix the cucumber and carrot in a large bowl. Add the salt and set aside for 10 minutes. Drain off the excess liquid.
2. In a small bowl, combine the chili, soy sauce, sugar, ginger juice, lime juice, and peanuts. Stir well and pour over the carrots and cucumber.
3. Transfer to a serving dish and sprinkle with the sesame seeds. Garnish with coriander leaves and serve.

Fresh Coriander Soup

Canh ngo ri

SERVES *4*

*C*anh is the general term used to describe the delicately flavored broth that is served as a part of most meals in Vietnam. Here, coriander blends with tamarind to create an aromatic, light soup.

1. In a saucepan, bring the vegetable stock and lemongrass to a boil, then turn the heat to medium and simmer for 4–5 minutes. Remove the lemongrass stalk.
2. Heat the oil in a saucepan and sauté the shallots and garlic until soft. Add the mushrooms and stir briefly. Add the contents of this pan to the vegetable stock.
3. Put the tamarind juice, sugar, soy sauce, pepper, and salt in the saucepan with the vegetable stock. Simmer for 3–4 minutes. Add the bean sprouts and fresh coriander and remove from heat. Garnish with coriander leaves.

4 cups (960ml) Vietnamese Vegetable Stock (see page 130)
1 stalk lemongrass, cut in two
1 tablespoon vegetable oil
2 shallots, thinly sliced
2 cloves garlic, minced
4 button mushrooms, thinly sliced
1 tablespoon tamarind juice
½ teaspoon castor sugar
2 tablespoons soy sauce
½ teaspoon freshly ground black pepper
½ teaspoon salt
1 cup (100g) bean sprouts
1 cup (20g) fresh coriander, with stems, chopped *
Fresh coriander leaves, for garnish

* Use the entire coriander, finely chopped, except the root. The coriander root can be added to the stock with the lemongrass and removed before use.

Tamarind Soup with Pineapple and Okra

Canh chua thom va dau bap

SERVES *4*   PHOTOGRAPH ON PAGE 103

*S*oup is a part of all Vietnamese meals, very often poured over rice. This famous sweet and sour soup has an interesting contrast of flavors, colors and textures.

1. In a saucepan, combine the tamarind juice, vegetable stock, oil, salt, sugar, soy sauce, ketchup, Spicy Chili Sauce, fried shallots, and fried garlic. Bring to a boil over medium heat and add the pineapple, okra, and celery. Simmer for 2–3 minutes.
2. Mix in the tomato, bean sprouts, scallions, and coriander stem. Remove from the heat and serve hot, garnished with coriander leaves.

½ cup (120ml) tamarind juice
4 cups (960ml) Vietnamese Vegetable Stock (see page 130), or water
2 teaspoons vegetable oil
1 teaspoon salt
1 teaspoon castor sugar
2 tablespoons soy sauce
1 tablespoon tomato ketchup
1 tablespoon Spicy Chili Sauce (see below)
1 tablespoon Crispy Fried Shallots (see page 131)
1 teaspoon Crispy Fried Garlic (see page 131)
Flesh of ¼ pineapple, cut into bite-sized chunks
4 okra, sliced diagonally
½ stick celery, sliced diagonally
1 tomato, cut into thin wedges
1 cup (100g) bean sprouts
½ small scallion, chopped
1 teaspoon coriander stem, chopped
Fresh coriander leaves, for garnish

Spicy Chili Sauce   *Nuoc cham cay*   MAKES *½ cup (120ml)*

3 fresh hot chilies, red or green, finely chopped
2 cloves garlic, finely chopped
3 tablespoons fresh coriander leaves, chopped
3 tablespoons lime juice

3 tablespoons soy sauce
3 tablespoons water
1 tablespoon castor sugar

The fresh chilies perk up this sauce, while the coriander leaves add an earthy flavor.

Using a mortar and pestle or a food processor, grind the chilies and garlic until smooth. Transfer to a small bowl. Add all the other ingredients and stir until the sugar has dissolved. Set aside for 10 minutes for the flavors to merge. Keeps refrigerated for about a week.

MAIN DISHES AND RICE

Pancakes Rolled with Vegetables   *Banh xeo chay*

2 cups (315g) rice flour
2 tablespoons cornstarch
½ teaspoon turmeric
3½ cups (840ml) coconut milk
½ teaspoon salt
Pinch of baking powder
2 tablespoons vegetable oil
1 small onion, sliced
2 cloves garlic, sliced
1¾ ounces (50g) daikon radish, julienned
1 carrot, julienned
1 cup (100g) bean sprouts
4 tablespoons chives, chopped
Vegetable oil for drizzling
Vietnamese Dipping Sauce (see page 134), to serve
Pickled Radish and Carrot (see below), to serve

* These pancakes are simply delicious when eaten wrapped in a rice paper roll. First soften the rice paper by spraying with water, then place on a dry plate. Place some lettuce, mustard leaves, and fresh herbs in the center of the rice paper. Place a piece of pancake over the leaves and herbs and roll up. Serve with Vietnamese Dipping Sauce or Pickled Carrot and Radish.

SERVES *4*

Vietnamese pizza! These savory pancakes filled with vegetables are chewy and slightly crispy at the ends. Enjoy them with Vietnamese Dipping Sauce or Pickled Radish and Carrot.

1. In a bowl, mix the rice flour, cornstarch, and turmeric with the coconut milk. Add the salt and the baking powder and stir until smooth. Set aside for 15 minutes.
2. Heat the oil in a saucepan and sauté the onion and garlic briefly. Add the daikon and carrot, stir over high heat for a minute, then remove with a slotted spoon and set aside. Reserve the oil.
3. Heat a frying pan and grease it with a little oil. Pour in a quarter of the rice-flour batter and spread it out to make an even layer. Take a quarter of each of the sautéed vegetables, bean sprouts, and chives and spread over the batter. Drizzle a little oil around the edges of the pancake and cook for 3–4 minutes, until the underside is golden brown.
4. Fold in half and slide onto a serving plate. Repeat with the remaining batter and vegetables. Serve with Vietnamese Dipping Sauce or Pickled Radish and Carrot.

Pickled Radish and Carrot   *Do chua*   MAKES *1 cup (150g)*

3½ ounces (100g) white radish	1 tablespoon castor sugar
1 carrot	1 tablespoon rice vinegar
1 teaspoon salt	1 tablespoon water

This dish can be made with julienned cucumber, sliced chilies, water spinach stem, or garlic cloves.

1. Slice the radish and carrot into julienne strips.
2. In a bowl, mix the salt, sugar, vinegar, and water and stir until the sugar has dissolved. Add the radish and carrot and leave to stand for at least 20 minutes before serving.

Rice Noodle Soup

Banh canh chay

SERVES *4*

This is usually eaten as breakfast food or as a snack after one's afternoon nap, often accompanied by Tapioca with Mung Beans (see page 138). For a fiery touch, add some Chili Lemongrass Sauté (see opposite).

1. Refresh the vermicelli by immersing in boiling water for one minute. Drain and set aside. Blanch the bean sprouts and set aside.
2. Place the shiitake, carrot, and tofu in a saucepan with the water, soy sauce, and sugar. Bring to a boil then lower the heat to medium and simmer for 4–5 minutes, until the liquid is almost absorbed.
3. In a separate saucepan, heat the Vietnamese Vegetable Stock.
4. Heat the oil in a frying pan and sauté the chilies and garlic until fragrant. Add to the vegetable stock and mix.
5. To serve, divide the blanched bean sprouts between 4 individual bowls. Divide the vermicelli into 4 equal portions and place over the bean sprouts. Evenly distribute the mushrooms, carrot, and tofu over the vermicelli. Sprinkle with the chives and finally pour the stock into the bowls.
6. Arrange the scallions, onion, coriander leaves, and Chili Lemongrass Sauté in separate bowls at the table to use as garnishes.

14 ounces (400g) rice vermicelli, cooked
1½ cups (150g) bean sprouts
4 dried shiitake mushrooms, soaked in hot water for 10 minutes and drained
1 carrot, sliced into 1-inch (3-cm) julienne
7 ounces (200g) atsuage deep-fried tofu, cut into strips
1½ cups (360ml) water
½ tablespoon soy sauce
1 teaspoon castor sugar
4 cups (960ml) Vietnamese Vegetable Stock (see page 130)
2 teaspoons vegetable oil
2 fresh red chilies, minced
2 cloves garlic, minced
Handful chives, chopped, for garnish
1 scallion, chopped, for garnish
¼ onion, thinly sliced, for garnish
Fresh coriander leaves, for garnish
Chili Lemongrass Sauté (see opposite), for garnish

Chili Lemongrass Sauté

Ot sate   MAKES **1½ cups (360ml)**

¼ cup (60ml) vegetable oil
8–10 cloves garlic, minced
10–12 fresh red chilies, minced
2 stalks lemongrass, minced
⅓ teaspoon salt

Every Vietnamese household has a ready supply of this delicious sauce ready to be mixed into noodle dishes.

Heat the oil in a saucepan and sauté the garlic for 3–4 minutes over medium heat until soft. Add the chilies, lemongrass, and salt. Stir for 4–5 minutes until fragrant. Remove from the heat and allow to cool. Store in an airtight jar. Keeps for about a week, refrigerated.

Stir-fried Eggplant and Tofu in Spicy Sauce

Ca tim xao dau hu

SERVES **4**   PHOTOGRAPH ON PAGE 103

14 ounces (400g) eggplant
7 ounces (200g) atsuage deep-fried tofu
3 tablespoons vegetable oil
2 cloves garlic, finely chopped
2 fresh hot chilies, green or red, finely chopped
4 shallots, finely sliced
4 dried shiitake mushrooms, soaked in hot water for
    10 minutes, drained, and diced finely
½ teaspoon salt
½ teaspoon freshly ground pepper
½ teaspoon castor sugar
1 teaspoon Spicy Chili Sauce (see page 132)
2 tablespoons soy sauce
1 tablespoon rice vinegar
½ cup (120ml) Vietnamese Vegetable Stock (see
    page 130)
2 tablespoons cashew nuts, fried
½ teaspoon sesame oil
Fresh coriander leaves, for garnish

This delicious main course is quick to make and an attractive addition to the table.

1. Cut the eggplant into 2-inch (5 cm) long slices. Cut the tofu into bite-sized pieces.
2. Heat the oil in a wok and sauté the garlic and chilies briefly over medium heat. Add the shallots, eggplant, tofu, and mushrooms. Stir-fry over high heat for 2–3 minutes, until the eggplants release some of their liquid.
3. Add the salt, pepper, sugar, Spicy Chili Sauce, soy sauce, vinegar, and vegetable stock and stir until the liquid is absorbed.
4. Sprinkle with the cashew nuts, drizzle with the sesame oil, and serve garnished with coriander leaves.

Vietnamese Fried Rice

Com chien thap cam

SERVES **4**   PHOTOGRAPH ON PAGE 103

3 tablespoons vegetable oil
2 cloves garlic, finely chopped
1 medium onion, finely chopped
1 carrot, shredded
1 cup (160g) cooked green peas
3 dried shiitake mushrooms, soaked in hot water for
    10 minutes, drained, and diced
1 tablespoon soy sauce
½ teaspoon salt
1 teaspoon castor sugar
½ teaspoon ground black or white pepper
4 cups (630g) cooked long-grain rice, cold
1 scallion with greens, finely sliced
Fresh coriander leaves, for garnish
Chopped chives, for garnish

Rice is an integral part of Vietnamese cuisine. This fried rice dish originated in China but is very popular in Vietnam. This is a great way to use leftover rice.

1. Heat the oil in a large wok and sauté the garlic and onion briefly over high heat. Add the carrot, peas, and mushrooms and stir to mix. Cook covered for 3–4 minutes, stirring occasionally.
2. Add the soy sauce, salt, sugar, and pepper and mix in the cooked rice. Cook until heated through, breaking up any lumps that may have formed.
3. Stir in the scallions and remove from the heat. Serve garnished with fresh coriander leaves and chives.

SIDE DISHES AND SNACKS

Fried Peanuts

Dau phong da ca

MAKES *2 cups*

These crunchy fried peanuts are available everywhere, from crowded shopping areas to movie theaters—wherever there are people, these peanuts are sure to go!

1½ cups (200g) raw peanuts
2 cups (315g) rice flour
1 tablespoon Spicy Chili Sauce (see page 132)
½ teaspoon salt
Pinch of baking powder
⅔ cup (160ml) water
Vegetable oil for deep-frying

1. Soak the peanuts in water for 30 minutes. Drain and set aside.
2. In a bowl, mix the rice flour with the Spicy Chili Sauce, salt, and baking powder. Add the peanuts and gradually add the water to make a coarse batter.
3. In a wok, heat the oil for deep-frying to 350°F (180°C). Take spoonfuls of the batter and deep-fry, in batches, until crisp and golden brown. Drain on kitchen paper and allow to cool before serving.

Mushroom Balls with Plum Sauce

Nam vien chen voi sot xi muoi

SERVES *4*

This is a popular takeout snack in the vegetarian shops and restaurants in the bustling business districts of Ho Chi Minh City.

8 dried shiitake mushroom caps, reconstituted and chopped
2 reconstituted, dried wood ear mushrooms, chopped
1¾ ounces (50g) straw mushrooms, halved
½ carrot, finely chopped
1 cup (125g) all-purpose flour
2 cloves garlic, finely chopped
½-inch (1-cm) cube fresh ginger, peeled and finely chopped
2 tablespoons soy sauce
2 fresh hot chilies, green or red, finely chopped
½ teaspoon castor sugar
½ teaspoon ground black pepper
½ teaspoon salt
⅔ cup (160ml) water
Vegetable oil for deep-frying
1 cup (100g) bread crumbs
1 cup (240ml) plum sauce, to serve

1. In a bowl, combine the mushrooms and carrot with the flour. Add the garlic, ginger, soy sauce, chilies, sugar, pepper, and salt. Gradually add the water, stirring to make a coarse mix.
2. In a wok, heat the oil for deep-frying to 350°F (180°C). Take spoonfuls of the mushroom mixture, roll in the bread crumbs, and shape into balls. Gently slide the balls into the hot oil and fry until golden brown, a few at a time. Drain on kitchen paper.
3. Place the bowl with the plum sauce in the center of a plate, arrange the mushroom balls around it, and serve.

Stir-fried Asparagus

Mang tay xao

1 pound (450g) fresh green asparagus
1 tablespoon sesame oil
2 cloves garlic, minced
3 shallots, sliced
4 tablespoons coconut milk
½ teaspoon castor sugar
½ teaspoon freshly ground pepper
Pinch of salt

Asparagus in Vietnamese cooking owes its presence to the French colonial influence. Here, the delicate asparagus is quickly stir-fried with garlic and soy sauce to make an attractive side dish.

1. Remove the hard ends from the asparagus and cut into 2-inch (5-cm) lengths.
2. Heat the oil in a frying pan and sauté the garlic and shallots over medium heat until fragrant. Add the asparagus and coconut milk stir-fry for 4–5 minutes until heated through.
3. Put the sugar, pepper, and salt in the pan with the asparagus, and stir. When the liquid has been fully absorbed, transfer to a serving dish.

Vietnamese Transparent Spring Rolls

Goi cuon

SERVES 4   PHOTOGRAPH ON PAGE 102

1¾ ounces (50g) dried rice vermicelli
8 dried shiitake mushroom caps, reconstituted .
3½ ounces (100g) atsuage deep-fried tofu
3½ ounces (100g) daikon radish
1 medium carrot
8 sheets spring roll wrappers
8 shiso leaves
½ cup (50g) bean sprouts
12–15 fresh basil leaves
8 chives
Fresh coriander leaves, for garnish
15–20 fresh mint leaves, for garnish
Spicy Peanut Sauce (see below), to serve

These crystal clear rolls, filled with thin slivers of vegetables, are easily one of the most popular Vietnamese dishes. I loved these rolls the first time I tried them and immediately became a fan of Vietnamese food.

1. Bring the vermicelli to a boil in a small saucepan and cook for 2–3 minutes until soft. Drain and set aside. Halve the shiitake caps and slice the tofu into thin strips. Slice the daikon and carrot into 2-inch (5-cm) julienne strips.
2. Use a water sprayer to wet the spring roll wrappers. Place on a flat surface.
3. Make a line of vegetables along the bottom half of the wrapper, starting with the shiso leaves and 2 pieces of shiitake. Place about two tablespoons of the other vegetables, some basil, chives, vermicelli, and tofu on top of the leaves and shiitake.
4. Spray a little more water over the wrappers if the edges seem dry. Roll over once to cover the filling and fold the sides in to secure the ends. Roll up to the end of the sheet. Repeat with the rest of the rice sheets until all the filling has been used.
5. To serve, slice each roll in half diagonally to display the colorful vegetable filling. Arrange over a bed of coriander and mint leaves and serve immediately with Spicy Peanut Sauce.

Spicy Peanut Sauce

Tuong dau phong cay   MAKES ½ cup (120ml)

½ cup (120ml) water
1 tablespoon castor sugar
2 tablespoons white miso
1½ tablespoons roasted peanuts, ground
2 fresh red chilies minced

This sauce can be used for any appetizer, and is often served with Vietnamese Transparent Spring Rolls.

In a small saucepan, bring the water to a boil. Add the sugar, miso, and peanuts, stir to mix, and remove from the heat. Allow to cool, then mix in the chilies.

DESSERTS

Corn in Coconut Milk

Che bap

SERVES *4*

1¼ cups (150g) cooked sweet corn kernels
3 cups (720ml) water
¾ cup (150g) castor sugar
2 teaspoons cornstarch dissolved in 3 tablespoons water
2 cups (480ml) coconut milk
Coconut cream, for drizzling

This typical Vietnamese dessert is often served at family gatherings.

1. Using a food processor, coarsely puree the corn. In a saucepan, bring the water to a boil. Add the pureed corn and sugar and stir over medium heat until the sugar dissolves.
2. Add the cornstarch-and-water mixture and stir continuously until the corn mixture thickens. Turn the heat to low and simmer for 2–3 minutes.
3. Pour in the coconut milk while stirring continuously. Remove from the heat and cool. Pour into individual bowls and serve warm or cold, drizzled with a little coconut cream.

Tapioca with Mung Beans

Che dau xanh

SERVES *4*

½ cup (100g) split mung beans
3 cups (720ml) water
⅓ cup (50g) tapioca pearls
¾ cup (150g) castor sugar
2 cups (480ml) coconut milk

In this classic cold sweet, the tapioca pearls and the mung beans swim in the coconut milk. It is usually eaten in the late afternoon as a snack with Rice Noodle Soup (see page 134) or simply by itself, but it can also be served as a dessert or as part of a buffet table setting.

1. Soak the mung beans in cold water for 10 minutes, then drain. In a large saucepan, bring the 3 cups water to a boil. Add the tapioca, turn the heat to low, and cook for 12–15 minutes until the tapioca pearls have turned soft and transparent.
2. Put the mung beans in the pan with the tapioca, turn the heat to medium, and cook for another 10–12 minutes, until the mung beans are tender. Add the sugar and stir until it dissolves.
3. Add the coconut milk and mix gently. Remove from the heat, transfer to a serving bowl, and set aside. This sweet may be served warm or thoroughly chilled.

Burma

I will never forget the first time I entered the Burmese restaurant in the small lanes of Hiroo, a posh residential neighborhood of Tokyo. I felt like I had entered a time machine. The serenity of the warm wooden interiors, comfortably simple and frugal, transported me to a land of orange-robed monks and golden pagodas.

The more I learned about Burma from the chef, Mo Ko Ko, the more mysterious and surreal it seemed. I listened, enthralled, as he spoke about his life in his home country, how meditation and discipline are a natural part of the peoples' upbringing, how every man must live the life of a monk for three three-week periods before they turn twenty-one. What brought me back to the present was the sight of the chef making a large bowl of the tomato salad, Kayenchinthi Thoat —a bowl full of shredded cabbage and tomato wedges, with red onion slices and rocket leaves, all flavored with gay abandon. I watched, dazed, as he threw in fried shallots and garlic, drizzled on some sweet soy sauce, shallot oil, and lemon juice, sprinkled it all with peanuts and ground sesame seeds, and hand mixed all of this with a tablespoon of toasted chickpea flour to give the final velvety touch to this amazing salad.

The first bite was an explosion of flavors and textures, and it was my first step on the journey to explore the hidden mysteries of Burmese cuisine. If you haven't had Burmese food before, your own journey can begin on the following page.

SOUPS AND SALADS

Bean Thread Noodle Salad with Potatoes

Kyar zan thoat

SERVES *4*

A famous Burmese salad made with boiled potatoes and the versatile bean thread noodles. Lemongrass adds a refreshing touch to this salad, which needs only a soup to make a complete meal.

1. Bring the 3 cups water to a boil in a saucepan, put in the noodles, and cook for 3–4 minutes. Drain and set aside to cool.
2. In a mixing bowl, combine the noodles with the potato, bean sprouts, and scallions. Add the toasted chickpea flour, crispy fried shallots, crispy fried garlic, shallot oil, salt, soy sauce, lemongrass, green chili, peanuts, and tamarind juice. Mix thoroughly.
3. Transfer to a serving bowl and garnish with cherry tomatoes and coriander leaves.

3 cups (720ml) water
1¾ ounces (50g) bean thread noodles
1 medium potato, boiled and sliced
½ cup (50g) bean sprouts, blanched
1 scallion, finely sliced
1 tablespoon Toasted Chickpea Flour (see below)
1 tablespoon Crispy Fried Shallots (see page 131)
1 tablespoon Crispy Fried Garlic (see page 131)
2 tablespoons Shallot Oil (see page 131)
¼ teaspoon salt
1 tablespoon soy sauce
½ stalk lemongrass, pureed
1 fresh hot green chili, finely chopped
1 tablespoon roasted peanuts, coarsely ground
2 teaspoons tamarind juice
Cherry tomatoes, halved, for garnish
Fresh coriander leaves, for garnish

* Wood ear mushrooms, reconstituted and chopped, and shredded white cabbage may be added to the salad.

Toasted Chickpea Flour *Besan*

1 cup (90g) chickpea flour

Place the chickpea flour in a frying pan and toast over medium-low heat for 2–3 minutes until the flour turns a shade darker. Remove from the heat and allow to cool. Store in an airtight container.

Ginger Salad

Gin thoat

SERVES *4*

This crisp, spicy salad was originally sustenance for monks who spend long hours in seated meditation.

1. (If using the pickled ginger, omit this first step.) Soak the julienned ginger in cold water for 10 minutes. Drain and set aside.
2. Place the ginger and cabbage in a mixing bowl. Add the nuts, sesame seeds, peanuts, and chilies. Toss to mix.
3. Add the lemon juice, soy sauce, salt, and toasted chickpea flour and drizzle with the sesame oil. Add the cherry tomatoes and mix thoroughly.
4. Arrange the lettuce on a serving dish and spoon the ginger salad over it.

1¾ ounces (50g) beni shoga pickled ginger, or fresh ginger, peeled and julienned
½ cup (25g) white cabbage, shredded
4 tablespoons mixed nuts
1 tablespoon black sesame seeds, crushed
1 tablespoon roasted peanuts, coarsely ground
2 fresh hot green chilies, thinly sliced
2 teaspoons lemon juice
2 teaspoons soy sauce
¼ teaspoon salt
1 teaspoon Toasted Chickpea Flour (see above)
2 teaspoons sesame oil for drizzling
4 cherry tomatoes, halved
Lettuce leaves, torn, to serve

Spicy Coconut and Vegetable Soup

Ohnnoh hi thizone hincho

SERVES *4*

2 cups (480ml) coconut milk
1 cup (240ml) water
5 lime leaves
2-inch (5-cm) piece lemongrass, crushed
2 tablespoons vegetable oil
1 medium onion, finely chopped
2 cloves garlic, finely chopped
½-inch (1-cm) cube fresh ginger, peeled and finely chopped
2 fresh hot green chilies, finely chopped
½ teaspoon paprika
½ teaspoon black pepper
3 tablespoons soy sauce
½ teaspoon salt
1 teaspoon lemon juice
4 broccoli florets, halved
4 cauliflower florets, halved
1 green or purple eggplant, sliced
1¾ ounces (50g) straw mushrooms, halved
1 tablespoon roasted peanuts, coarsely ground
3 tablespoons Toasted Chickpea Flour (see opposite)
Fresh coriander leaves, for garnish

This popular soup is sold at cafes and by roadside vendors all over the country. The small round green variety of eggplant widely used in southeast Asian cuisine works well in this dish if you can get hold of any.

1. Put the coconut milk, water, lime leaves, and lemongrass in a saucepan and bring to a boil. Turn the heat to low and simmer for 5–7 minutes.
2. Meanwhile, heat the oil in a saucepan and sauté the onion, garlic, ginger, and chilies over medium heat for 2–3 minutes. Add the paprika, black pepper, soy sauce, salt, and lemon juice. Turn the heat to high, and stir for 1 minute.
3. Add the broccoli, cauliflower, eggplant, and mushrooms and mix well.
4. Put the vegetable mixture in the saucepan with the coconut milk mixture and bring to a boil.
5. Put the peanuts and the toasted chickpea flour in the saucepan and simmer for 3–4 minutes, stirring continuously until the mixture thickens.
6. Garnish with coriander leaves and serve hot.

Tomato Salad

Kayenchinthi thoat

SERVES *4*

Lettuce leaves, roughly torn, for garnish
1 cup (45g) white cabbage, shredded
½ red onion, thinly sliced
1 cup (20g) arugula leaves, torn
1 tablespoon Crispy Fried Shallots (see page 131)
1 tablespoon Crispy Fried Garlic (see page 131)
2 tablespoons Shallot Oil (see page 131)
1 tablespoon roasted peanuts, coarsely ground
½ teaspoon dried basil
1 tablespoon crushed black sesame seeds
1 teaspoon lemon juice
1 teaspoon soy sauce
1 teaspoon sweet soy sauce
½ teaspoon salt
1 tomato, sliced into thin wedges
1 teaspoon Toasted Chickpea Flour (see opposite)
Fresh coriander leaves, for garnish

* Long Bean Salad is another popular Burmese dish. Follow the recipe for Tomato Salad, substituting blanched long beans for the tomatoes.

This is one of my favorite Burmese salads. The fried shallots and garlic with the peanuts and sesame seeds add delicious flavor and crunch to this exotic salad. For a colorful variation, replace the tomato with sliced avocado and a few cherry tomatoes.

1. Make a bed of lettuce leaves on a serving dish.
2. In a deep bowl, combine the cabbage, red onion, and arugula. Add the crispy fried shallots, crispy fried garlic, shallot oil, peanuts, basil, and sesame seeds. Toss to mix.
3. Add the lemon juice, soy sauce, sweet soy sauce, salt, and tomato wedges. Finally, add the toasted chickpea flour and toss again.
4. Place the tossed salad on the bed of lettuce and serve.

MAIN DISHES

Cauliflower Coconut Curry with Noodles

Ban gobi ohnnoh khaukswe

SERVES **4**

PHOTOGRAPH ON PAGE 104

This delicately spiced curry is poured over a bowl of wheat noodles and served with a variety of accompaniments that lend contrasting flavors and textures to the dish and allow the taste to be adjusted to the diner's mood. I have used cauliflower as the main vegetable because it absorbs the flavors of the soup beautifully.

1. Blanch the cauliflower and carrot. Drain, mix with the green peas and set aside.
2. Heat the oil in a saucepan and sauté the onion for 5–6 minutes over medium heat, until lightly browned. Add the Thai Soup Paste, cauliflower, carrot, and peas. Stir-fry for 1 minute. Add the sugar and salt.
3. Put the water and coconut milk into the saucepan with the vegetables and bring to a boil. Turn down the heat and simmer for 4–5 minutes, stirring occasionally.
4. Divide the noodles between individual bowls and pour a ladleful of the cauliflower coconut curry over each. Serve with the accompaniments and make sure that your guests add a little of everything to the soup.

11 ounces (310g) cauliflower florets
1 carrot, sliced diagonally
½ cup (80g) cooked green peas
4 tablespoons vegetable oil
1 medium onion, grated
4 tablespoons Thai Soup Paste (see page 115)
1 teaspoon castor sugar
1 teaspoon salt
3 cups (720ml) water
3 cups (720ml) coconut milk
1 pound (450g) wheat flour noodles or spaghetti, cooked

FOR THE ACCOMPANIMENTS

4 Split Pea Fritters (see page 148)
Toasted Chickpea Flour (see page 140)
Crispy Fried Shallots (see page 131)
Crispy Fried Garlic (see page 131)
Fresh coriander leaves
Fresh parsley
Finely sliced scallions
Ramen noodles, deep-fried and broken
Red chili flakes
Lemon wedges

Curry with Split Pea Fritters

Pe kyaw chet

SERVES **4**

Split Pea Fritters are a popular snack in Burma, but they become a delicious and hearty meal when served with curry sauce and piping hot rice.

1. Heat the oil in a saucepan and sauté the onion, garlic, and ginger for 2–3 minutes over medium heat. Add the tomatoes, salt, curry powder, and water. Bring to a boil.

2 tablespoons vegetable oil
1 onion, finely chopped
2 cloves garlic, finely chopped
1 pea-sized piece fresh ginger, peeled and finely chopped
2 medium tomatoes, chopped
½ teaspoon salt
½ teaspoon curry powder
1 cup (240ml) water
4 Split Pea Fritters (see page 148), broken into pieces
Fresh coriander leaves, for garnish

2. Turn the heat to medium-low, put the broken split pea fritters in the saucepan, and simmer for 4–5 minutes. Sprinkle with coriander leaves and serve with rice.

Stir-fried Spinach with Mushrooms

Kazunyeat hmo kyaw

SERVES *4*   PHOTOGRAPH ON PAGE 105

11 ounces (310g) spinach
7 ounces (200g) enoki mushrooms
2 teaspoons vegetable oil
½ medium onion, finely sliced
2 cloves garlic, thinly sliced
1 red bell pepper, thinly sliced
1 teaspoon sweet soy sauce
1 teaspoon soy sauce
Pinch of salt
¼ teaspoon black pepper
White sesame seeds, toasted, for garnish (see page 47)

Tender enoki mushrooms add a subtle taste to this popular preparation. Water spinach (also known as morning glory) can be substituted for regular spinach.

1. Rinse the spinach under running water. Trim the base of the enoki clusters, and separate the mushrooms.
2. Heat the oil and sauté the onion and garlic for 1 minute over medium heat, until the onions are soft.
3. Add the enoki and red pepper and stir briefly. Add the spinach and mix. Add the sweet soy sauce, soy sauce, salt, and pepper. Stir for 2 minutes over high heat and transfer to a serving dish. Serve garnished with the sesame seeds.

Tofu and Pickled Mustard Stir-fry

Tayoke pepyar kyamasui monnyinchin tof kyaw

SERVES *4*

14 ounces (400g) firm tofu
2 tablespoons vegetable oil
2 cloves garlic, finely chopped
1 cup (100g) pickled mustard greens, chopped
2 fresh hot green chilies, finely sliced
1 teaspoon lemon juice
2 tablespoons soy sauce
¼ teaspoon salt

This is an example of Chinese-Burmese fusion cooking. The prefix *tayoke* is added to dishes of Chinese origin. Chinese pickled mustard greens are available from Asian supermarkets.

1. Drain the tofu, wrap in a dish towel, and place a weight, such as a dinner plate, on top. Set aside for 10 minutes. Cut into ¾-inch (2-cm) dice.
2. Heat the oil and sauté the tofu for 3–4 minutes over medium heat, until crisp and brown. Add the garlic and sauté until fragrant.
3. Add the pickled mustard leaves and green chilies, turn the heat to high, and stir-fry for 1–2 minutes.
4. Sprinkle with the lemon juice, soy sauce, and salt. Toss to mix. Transfer to a dish and serve with hot rice.

RICE AND NOODLES

Chili Rice

Ngayoak thi tamin soat

SERVES *4*

3 cups (550g) cooked short-grain rice
1 tablespoon Chilies in Oil (see page 148)
1 tablespoon soy sauce
1 tablespoon roasted peanuts, crushed
1 tablespoon Garlic Oil (see page 131)
1 teaspoon sweet soy sauce

This delicious spicy rice, ready in just a few minutes, is similar to the Korean Kimchi Rice (see page 177). In Burma, the rice is mixed by hand to ensure a thorough blending of flavors. Chilies in Oil, a staple of every Burmese kitchen, are a key ingredient in this dish.

In a bowl, mix all the ingredients together. Transfer to a serving dish and serve with pickles and a soup.

Stir-fried Noodles

Kyarzan kyaw

SERVES *4*

5 ounces (140g) rice vermicelli
1 tablespoon vegetable oil
1 medium onion, sliced
2 cloves garlic, finely chopped
3 tablespoons carrot, julienned
3 tablespoons snow peas, halved diagonally
1 cup (45g) white cabbage, shredded
2 cups (90g) Chinese cabbage, cut into 1¾-inch (3-cm) pieces
½ cup (20g) bok choy leaves, cut into long strips
1 tablespoon soy sauce
1 tablespoon sweet soy sauce
Pinch of salt
1 teaspoon sesame oil
Chilies in Oil (see page 148), to serve

Rice vermicelli is used in stir-fried dishes, and bean noodles are generally used in soups and salads. The sesame oil drizzled onto the vermicelli at the end of cooking time adds a delicious flavor.

1. Soak the vermicelli in water for at least an hour. Drain and set aside.
2. Heat the vegetable oil in a large saucepan and sauté the onion and garlic for 2–3 minutes over high heat, stirring all the time.
3. Add the carrot, snow peas, white cabbage, Chinese cabbage, and bok choy and stir-fry over high heat for 3–4 minutes, until the vegetables are glazed.
4. Add the vermicelli, soy sauce, sweet soy sauce, salt, and sesame oil and toss to mix. Transfer to a serving dish and serve with Chilies in Oil.

SIDE DISHES

Bamboo Shoot and Green Pea Stir-fry

Mhyit gyaw

SERVES *4*

4 tablespoons vegetable oil
1 medium onion, sliced
9 ounces (255g) cooked bamboo shoots, sliced
1 cup (160g) cooked green peas
½ teaspoon salt
1 tablespoon soy sauce
1 tablespoon sweet soy sauce
½ teaspoon paprika

An easy-to-make accompaniment to a meal, this stir-fry can be served with a slice of toast for breakfast, or with steamed rice for lunch. Chickpeas can be used instead of green peas.

1. Heat the oil in a saucepan and sauté the onion over medium heat for 7–8 minutes, until crisp. Add the bamboo shoots, turn the heat to high, and stir-fry for 2–3 minutes until lightly browned.
2. Put the green peas, salt, soy sauce, sweet soy sauce, and paprika in the pan. Toss briefly and transfer to a serving dish.

Braised Bitter Gourd

Chathin kyathi nhut

SERVES *4*

2 bitter gourds, about 3½ ounces (100g) each
1 teaspoon salt
2 tablespoons vegetable oil
1 large onion, minced
2 cloves garlic, finely chopped
½ cup (60g) roasted peanuts, coarsely ground
2 fresh hot green chilies, finely chopped
½ teaspoon paprika
½ teaspoon turmeric
¼ teaspoon salt
2 teaspoons vegetable oil
½ cup (120ml) water

Braising is a popular method of cooking in Burma, where the cooking until recently has been done on charcoal or wood. Braising leaves the cooking pan dry and ready to use for the next dish without wasting time and precious fuel. In this delicious dish, bitter gourd (also known as bitter melon) is stuffed with onion, garlic, chilies, and peanuts, then braised.

1. Cut each bitter gourd in half lengthwise, and spoon out the seeds. Bring a pan of water to a boil and add the salt. Immerse the bitter gourd shells into the boiling water for 2–3 minutes until the water turns green. Drain and set aside to cool.
2. Heat the 2 tablespoons vegetable oil in a saucepan and sauté the onion and garlic for 4–5 minutes over medium heat until the onions are lightly browned. Add the peanuts, chilies, paprika, turmeric, and salt. Stir briefly and remove from the heat.
3. Fill the bitter gourd shells with the spice mixture. Heat the 2 teaspoons oil in a saucepan, then add the stuffed bitter gourd. Pour ½ cup water into the pan and cook covered for 8–10 minutes over medium heat, stirring occasionally, until the water has been absorbed. Serve with steamed rice.

Deep-fried Vegetables in Batter

Ahkyaw soun

SERVES *4*

Vegetable oil for deep-frying
1 small eggplant, sliced into thin rounds
2 eringi mushrooms, halved lengthwise
1 green bell pepper, cut into 4 pieces
1 medium onion, sliced into thin rings
1½ cups (360ml) Spicy Besan Batter (see below)

Fritters are sold on every street corner of Mandalay and Rangoon. In Burma the locals rarely make these at home, opting to buy them from the street vendors or local shops where they are assured of taste and freshness. This crispy appetizer reminds me of Japanese tempura, but while tempura is made with all-purpose flour, the Burmese recipe calls for chickpea flour and rice flour. Make sure you put plenty of these deep-fried battered vegetables on your table—they disappear faster than you would think possible!

1. In a wok, heat the oil for deep-frying to 350°F (180°C). Dip the vegetable pieces in the batter and slide into the hot oil, a few at a time. Deep-fry until golden brown, and drain on kitchen paper.
2. Transfer to a serving dish and serve with Sweet Mango Chutney or Hot and Sour Dip (see below).

Spicy Besan Batter for Deep-fried Vegetables

Pemonh asut anhit   MAKES *1½ cups (360ml)*

½ cup (45g) Toasted Chickpea Flour (see page 140)
½ cup (75g) rice flour
Pinch of baking powder, optional
¼ teaspoon turmeric
¼ teaspoon paprika
1 teaspoon Ginger Garlic Paste (see page 18)
2 tablespoons fresh coriander leaves, with stalks, chopped
1 teaspoon corn oil
½ cup (120ml) cold water
½ teaspoon salt

Combine all the ingredients and mix until smooth. The batter should not be too thin. Baking powder gives the batter a crisp texture.

Sweet Mango Chutney

Tayet ti ta nut acho   MAKES *1½ cups (360ml)*

2 large ripe mangoes
2 tablespoons castor sugar
2 teaspoons Ginger Juice (see page 43)
½ teaspoon salt
2 tablespoons lemon juice

1. Peel and dice the mangoes and place in a saucepan. Add the sugar, ginger juice, salt, and lemon juice. Bring to a boil and simmer for 4–5 minutes over medium heat. Use a flat spoon to mash coarsely.
2. Transfer to a bowl and allow to cool. Serve with Burmese appetizers. Store in an airtight jar in the refrigerator. Keeps for about a week.

Hot and Sour Dip

Achin   MAKES *¼ cup (60ml)*

3 cloves garlic, grated
¾-inch (2-cm) cube fresh ginger, peeled and grated
2 tablespoons tamarind paste
2 tablespoons soy sauce
4 tablespoons water
1½ tablespoons castor sugar
1 teaspoon red chili flakes
½ teaspoon paprika
½ teaspoon salt
1 teaspoon white sesame seeds, toasted (see page 42)

This sauce is especially good with Deep-fried Winter Squash (see opposite) and Deep-fried Vegetables in Batter (see above). Tamarind is the most commonly used souring agent used in Burmese cuisine. Use lemon juice if you can't get hold of tamarind.

Combine all the ingredients to make a smooth sauce. Store in an airtight jar in the refrigerator. Keeps for several weeks.

SNACKS

Deep-fried Winter Squash
Bu te kyaw

SERVES *4*

1 pound (450g) winter squash
1½ cups (225g) rice flour
½ cup (75g) glutinous rice flour
1 medium onion, grated
1 teaspoon Ginger Garlic Paste (see page 18)
⅔ tablespoon salt
¼ teaspoon baking soda
1½ cups (360ml) water
Vegetable oil for deep frying
Hot and Sour Dip (see opposite), to serve

These savory snacks are sold in little thatched huts by hawkers who make them fresh to order. The tired traveler can take a breather under the trees, where a few stools are placed around a makeshift table. Glutinous rice flour gives the deep-fried squash a crispy texture. In Burma, a pale green bottle-shaped squash known as bottle gourd is used for this dish.

1. Peel the squash and remove the seeds. Cut into 2-inch (5-cm) long strips and set aside.
2. In a bowl, combine the rice flour and the glutinous rice flour with the onion, Ginger Garlic Paste, salt, and baking soda. Add the water gradually, mixing all the time to make a smooth batter.
3. Heat the oil to 350°F (180°C). Dip each strip of squash in the batter and slide into the hot oil, in small batches. Deep-fry until golden brown. Remove with a slotted spoon, drain on kitchen paper, then transfer to a serving dish. Serve with Hot and Sour Dip.

* Make banana fritters by substituting bananas for the squash.

Oriental Vegetable Crepes
Mohnpiketalet

SERVES *4*

2 cups (315g) rice flour
½ cup (60g) all-purpose flour
½ teaspoon salt
½ teaspoon baking powder
1½ cups (360ml) water
2 tablespoons black sesame seeds
2 tablespoons white sesame seeds
½ teaspoon salt
1 cup (100g) cooked green-pea sprouts
1 cup (45g) white cabbage, shredded
2 scallions, sliced
Sesame oil for drizzling
Dash of black pepper
Chilies in Oil (see page 148), to serve

My friend Mo Ko Ko remembers going to pagoda festivals in Rangoon as a child, where bustling stalls sold an array of food. Delicious sweet and savory crepes were his family's favorite festival snack, prepared on hand-carried stoves, and served folded up on a piece of paper. Here is an exotic version of the savory crepe.

1. In a bowl, combine the rice flour, all purpose flour, ½ teaspoon salt, and baking powder. Add the water and mix into a smooth, thin batter.
2. Toast the black and white sesame seeds and ½ teaspoon salt together in a dry saucepan over low heat, stirring constantly for 2–3 minutes until fragrant. Grind to a coarse mixture in a food processor.

147

3. In a bowl, combine the sprouts, cabbage, and scallions.

4. Grease a hot frying pan. Over medium-high heat, pour in a ladle-ful of the batter and spread evenly to make a crepe about 4 inches (10 cm) in diameter. Turn the heat to medium. Drizzle a little sesame oil around the sides of the pan.

5. Scatter 2 tablespoons of the sprout, cabbage, and scallion mixture over the crepe and press gently with a spatula. Sprinkle with a tea-spoon of the ground sesame seed mixture and a dash of pepper. Cook for 3–4 minutes until the base is lightly browned and the edges are crisp. Flip over and cook the other side for 3–4 minutes on medium heat. Fold the pancake in half and slide on to a serving dish.

6. Repeat this process until all the batter and vegetables have been used. Serve with Chilies in Oil.

Chilies in Oil *Balechaung* MAKES *1 cup (240ml)*

This spicy chili sauce is served as an accompaniment to rice and other Burmese dishes.

¼ cup (60ml) vegetable oil
1 medium onion, chopped
3 cloves garlic, finely chopped
20 dried red chilies, thinly sliced

½ teaspoon salt
2 tablespoons roasted peanuts, crushed, optional

1. Heat the oil in a saucepan and stir-fry the onion and garlic over medium heat for 3–4 minutes until crisp.
2. Add the chilies and salt and sauté for 2 minutes until the chilies are crisp.
3. Add the peanuts and mix well. Remove from the heat and transfer to a bowl to cool. Store in an airtight jar in the refrigerator. Will keep for about a month.

Split Pea Fritters

Kalar peya kyaw

SERVES *4*

PHOTOGRAPH ON PAGE 105

3 cups (500g) split yellow lentils
1 medium onion, finely chopped
2 fresh hot green chilies, finely chopped
½ cup (10g) fresh coriander leaves, with stalks, finely chopped
⅔ teaspoon salt
Vegetable oil for deep-frying
Handful fresh basil leaves, for garnish
Lemon wedges, to serve

In Burma, the prefix *kalar* is added to all dishes of Indian origin, and the stalls selling these fritters are Indian owned. The vendor makes a cone out of an old newspaper, throws in a dozen fritters, and the customer walks off happily eating them. The original Indian version includes minced ginger and coriander seeds. Either version is a deli-cious crunchy snack or accompaniment to a meal.

1. Wash the lentils and leave to soak in a deep bowl of water for 3–4 hours. Drain, and blend to a coarse puree in a food processor. Trans-fer to a bowl and add the onion, chilies, fresh coriander, and salt. Mix well and make round flat patties of about 1½ inches (4 cm) in diameter.

2. Heat the oil for deep-frying to 350°F (180°C) and slide in the pat-ties, a few at a time. Fry for 2–3 minutes over medium heat until golden brown. Remove from the oil with a slotted spoon and drain on kitchen paper.

3. Arrange on a serving dish, garnished with basil. Serve with lemon wedges and sprinkle with lemon juice before eating.

Indonesia

Satay, Gado Gado, Soto, Sayur Lodeh, Sambal Terong, Nasi Goreng, Sambal, Bakvan, Sambal Goreng Tempeh. These exotic sounding names could well be the vocal accompaniment to the lilting Indonesian gamelan music. They are, instead, the fabulous dishes that make up the Indonesian culinary repertoire.

On my first visit to Indonesia, I was fascinated by the array of dishes brought out in front of me as I dined with my friend Putri at a quiet restaurant in Jakarta. I was mesmerized by the atmosphere as fresh banana leaves were laid out with Indonesian music wafting in the background. Two waiters appeared from either side of the room with a tray of eight or ten dishes of food delicately balanced on each hand, which they placed in front of us with surprising ease. The table was soon overflowing with over twenty dishes of colorful and aromatic foods, many of them tailor-made to my vegetarian tastes.

The chef, a friend of my host, sat with us and shared the joys of the cuisine with me. Some of his insightful advice I take great pleasure in sharing with you, along with my own Indonesian vegetarian recipes.

Indonesian food is a great awakening for your taste buds. Indonesia—the Spice Islands—is home to many of the spices we use in the West today. Fresh spices are a part of everyday cooking, making the food is as multifaceted as its many islands.

SOUPS AND SALADS

Mixed Vegetable Salad with Peanut Sauce

Gado gado

SERVES *4*   PHOTOGRAPH ON PAGE 106

The signature dish of Indonesia, Gado Gado, is part of the daily diet as it is made from affordable ingredients. My Indonesian friend Nancy recommends mixing the peanut sauce with the vegetables before serving, for a harmonious blend of flavors. The finest Gado Gado is served wrapped in a banana leaf.

1. Arrange the vegetables on a serving platter and set aside.
2. For the sauce, heat the oil in a saucepan and sauté all the sauce ingredients for 2–3 minutes. Add ¼ cup water and simmer for a further 3–4 minutes over high heat. Remove from the heat and allow to cool. Transfer to a food processor and blend to a smooth paste.
3. To serve, pour the peanut sauce over the vegetable platter, scatter with tofu strips and fried shallots, and serve with krupuk.

1 cup (100g) bean sprouts, blanched
3 cups (135g) white cabbage, cut into bite-sized pieces, blanched
1 carrot, julienned and blanched
1 cucumber, sliced diagonally
1 medium potato, fried and cut into chunks
1 cup (50g) spinach leaves
½ cup (50g) green beans, blanched and cut into bite-sized pieces
7 ounces (200g) atsuage deep-fried tofu, cut into strips
Crispy Fried Shallots (see page 131), to serve
Krupuk deep-fried crackers, to serve

FOR THE SAUCE

3 teaspoons peanut oil
2 cups (250g) deep-fried peanuts
3 cloves garlic
6 fresh red chilies
3 kaffir lime leaves
¼ cup (50g) palm sugar
1 teaspoon salt
1 teaspoon tamarind juice

Pickled Vegetable Salad

Achar kuning

SERVES *4*

This is a tantalizing and aromatic Javanese salad, a regular feature of Indonesian home cooking. It is a great accompaniment to rice and stir-fried dishes.

1. Soak the carrot, green beans, and cucumber for 10 minutes in 2 cups water to which ½ teaspoon salt and 1 tablespoon vinegar have been added, then drain. Blanch the green beans and carrots.
2. In a food processor, blend the candlenuts, turmeric, garlic, shallots, galangal, salt, and sugar to a smooth paste.
3. Heat the oil in a saucepan and sauté the candlenut paste for 2–3 minutes over medium heat. Add the peanuts, lemongrass, and salam leaves and stir briefly.
4. Add the carrot, green beans, cucumber, ¼ cup water, vinegar, salt, and sugar. Stir continuously over high heat until the water has been absorbed. Transfer to a serving bowl.

1 carrot, julienned
2 cups (200g) green beans, halved
2 cucumbers, julienned
2 cups (480ml) water
½ teaspoon salt
1 tablespoon rice vinegar
8 candlenuts
½ teaspoon turmeric
4 cloves garlic
6 shallots, halved
1 slice galangal
½ teaspoon salt
1 teaspoon castor sugar
1 tablespoon peanut oil
½ cup (60g) raw peanuts, boiled
1 stalk lemongrass
2 salam leaves
¼ cup (60ml) water
1 tablespoon rice vinegar
½ teaspoon salt
1 teaspoon castor sugar

FOR THE SOUP

5 cups (1.2 L) water
2 stalks lemongrass, halved
3 kaffir lime leaves
1 slice galangal
2 salam leaves
¼ teaspoon white pepper
1 teaspoon salt

FOR THE SOTO SPICE PASTE

8 candlenuts	2 fresh red chilies
4 cloves garlic	½ teaspoon turmeric
8 shallots	¼ teaspoon nutmeg
1 slice galangal	2 tablespoons water

VEGETABLES

3 tablespoons celery, with leaves, sliced diagonally
2 cups (200g) bean sprouts, blanched
3½ ounces (100 g) bean thread noodles, cooked
1 cup (45g) shredded white cabbage
2 medium potatoes, diced and deep-fried
2 medium tomatoes, cut into wedges
1 cup (240ml) Crispy Fried Shallots (see page 131)

GARNISHES

Kecap manis	Lime wedges
Sambal	Krupuk deep-fried crackers

Vegetable Soup

Soto

SERVES *4*　　　　　　　　　　　　　　　　PHOTOGRAPH ON PAGE 107

This robust noodle and vegetable soup makes an interesting start to a meal. The vegetables are all arranged on a large platter and placed on the table. When ready to serve, spoonfuls of the vegetables are placed in each serving bowl, and the flavored hot broth is poured over them. A colorful dish, it is usually eaten with rice and sambal.

1. Place the soup ingredients in a saucepan, bring to a boil over medium heat, then simmer for 10 minutes.
2. Using a food processor, blend the Soto spice paste ingredients together. Add the spice mixture to the soup and simmer for a further 5–7 minutes over medium heat.
3. To prepare the vegetables, place a bowl of fried shallots in the middle of a serving dish, and arrange the other vegetables around the bowl. Keep at the table.
4. To serve, place spoonfuls of noodles and vegetables in individual bowls, and pour a ladleful of soup into each. Garnish according to individual taste.

3 cups (720ml) water
¾ cup (100g) raw peanuts
3 baby corn ears, sliced
8 green beans, cut into 1-inch (3-cm) lengths
2 salam leaves
2 slices galangal
5 shallots
5 candlenuts
1 teaspoon salt
1 teaspoon cayenne pepper
1 tablespoon turmeric
1 tablespoon palm sugar
Crispy Fried Shallots (see page 131), for garnish

Vegetable Soup from Jakarta

Sayur asem

SERVES *4*

Turmeric, called *asem* in Indonesia, lends a beautiful golden color to this light and spicy soup.

1. Bring the 3 cups water to a boil in a saucepan. Add the peanuts, baby corn, green beans, salam leaves, and galangal and simmer for 5–7 minutes, until the vegetables are tender.
2. Using a food processor, grind the shallots, candlenuts, salt, and cayenne pepper to a paste.
3. Add the paste, turmeric, and palm sugar to the soup. Bring to a simmer for 3–4 minutes, then remove from the heat. Serve hot, garnished with fried shallots.

MAIN DISHES

Mixed Vegetable Coconut Curry *Sayur lodeh*

SERVES *4*   PHOTOGRAPH ON PAGE 107

Indonesian curries have a coconut base and are usually thin. The various sambal sauces at the table give the diner plenty of opportunities to spice it up.

1. Put the coconut milk and water in a large saucepan and bring to a boil. Add the salam leaves, galangal, palm sugar, and salt.
2. Using a food processor, blend the Lodeh paste ingredients together.
3. Heat the oil in a saucepan and sauté the Lodeh paste and coriander powder for 2–3 minutes over medium heat. Add the tempeh, carrot, tofu, radish, eggplant, baby corn, green beans, and cabbage. Stir-fry over high heat for 1 minute.
4. Put the tempeh, tofu, and vegetable mixture in the saucepan with the coconut milk mixture and bring to a boil. Simmer for 8–10 minutes over medium heat until the vegetables are tender. Serve with rice, pickles, and a selection of sambals.

2 cups (480ml) coconut milk
1 cup (240ml) water
2 salam leaves
2 slices galangal
2 tablespoons palm sugar
1 teaspoon salt
2 tablespoons peanut oil
1 teaspoon coriander powder
7 ounces (200g) tempeh, cut into 8 pieces
1 carrot, cut into bite-sized pieces
7 ounces (200g) atsuage deep-fried tofu, cut into 8 pieces
5 ounces (140g) white radish, cut into 8 pieces
2 small eggplants, quartered
4 baby corn ears, halved
½ cup (50g) green beans, cut into bite-sized pieces
2 cups (90g) white cabbage, cut into bite-sized pieces
Sambal (see page 157), to serve

FOR THE LODEH PASTE

4 fresh red chilies	3 shallots
8 candlenuts	1 teaspoon cumin seeds
3 cloves garlic	1 teaspoon coriander seeds
2 slices fresh ginger, peeled	¼ teaspoon nutmeg

Spicy Eggplant *Sambal terong*

SERVES *4*

Indonesian eggplants, like the Japanese ones, are small and tender and do not require salting. The spongy eggplant easily absorbs the flavors of the cooking sauce, making this dish a quick and spicy complement to rice.

1. Heat the oil in a saucepan and sauté the shallots, garlic, and ginger over medium heat for 2 minutes until fragrant.
2. Add the eggplant and stir briefly. Add the water, salt, and turmeric and cook covered for 8–10 minutes until the eggplant is tender.
3. Add the Tomato Sambal and stir to mix. Heat through and transfer to a serving dish. Garnish with scallions and celery leaves.

4 tablespoons peanut oil
6 shallots, sliced
2 cloves garlic, finely chopped
½-inch (1-cm) cube fresh ginger, peeled and minced
5–6 small eggplants halved lengthwise
1 cup (240ml) water
1 teaspoon salt
½ teaspoon turmeric
1 cup (240ml) Tomato Sambal (see page 157)
Scallions, sliced, for garnish
Celery leaves, chopped, for garnish

Spicy Fried Tempeh

Sambal goreng tempeh

SERVES 4

PHOTOGRAPH ON PAGE 106

2 tablespoons peanut oil
3 shallots, sliced
3 cloves garlic
1 medium tomato, chopped
4 dried red chilies, sliced
4 fresh hot green chilies, sliced
2 slices galangal
4 tablespoons palm sugar
2 salam leaves
¼ cup (60ml) water
1 tablespoon tamarind juice
½ teaspoon salt
14 ounces (400g) tempeh, sliced into thin strips, deep-fried
1 cup (125g) peanuts, deep-fried
2 tablespoons kecap manis
Celery leaves, for garnish
Red bell pepper, sliced, for garnish

When I tried this Javanese favorite for the first time, I was surprised at the chewy texture of the tempeh. This dish, with its combination of sweet palm sugar, hot chilies, and fried peanuts, is the perfect accompaniment to rice.

1. Heat the oil in a saucepan and sauté the shallots, garlic, tomato, chilies, and galangal for 2–3 minutes over medium heat.
2. Add the palm sugar, salam leaves, water, tamarind juice, and salt. Stir over medium heat until the palm sugar has dissolved.
3. Add the deep-fried tempeh, deep-fried peanuts, and kecap manis. Stir constantly over high heat until the sauce has caramelized.
4. Serve with rice, garnished with celery leaves, and red pepper.

Stir-fried Tempeh in Coconut Milk

Tumis tempeh santan

SERVES 4

3 tablespoons peanut oil
8 shallots, thinly sliced
3 cloves garlic, thinly sliced
5 fresh red chilies, sliced
3 fresh hot green chilies, sliced
2 salam leaves
2 slices galangal, crushed
2 medium tomatoes, each cut into 8 wedges
11 ounces (310g) tempeh, sliced and briefly shallow-fried in peanut oil
2 cups (480ml) coconut milk
2 tablespoons kecap manis
1 tablespoon soy sauce
½ teaspoon salt
1 teaspoon palm sugar
½ cup (50g) snow peas, sliced diagonally

The basic spices and condiments used in this dish are always on hand in Indonesian homes. Tempeh and coconut milk are a staple too, making this an easy and popular accompaniment to rice.

1. Heat the oil in a saucepan and sauté the shallots, garlic, and chilies over medium heat for 2–3 minutes. Add the salam leaves, galangal, and tomato. Stir briefly.
2. Add the tempeh, coconut milk, kecap manis, soy sauce, salt, and palm sugar. Simmer for 2–3 minutes, until the sauce has thickened. Mix in the snow peas.
3. Transfer to a serving dish and serve with Indonesian Fried Rice or Yellow Rice (see page 155).

Tofu Satay

Sate tahu

SERVES *4*

The Satay Sauce can be prepared ahead of time to reduce cooking time. This dish is a great addition to a Sunday afternoon brunch or dinner.

1. Using a food processor, grind the marinade ingredients to a paste.
2. Heat the oil in a saucepan and sauté the marinade paste, salam leaves, and lemongrass for 2–3 minutes over medium heat. Transfer the mixture to a bowl and allow to cool.
3. Put the tofu and eringi mushrooms in the bowl with the marinade and mix. Leave to marinate at room temperature for 2 hours, then remove the salam leaves and lemongrass.
4. Thread the tofu and eringi on skewers.
5. Heat a frying pan and drizzle a little oil into it. Place the tofu and eringi skewers in the pan, and brown for 4–5 minutes, turning occasionally. Repeat the process until all the skewers have been browned. The skewers can be grilled instead of fried.
6. Place a bowl of Satay Sauce in the centre of a large plate. Arrange the tofu and eringi skewers all around it. Serve with the lemon wedges.

2 tablespoons peanut oil
2 salam leaves
1 stalk lemongrass, halved and crushed
14 ounces (400g) atsuage deep-fried tofu, cut into ¾-inch (2-cm) dice
3 eringi mushrooms, cut into ¾-inch (2-cm) pieces
Peanut oil for drizzling
Satay Sauce (see below), to serve
Lemon wedges, for garnish

FOR THE MARINADE

8 candlenuts
6 fresh hot green chilies
5 fresh red chilies
8 shallots
5 cloves garlic
1-inch (3-cm) cube fresh ginger, peeled
1 teaspoon coriander seeds
1 teaspoon whole black peppercorns
3 tablespoons palm sugar

Satay Sauce *Base satay*

MAKES *4 cups (960ml)*

1½ cups (185g) raw peanuts, deep-fried
4 cloves garlic
8 shallots, sliced
8 fresh hot green chilies
½ cup (100g) palm sugar

2 cups (480ml) coconut milk
3 tablespoons kecap manis
1 tablespoon lime juice
1 tablespoon Crispy Fried Shallots (see page 131)

This sweet and nutty sauce forms the base for most satay dishes and can also be used as a dip.

1. In a food processor, combine the peanuts, garlic, shallots, chilies, and palm sugar and blend to a smooth paste. Add a little of the coconut milk if the mixture is too dry. Transfer to a saucepan.
2. Transfer the paste to a saucepan and add the coconut milk, kecap manis, and lime juice. Bring to a simmer over medium heat, stirring all the time until the sauce thickens. Before serving, stir in the fried shallots.
3. The sauce keeps for a week, refrigerated.

RICE DISHES

Indonesian Fried Rice
Nasi goreng

SERVES *4*

3 tablespoons peanut oil
1 medium onion, finely chopped
6 shallots, sliced
3 cloves garlic, sliced
½-inch (1-cm) cube fresh ginger, peeled and finely chopped
2 fresh red chilies, finely chopped
2 scallions, with greens, finely chopped
1 cup (100g) bean sprouts
6–8 snow peas, halved diagonally
½ red bell pepper, sliced
½ green bell pepper, sliced
4 cups (630g) cooked long-grain rice
3 tablespoons kecap manis
1 tablespoon soy sauce
Sambal (see page 157), to serve
Sliced cucumber, to serve
Tomato wedges, to serve
Krupuk deep-fried crackers, to serve

Nasi Goreng is one of Indonesia's best-known dishes. There are subtle differences in the way it is prepared throughout the country, depending on the origin of the people and the availability of the ingredients. This is the way I made it for my family when I first made them an Indonesian meal. My daughter loved the flavor of the kecap manis and it has since become a staple of my kitchen pantry.

1. Heat the oil in a saucepan and sauté the onion, shallots, and garlic for 3–4 minutes over medium heat, until fragrant.
2. Add the ginger and chilies and mix. Add the scallions, bean sprouts, snow peas, and red and green pepper and stir quickly over high heat for 2–3 minutes.
3. Add the rice, kecap manis, and soy sauce and mix thoroughly. Serve with sambal, sliced cucumber, tomato wedges, and krupuk.

Yellow Rice
Nasi kuning

SERVES *4*

1½ cups (280g) long-grain rice
1 teaspoon turmeric
2½ cups (600ml) coconut milk
1 salam leaf
1 pandan leaf
1 stalk lemongrass, halved and crushed
2 slices galangal

Yellow is an auspicious color in Indonesia and is also the color of royalty. Nasi Kuning is served at festivals and celebrations, usually shaped into a cone to represent the mythical Hindu mountain, Meru. This dish goes well with Mixed Vegetable Coconut Curry (see page 152).

1. Wash the rice and soak in water for 10 minutes. Drain and set aside.
2. Combine the rice with the turmeric, coconut milk, salam leaf, pandan leaf, lemongrass, and galangal. Transfer to a rice cooker and cook in the usual way. If cooking in a saucepan, place over medium heat for the first 5 minutes. Stir once, then turn the heat to low for another 5–7 minutes until the liquid is absorbed. Remove from the heat and keep covered for 10 minutes.
3. Before serving, remove the salam leaf, pandan leaf, lemongrass, and galangal. The rice can be pressed into a cone shape if desired.

SNACKS AND SIDE DISHES

Assorted Vegetable Fritters   *Bakvan*

SERVES *4*

Many homes in Indonesia, especially in Java, have fried snacks and tempeh at the table throughout the day, along with sambal sauce. These tasty fritters are seasoned simply with garlic, salt and pepper and served with spicy sambal and kecap manis.

1. In a deep mixing bowl, combine the cabbage, scallions, carrot, and sweet corn with the flour.
2. Add the garlic, baking soda, salt, and pepper. Gradually pour in the water, stirring all the time, until you have a thin batter.
3. Heat the oil for deep-frying to 350°F (180°C). Take a ladleful of the vegetable batter and slide into the hot oil, in small batches. Deep-fry over medium heat, turning once until crisp and golden brown on both sides.
4. Drain on kitchen paper and transfer to a serving dish. Serve hot with sambal and kecap manis.

3 cups (135g) white cabbage, shredded
2 scallions, thinly sliced
1 carrot, grated
1 cup sweet corn kernels, cooked
3 cups (380g) all-purpose flour
2 teaspoons garlic, grated
Pinch of baking soda
½ teaspoon salt
½ teaspoon ground white pepper
1½ cups (360ml) water
Vegetable oil for deep-frying

Deep-fried Battered Tofu   *Tahu goreng tapung*

SERVES *4*

Tofu is widely used in Indonesian home cooking. This deep-fried tofu dish makes an ideal accompaniment to a drink and is a favorite beer garden snack.

1. Slice the tofu into thin 1½-inch (4-cm) long strips.
2. In a mixing bowl, combine the flour, coriander powder, cardamom, garlic, salt, and water. Mix to a thick, smooth batter.
3. In a wok, heat the oil for deep-frying to 350°F (180°C). Dip the tofu strips in the batter and coat generously. Slide the tofu strips into the hot oil and deep-fry until golden brown. Drain on kitchen paper and transfer to a serving dish.
4. Garnish with slivers of red and green chilies and serve with the sambal of your choice.

11 ounces (310g) firm tofu, drained
2 cups (315g) rice flour
1 tablespoon coriander powder
1 teaspoon cardamom, ground
2 cloves garlic, grated
½ teaspoon salt
½ cup (120ml) water
Peanut oil for deep-frying
Fresh red and green chilies, slivered, for garnish
Sambal (see opposite), to serve

■ SAMBALS

Tomato Sambal

Sambal tomat   MAKES *1 cup (240ml)*

8 fresh red chilies   ½ teaspoon salt
10 shallots, sliced   2 tablespoons peanut oil
4 cloves garlic   2 medium tomatoes,
3 slices galangal   chopped
2 teaspoons lime juice

Sambal is a spicy, tangy relish, often made with fruit, but tomato sambal is the most widely used. My Indonesian friend Rusi taught me this recipe, and I've found that it goes well with Indian and Thai snacks too.

1. Using a food processor, blend the chilies, shallots, garlic, galangal, lime juice, and salt to a paste. Transfer to a small bowl.
2. Heat the oil in a saucepan and sauté the paste for 2–3 minutes, until fragrant.
3. Add the tomato and stir to mix. Cook covered for 3–4 minutes over medium heat. Mash coarsely while mixing. Stir until most of the liquid has been absorbed. The sambal should not be runny. Keeps refrigerated for 3–4 days.

Mango Sambal

Sambal mangga   MAKES *about 1½ cups (360ml)*

3 raw green mangoes   4 fresh hot green chilies
1 teaspoon salt   4 tablespoons peanut oil
8 shallots   A few basil leaves, torn
4 fresh red chilies

This sambal reminds me of a green mango pickle we make in India. My mother's recipe includes ground dried red chilies, mustard seeds, and fenugreek seeds.

1. Peel the mangoes and chop the flesh finely. Sprinkle with salt and set aside for 5–7 minutes. Squeeze out the excess liquid and place in a bowl.
2. Using a mortar and pestle or a food processor, grind the shallots and red and green chilies to a paste.
3. Heat the oil in a saucepan and sauté the paste for 2–3 minutes over medium heat. Transfer to a bowl and allow to cool. Add the mango and basil, and mix well. Store in an airtight jar in the refrigerator. Keeps refrigerated for 3–4 days.

Manado Sambal

Sambal dabu dabu kenari   MAKES *2 cups (480ml)*

1 cup (100g) bean sprouts,   3 tablespoons water
   blanched   3 tablespoons kenari nuts
1 cucumber, julienned   or cashews
4 shallots, finely sliced   2 tablespoons tamarind
4 fresh red chilies, finely   juice
   sliced   1 teaspoon castor sugar
6–8 basil leaves   ½ teaspoon salt

This sambal originated in the Manado region of Java. The bean sprouts and cucumber add a delightful crunch.

In a mixing bowl, combine the bean sprouts, cucumber, shallots, and chilies. In a food processor, blend the basil, 3 tablespoons water, kenari nuts, tamarind juice, sugar, and salt. Spoon out the sauce and pour over the cucumber and bean sprouts. Serve at room temperature. Keeps refrigerated for 3–4 days.

6–8 fresh red chilies
3 cloves garlic
4 shallots
1 slice galangal
3 kaffir lime leaves
½ teaspoon salt
½ cup (120ml) water
11 ounces (310g) tempeh, mashed
Peanut oil for deep-frying
Kecap manis, to serve
Sambal (see above), to serve

Tempeh Fritters   *Perkedal tempeh*

SERVES 4

Fried snacks are eaten in the afternoon with tea and as an accompaniment to meals.

1. Using a food processor, grind the chilies, garlic, shallots, galangal, lime leaves, salt, and water to a smooth paste.
2. Combine the mashed tempeh with the spice paste and mix until smooth. Divide into 8 discs and flatten slightly.
3. Heat the oil for deep-frying to 350°F (180°C) and deep-fry the tempeh discs, a few at a time, until crisp and golden brown. Drain on kitchen paper and transfer to a serving dish. Serve with kecap manis and a selection of your favorite sambals.

DRINKS AND DESSERTS

Avocado Espresso Shake   *Es apokat espresso*

SERVES *4*

This unusual yet typically Indonesian drink has to be tried to be believed. It is simply delicious!

Using a food processor, all the ingredients until smooth. Pour into individual glasses and serve.

4 ripe avocados, roughly chopped
½ cup (120ml) palm syrup
1 shot espresso or ½ cup (120ml) coffee
½ cup (120ml) soy milk
2 cups crushed ice

* This is also a delicious drink without the espresso.

Deep-fried Banana   *Pisang goreng*

SERVES *4*

This delicious deep-fried dish is a popular sweet snack in Indonesia. It resembles the Thai banana dessert, kwai kek, which is made in a similar manner.

1. Slice the banana diagonally into chunks.
2. In a small bowl, combine the flour with the coconut milk, sugar, salt, and sesame seeds. Add the banana chunks and mix to coat with the batter.
3. Heat the oil for deep-frying to 350°F (180°C) and fry the bananas, a few at a time, until crisp and golden brown. Drain on kitchen paper and serve.

4 small or 2 large bananas
2 tablespoons rice flour
½ cup (120ml) coconut milk
1 tablespoon castor sugar
Pinch of salt
1 teaspoon white sesame seeds, toasted (see page 42)
Vegetable oil for deep-frying

Fruit in Coconut Milk   *Es kolak*

SERVES *4*

This typical Indonesian sweet snack is like a fruit salad, perfect for a hot summer afternoon.

Combine all the ingredients in a deep bowl. Mix thoroughly and serve in individual dishes.

2 small bananas, sliced
½ apple, diced
⅔ cup (100g) sweet potato, boiled and diced
¼ cup (60ml) palm syrup
3 cups (720ml) coconut milk
Pinch of salt
2 slices canned jackfruit, diced
1 cup crushed ice

Malaysia

One of my most memorable meals took place in the old town of Georgetown in Penang, at a night food stall. These outdoor dining places burst into life at sundown. As my Malaysian friend and I walked through the maze of stalls selling satays, curries, and noodles, the smell of burning charcoal and the foods roasting over it assailed our senses.

Soon we were seated on a humble wooden bench, bent over our bowls of classic Laksa Penang. As the fresh lemongrass, spices, and tamarind gave our appetites a kick, we began to hungrily eye the Indian food displayed in the stall across the way. Instantly we were surrounded by young boys from the stall. One brought us kari and fragrant basmati rice, another rushed over with a plate full of kari puffs and peanut sauce. It was not, I have to admit, a night of restraint.

Since so much of Malaysia's cuisine is influenced by its neighbors—Thailand, Singapore, and Indonesia—and its immigrant population of Chinese and south Indians, the country deserves its reputation as the melting pot of Asia's culinary treasures. While the food in the northern states of Malaysia includes the flavors of chili, lemongrass, and tamarind because of its proximity to Thailand, the rest of Malaysia uses coconut milk and spices.

I have included a selection of recipes for both styles of food, but as an Indian, I am most proud to introduce some of the many dishes whose origins can be traced back to my country.

MAIN DISHES

Chili Eggplants with Fresh Basil

Terung berempah dengan basil

SERVES *4*

A quick and easy eggplant preparation that is a popular addition to a meal in both Malaysia and Indonesia. In Indonesia the eggplants in this dish are stir-fried, but in this Malaysian version of the recipe, they are deep-fried.

1. Cut the eggplants into bite-sized pieces.
2. In a wok, heat the oil for deep-frying to 350°F (180°C). Deep-fry the eggplant until crisp and golden. Drain on kitchen paper and set aside.
3. Heat the 1 tablespoon vegetable oil in a saucepan and sauté the Tomato Sambal for 2–3 minutes over medium heat. Put in the basil leaves, salt, and sugar and stir to mix. Add the fried eggplant and mix gently.
4. Remove from the heat and transfer to a serving dish.

5 small eggplants
Vegetable oil for deep-frying
1 tablespoon vegetable oil
1 cup (240ml) Tomato Sambal (see page 157)
1 cup (20g) fresh basil leaves, chopped
½ teaspoon salt
1 teaspoon castor sugar

Fiery Potato Curry

Kari pedas kentang

SERVES *4*

This spicy curry of Indian origin has been adapted to the Malaysian palate with the addition of lemongrass and vinegar. Great served simply with fluffed-up plain white rice.

1. Heat 2 tablespoons vegetable oil in a saucepan and sauté the onion, garlic, ginger, and chilies for 2–3 minutes over medium heat.
2. Using a food processor, grind the spice paste ingredients until smooth, using a little water if necessary.
3. Heat 2 tablespoons vegetable oil in a saucepan and sauté the ground spice paste for 2–3 minutes over medium heat.
4. Add the potatoes, salt, soy sauce, vinegar, sugar, and water. Mix in the sautéed onion-and-garlic mixture. Cook for 2–3 minutes and transfer to a serving dish. Serve hot with rice.

2 tablespoons vegetable oil
1 medium onion, finely chopped
3 cloves garlic, finely chopped
¾-inch (2-cm) cube fresh ginger, peeled and julienned
2 red fresh chilies, seeds removed, thinly sliced
2 tablespoons vegetable oil
1 pound (450g) baby potatoes, boiled, peeled and halved
1 teaspoon salt
1 teaspoon soy sauce
2 tablespoons rice vinegar
2 teaspoons castor sugar
1 cup (240ml) water

FOR THE SPICE PASTE

2 tablespoons poppy seeds, soaked in water for 5 minutes
1 teaspoon mustard seeds, soaked in water for 5 minutes
8 dried red chilies, soaked in water for 5 minutes
2 stalks lemongrass, chopped
2 slices galangal
1 teaspoon turmeric
10 shallots, peeled

Indian Vegetable Curry

Sayur kari

SERVES 4

Vegetable oil for deep-frying
10 okra, topped, tailed, and halved
3 small eggplants, halved, cut into bite-sized pieces
2 medium potatoes, peeled and julienned
1 medium carrot, julienned
Coriander leaves for garnish

FOR THE CURRY BASE

2 tablespoons vegetable oil
1 teaspoon mustard seeds
1 teaspoon fennel seeds
1 teaspoon fenugreek seeds
1 teaspoon cumin seeds
4 dried red chilies
4–5 curry leaves
3 cloves garlic, sliced
1 medium onion, sliced
5 shallots, sliced
2 medium tomatoes, chopped
Pea-sized piece fresh ginger, peeled and finely chopped
1 teaspoon salt
1 teaspoon turmeric
2 teaspoons coriander powder
1 teaspoon cayenne pepper
1 teaspoon garam masala (see page 16)
2 cups (480ml) water
1 tablespoon tamarind juice
1 teaspoon castor sugar

A Malaysian version of the robust Indian curry, which is delicious served with Spicy Basmati Rice with Whole Spices (see page 162). The curry base can be prepared ahead of time. Do not let the long list of ingredients deter you as most of them are used together in the seasoning.

1. Heat the oil for deep-frying to 350°F (180°C). Deep-fry the okra, eggplant, potato, and carrot until well browned. Drain on kitchen paper and set aside.
2. For the curry base, heat the oil in a saucepan over medium heat, and add the mustard seeds, fennel seeds, fenugreek seeds and cumin seeds. When the mustard seeds start to splutter, add the chilies, curry leaves, garlic, onion, and shallots. Sauté for 3–4 minutes until fragrant. Mix in the tomato and ginger and stir briefly. Add the salt, turmeric, coriander powder, cayenne pepper, and garam masala and bring to a simmer. Add the water, tamarind juice, and sugar and bring to a boil.
3. Add the fried vegetables and mix thoroughly. Simmer for 6–8 minutes until the spices are well blended with the vegetables. Garnish with coriander leaves and serve with rice.

Stir-fried Sugar Snap Peas and Baby Corn

Kacang pea dan jagung muda masak campur

SERVES 4

2 tablespoons sesame oil
4 cloves garlic, sliced
7 ounces (200g) sugar snap peas, blanched
4 baby corn ears, sliced in half diagonally, blanched
½ carrot, sliced diagonally, blanched
¼ cup (60ml) water
1 tablespoon sake
1 tablespoon soy sauce
¼ teaspoon castor sugar
¼ teaspoon salt
¼ teaspoon ground white pepper
1 teaspoon cornstarch mixed with 2 tablespoons water
2 fresh red chilies, sliced, for garnish
Daily Chili Sambal (see page 163), to serve

One of the many dishes served with rice, especially popular with the Malaysian Chinese during their New Year.

1. Heat the oil in a saucepan and sauté the garlic for 8–10 seconds over medium heat.
2. Add the sugar snap peas, baby corn, and carrot and stir-fry over high heat for one minute.
3. Add the water, sake, soy sauce, sugar, salt, and pepper. Bring to a simmer over high heat.
4. Add the cornstarch-and-water mixture and stir until the sauce thickens. Transfer to a serving dish and garnish with the sliced chilies. Serve with fluffy hot rice and Daily Chili Sambal.

RICE DISHES

Fragrant Lemongrass Rice

Nasi campor serai

SERVES *4*   PHOTOGRAPH ON PAGE 108

A deliciously aromatic rice cooked in coconut milk with lemongrass, lime leaves, and galangal, and served with an array of fresh herbs.

1. Heat the oil in a saucepan and sauté the rice for 2–3 minutes over medium heat, until translucent.
2. Add the coconut milk, salt, lemongrass, lime leaves, and galangal. Transfer to a rice cooker, if using, and cook in the usual way. If cooking in the saucepan, bring to a boil once and reduce the heat to medium. Simmer for 10 minutes, covered, stirring occasionally. Cook on low heat for another 5 minutes. Remove from the heat and keep covered for 5 minutes.
3. Remove the lemongrass, lime leaves, and galangal. Fluff up the rice with a fork and scatter the red bell pepper over it. Place the rice in the centre of a serving dish and arrange the herbs around it in separate groups (see photograph on page 108).

2 tablespoons peanut oil or vegetable oil
2½ cups (455g) long-grain rice, soaked for 10 minutes, and drained
4 cups (960ml) coconut milk
½ teaspoon salt
1 stalk lemongrass, halved and crushed
3 kaffir lime leaves
1 slice galangal
1 red bell pepper, chopped
Crispy Fried Shallots (see page 131), for garnish

HERBS FOR GARNISH

Scallions, finely sliced
Fresh coriander leaves
Fresh dill
Fresh mint leaves
Fresh parsley
Fresh basil
Chives, chopped

Spicy Basmati Rice with Whole Spices

Beras basmati berempah

SERVES *4*

Fragrant and spicy, this rice is a wonderful complement to Indian Vegetable Curry (see page 161).

1. Heat the oil in a saucepan and add the cumin seeds, cinnamon, cloves, and cardamom. Stir briefly over medium heat until fragrant.
2. Add the shallots and sauté for 2–3 minutes until soft.
3. Add the cayenne pepper, turmeric, garam masala, and salt. Stir to mix.
4. Add the rice and stir for a minute to coat with the spices.
5. Add the water and transfer to a rice cooker, if using, and cook in the usual way. If cooking in the saucepan, cook covered for 5 minutes over high heat. Reduce the heat to medium and cook for a further 10–12 minutes, stirring occasionally, until all the water is absorbed. Remove from the heat and keep covered for another 5 minutes.
6. Fluff up the rice with a fork and garnish with almonds and raisins.

2 tablespoons vegetable oil
1 teaspoon cumin seeds
1 stick cinnamon
4–5 cloves
2 cardamom pods
6 shallots, sliced
½ teaspoon cayenne pepper
½ teaspoon turmeric
½ teaspoon garam masala (see page 16)
1 teaspoon salt
2 cups (370g) long-grain basmati rice, washed and drained
4 cups (960ml) water
10–12 almonds, slivered, for garnish
10–12 raisins, for garnish

NOODLES

2 tablespoons sesame oil
4 cloves garlic, finely chopped
2 medium leeks, with greens, chopped
2 tablespoons Daily Chili Sambal (see below)
2 cups (480ml) water
2 tablespoons kecap manis
2 tablespoons soy sauce
½ teaspoon ground white pepper
2 cups (90g) Chinese cabbage, chopped
2 cups (100g) spinach leaves, chopped
1 cup (100g) bean sprouts
1 tablespoon cornstarch mixed with 4 tablespoons water
9 ounces (255g) ramen noodles, deep-fried
2 fresh red chilies, sliced, for garnish
Fresh coriander leaves, for garnish

Daily Chili Sambal
Sambal chili   MAKES ½ cup (120ml)

6 fresh red chilies, seeded	Blend to a
4 tablespoons water	paste in a food
3 tablespoons rice vinegar	processor.
1½ tablespoons castor sugar	
½ teaspoon salt	

FOR THE SPICE PASTE

1 tablespoon coriander seeds	2 cloves garlic, crushed
1 tablespoon cumin seeds	¾ inch (2-cm) cube galangal, sliced
6 candlenuts or cashews	½ teaspoon turmeric
5 fresh red chilies	¼ teaspoon nutmeg

FOR THE SOUP

3 tablespoons peanut oil or vegetable oil	2 cups (480ml) coconut milk
1 stalk lemongrass, halved and crushed	1 cup (240ml) water
3 kaffir lime leaves	⅔ teaspoon salt
2 slices galangal	1 medium tomato, cut into 8 wedges
7 ounces (200g) atsuage deep-fried tofu, sliced	11 ounces (310g) wheat flour noodles or thin spaghetti, cooked

Crispy Noodles with Spicy Sauce *Mee rangup dan sayur*

SERVES *4*

This is a Malay version of a famous Chinese dish. Sweet and spicy sauce is poured over crisp noodles and served immediately.

1. Heat the oil in a saucepan and sauté the garlic and leek over medium heat for one minute. Add the Daily Chili Sambal and stir to mix.
2. Add the water, kecap manis, soy sauce, and pepper and bring to a boil.
3. Add the cabbage, spinach, and bean sprouts and simmer for one minute.
4. Stir in the cornstarch-and-water mixture, reduce the heat, and keep stirring until the sauce thickens.
5. Arrange the noodles on a serving dish and pour the sauce over them. Alternatively, place the noodles in individual bowls and pour the sauce over each portion. Garnish with chilies and coriander.

Noodles in Spicy Coconut Soup *Laksa lemak*

SERVES *4*   PHOTOGRAPH ON PAGE 109

This is the vegetarian version of the famous Malay dish known as Laksa Lemak, which originated in Melaka. Spicy hot coconut broth is poured over the noodles and served with an assortment of garnishes.

1. Using a food processor, grind the spice paste ingredients together until smooth, using a little water if needed.
2. For the soup, heat the oil in a saucepan and sauté the ground spice paste for 2–3 minutes over medium heat, until fragrant. Stir in the lemongrass, lime leaves, galangal, and tofu.
3. Add the coconut milk, water, and salt. Bring to a boil and simmer over low heat for 6–8 minutes. Add the tomato to the simmering broth.

4. Arrange the garnishes on the table. Immerse the noodles in boiling water for a few seconds. Drain and divide between individual bowls. Pour a ladleful of the hot coconut broth into each bowl. Invite your guests to add their favorite garnishes.

2 scallions, finely sliced	Lettuce leaves, shredded
½ cucumber, sliced	Sambal (see page 157)
Celery leaves	Krupuk deep-fried
Bean sprouts	crackers

Penang Noodles with Sour Soup   *Penang laksa*

SERVES *4*

This fragrant vegetarian version of the famous Penang Laksa reminds me of the Vietnamese tamarind soup and the Thai tom yum soup, once again proving that all the Southeast Asian countries are connected by a transparent culinary thread. This dish is a complete contrast to the spicy coconut Laksa Lemak.

1. In a large saucepan, bring the vegetable stock to a boil. Add the tamarind juice, galangal, lime leaves, sugar, and Thai Soup Paste. Simmer for 5–6 minutes over medium heat.
2. Refresh the noodles by boiling them in 5 cups water for 3–4 minutes. Drain and divide between individual bowls.
3. Pour a ladleful of the soup into each bowl of noodles and sprinkle with a generous helping of each of the toppings. Serve with Daily Chili Sambal, which can be mixed into individual bowls for an extra touch of spice.

6 cups (1.5 L) Thai Vegetable Stock (see page 117)
4 tablespoons tamarind juice
3 slices galangal
3 kaffir lime leaves, chopped, optional
1 tablespoon castor sugar
3 tablespoons Thai Soup Paste (see page 115)
14 ounces (400g) rice noodles, cooked
5 cups (1.2 L) water

FOR THE TOPPINGS

1 cucumber, sliced into thin rounds
1 medium leek, sliced diagonally
2 cups (200g) bean sprouts, blanched
3 shallots, sliced
8–10 chunks fresh pineapple
Mint leaves
Fresh basil
2 fresh red chilies, sliced
Crispy Fried Shallots (see page 131)
Crispy Fried Garlic (see page 131)
Daily Chili Sambal (see page 163), to serve

Stir-fried Noodles with Vegetables   *Mee Goreng*

SERVES *4*   PHOTOGRAPH ON PAGE 109

There are as many versions of Mee Goreng in Malaysia as there are cooks, with each version giving its own unique twist to this classic dish. The only common ingredient is noodles—all else is left to the mood and the imagination of the chef. This spicy Indian version is my favorite hawker food in Singapore.

1. Heat the oil in a saucepan and sauté the garlic, shallots, and leek briefly. Add the Daily Chili Sambal and stir for 10 seconds over medium heat.
2. Add the tofu, cabbage, bean sprouts, and mustard greens. Sauté over high heat for 2–3 minutes.
3. Add the tomato, garlic stems, chilies, and tomato puree and stir to mix.
4. Add the noodles, soy sauce, and pepper and stir until well mixed.
5. Sprinkle with coriander leaves and remove from the heat. Transfer to a serving dish and serve garnished with tomato and cucumber.

2 tablespoons vegetable oil
2 cloves garlic, finely chopped
4 shallots, sliced
2 medium leeks, chopped
1 tablespoon Daily Chili Sambal (see page 163)
7 ounces (200g) atsuage deep-fried tofu, cut into strips
2 cups (90g) white cabbage, shredded
2 cups (200g) bean sprouts
2 cups (110g) mustard greens, chopped
1 medium tomato, chopped
5 garlic stems, chopped
3 fresh red chilies, sliced
1 tablespoon tomato puree
14 ounces (400g) yakisoba noodles, cooked
2 tablespoons soy sauce
½ teaspoon ground white pepper
Handful fresh coriander leaves
Cherry tomatoes, for garnish
Cucumber, sliced diagonally, for garnish

* Use 3 cups cooked long-grain rice instead of noodles to make a delicious Nasi Goreng.

SIDE DISHES AND SNACKS

Curry Puffs

Kari pap

SERVES *24*

FOR THE PASTRY

2 cups (250g) all-purpose flour
2 tablespoons vegetable oil
½ cup (120ml) water
¼ teaspoon salt

FOR THE FILLING

2 tablespoons vegetable oil
1 teaspoon cumin seeds
1½-inch (4-cm) cube fresh ginger, peeled and grated
2 fresh hot green chilies, finely chopped
1 medium onion, finely chopped
2 teaspoons coriander powder
½ teaspoon turmeric
½ teaspoon cayenne pepper
2 teaspoons curry powder
1 pound (450g) potatoes, boiled, peeled, and diced
1 cup (160g) green peas, cooked
1 teaspoon salt
Handful fresh coriander leaves, chopped

Flour for dusting
Vegetable oil for deep-frying

An all-time favorite snack of the Malay people, these curry puffs were introduced by Indian vendors. The locals pick up these puffs on way to work early in the morning, or eat them with piping hot spiced tea as an afternoon snack, accompanied by spicy sambal.

1. In a deep bowl, combine all the pastry ingredients and knead to a smooth dough. Cover with a damp cloth and set aside for 10 minutes.
2. For the filling, heat the vegetable oil in a saucepan over medium heat and add the cumin seeds. When the cumin seeds start to sizzle, put in the ginger, chilies, and onion. Sauté for 3–4 minutes until the onions are soft.
3. Put in the coriander powder, turmeric, cayenne pepper, and curry powder, and stir briefly until fragrant. Add the potato, green peas, and salt, stir to mix, and heat through. Sprinkle the coriander leaves into the pan and remove from the heat. Transfer to a bowl and allow to cool.
4. Divide the dough into 24 balls. Dust with flour and roll into 2 inch (5-cm) discs.
5. Place a spoonful of the filling onto the center of the disc and fold the dough to make a crescent shape. Press the edges into a wave pattern to seal. Repeat this process with the remaining dough and filling.
6. Heat the oil for deep-frying to 350°F (180°C) and slide in the curry puffs, a few at a time. Deep-fry until crisp and golden brown. Alternatively bake the curry puffs in a preheated oven for 20 minutes, turning occasionally, until evenly browned.

Green Papaya Pickle

Achar betik muda

SERVES *4*

1 small raw green papaya, about 12 ounces (340g)
2 tablespoons vegetable oil
1 tablespoon mustard seeds
2 tablespoons chickpea flour
3 fresh red chilies, sliced
1 teaspoon coriander powder
½ teaspoon turmeric
¼ teaspoon salt
1 tablespoon lemon juice

This interesting pickle of Indian origin is as popular in India as in Malaysia. Served with freshly fried snacks and fritters, it is a beautiful complement to both.

1. Peel the papaya, halve lengthwise, remove the seeds, and slice thinly.

2. Heat the oil in a saucepan over medium heat and add the mustard seeds. When they start to splutter, add the chickpea flour and sauté for one minute until fragrant.
3. Add the chilies, coriander powder, turmeric, and salt. Stir briefly, then mix in the papaya slices and cook for 2–3 minutes over medium heat.
4. Drizzle the lemon juice into the pan, then remove from heat and transfer to a serving bowl.

Red Lentil Fritters

Kacang merah goreng

SERVES *4*

Red lentils can be used after only fifteen minutes of soaking, making these crunchy fritters a quick addition to a meal.

1. Wash the red lentils and soak in water for 15 minutes. Drain and grind to a coarse puree, using a food processor.
2. In a deep bowl, mix the garlic, lemon rind, ginger, coriander powder, turmeric, palm sugar, and salt. Add the pureed lentils and mix well.
3. Heat the oil for deep-frying to 350°F (180°C). Take spoonfuls of the lentil mixture and flatten slightly by hand to make a thick disc. Slide into the hot oil in small batches. Deep-fry until golden brown. Drain on kitchen paper.
4. Heat the 2 tablespoons peanut oil in a saucepan and sauté the leeks and coconut. Add the fritters and toss to mix. Serve garnished with fresh coriander.

2 cups (340g) red lentils
2 cloves garlic, crushed
2 teaspoons grated lemon rind
½-inch (1-cm) cube fresh ginger, peeled and grated
2 teaspoons coriander powder
½ teaspoon turmeric
2 teaspoons palm sugar
⅔ teaspoon salt
Peanut oil for deep-frying
2 tablespoons peanut oil
3 leeks, including green part, thinly sliced diagonally
½ cup (40g) fresh grated coconut
Fresh coriander, for garnish

* The fritters can be broken into pieces in the final mixing process. This will add to the flavor and the texture of the dish.

Stuffed Chili Pickles

Jeruk chili

SERVES *4*

Surprisingly easy to make, these stuffed chilies will surely spice up any meal. Bite on them with spoonfuls of rice or mouthfuls of noodles.

1. Make a lengthwise slit along each chili, keeping both ends intact. Remove the seeds.
2. In a small bowl, combine the ground mustard seeds, ground fenugreek seeds, coriander powder, cayenne pepper, and salt.
3. Fill each chili with a teaspoonful of the spice mixture.
4. Heat the oil in a saucepan and put in the whole mustard seeds. When they start to splutter, put in the stuffed chilies and cook for 2–3 minutes over medium heat until lightly browned. Sprinkle with the lemon juice and remove from the heat. Transfer to a serving bowl and allow to cool before eating.

8 long fresh hot green chilies, with stalks
1 tablespoon mustard seeds, ground
1 teaspoon fenugreek seeds, ground
1 tablespoon coriander powder
½ teaspoon cayenne pepper
½ teaspoon salt
1 tablespoon vegetable oil
1 teaspoon whole mustard seeds
1 tablespoon lemon juice

Korea

With each country so far in this book, I have organized the dishes in categories as close as possible to the Western concept of a meal—soups, salads, main dishes, and so on—for the convenience of meal planners. But I've found the Korean dining style is quite difficult to fit into the conventional mold, so you'll notice a slight difference here.

A typical Korean table consists of colorful bowls of kimchi, the simple vegetable dishes known as *namul* and *chorim*, a spicy soup, and sometimes noodles, all arranged beautifully and served with a heaping bowl of piping hot white rice.

Having lived in Japan and cooked Japanese food for more than half my life, I thought I knew all about shredding and slicing and the use of soy sauce and sesame oil. I was mistaken. I had no idea how finely food has to be shredded for cooking in the Korean way. On my first of many visits to her home, I watched, enthralled, as my Korean friend Soo Young worked her deft, nimble hands to turn out incredibly thin slivers of vegetables and tofu, which were remarkably uniform in size.

But it is the chili pepper and the enthusiasm with which it is used that sets Korean cuisine apart from other cuisines. It is the soul of Korean cooking, transforming even the most mundane and basic ingredients into hearty, mouthwatering dishes. Don't hesitate when using it.

SOUPS AND SALADS

Mushroom Soup

Bosot tang

SERVES *4*

11 ounces (310g) assorted fresh mushrooms (button mushrooms, wood ear mushrooms, etc)
6 dried shiitake mushrooms, soaked in hot water for 10 minutes and drained
1 piece burdock, about 5 inches (12.5 cm) long
1 tablespoon rice flour
¼ cup (60ml) Konbu Dashi (see page 40)
1 tablespoon sesame oil
4 cups (960ml) Konbu Dashi (see page 40)
6 tablespoons white sesame powder
Salt to taste
Dash of pepper

Korean soups can be thin and light or thick and hearty. This substantial and mildly flavored soup is a great accompaniment to a spicy kimchi and rice.

1. Cut the assorted fresh mushrooms into bite-sized pieces. Slice the reconstituted shiitake thinly. Slice the burdock into thin julienne strips.
2. In a small bowl, dissolve the rice flour in the ¼ cup konbu dashi.
3. Heat sesame oil in a saucepan and sauté the fresh mushrooms briefly. Add the shiitake and burdock and stir to mix. Add the 4 cups konbu dashi and sesame powder and season with salt and pepper. Bring to a boil. Add the rice flour and dashi mixture from step 2, and simmer for 2–3 minutes over medium heat. Serve hot.

Vegetable Salad with Sesame Almond Dressing

Ta tu tan yatche salada

SERVES *4*

3 cups (720ml) water
7 ounces (200g) fresh green asparagus, cut into 1-inch (3-cm) pieces
1 cup (100g) broccoli florets
1 medium zucchini, thinly sliced
1 medium carrot, thinly sliced
1 red bell pepper, deseeded and sliced

FOR THE DRESSING
2 tablespoons sesame paste
1 tablespoon sesame oil
1 tablespoon rice vinegar
2 tablespoons soy sauce
1 tablespoon water
2 tablespoons almonds, roasted and crushed
1 teaspoon kuko seeds

An example of Korean fusion cooking, this salad beautifully blends traditional ingredients with ingredients imported from the West. For an easy variation, grill the vegetables instead of boiling.

1. Bring the 3 cups water to a boil in a large saucepan. Put in the hard ends of the asparagus and the broccoli florets. Cook for 2 minutes then add the remaining asparagus, the zucchini, and the carrot. Boil for a further 2 minutes. Briefly immerse the red pepper slices in the boiling water, then remove the pan from the heat. Drain the vegetables and refresh under running water. Drain and transfer to a serving plate.
2. In a bowl, mix the dressing ingredients and stir until smooth. Serve as a separate dipping sauce, or drizzle over the vegetables before serving.

MAIN MEALS

Asparagus Namul

Asparagus namul

SERVES *4 as a shared side dish*

2 cups (480ml) water
14 ounces (400g) fresh green asparagus, cut into
    diagonal ¾-inch (2-cm) lengths
2 tablespoons rice vinegar
1 teaspoon red chili flakes
2 teaspoons white sesame seeds
2 teaspoons sesame oil
¼ teaspoon salt

Namul are quick vegetable-based dishes that use simple seasonings such as sesame oil, vinegar, Korean red pepper powder, sesame powder, and sesame seeds. There are usually a variety of namul dishes at the table to be shared by everyone.

Bring the 2 cups water to a boil in a saucepan and cook the asparagus for 3–4 minutes, until tender. Rinse under running water. Drain and transfer to a bowl. Add the vinegar, chili flakes, sesame seeds, sesame oil, and salt. Toss to mix and transfer to a serving bowl.

Bean Sprout Namul

Kong namul

SERVES *4 as a shared side dish*

3 cups (720ml) water
4 cups (400g) bean sprouts
2 tablespoons rice vinegar
2 tablespoons sesame oil
3 tablespoons soy sauce
1 scallion, finely chopped
¼ teaspoon salt
½ teaspoon chili flakes
1 teaspoon castor sugar
1 clove garlic, grated

Bring the 3 cups water to a boil in a large saucepan. Drop in the bean sprouts for 3–4 minutes until soft. Drain and transfer to a deep bowl. Add all the other ingredients, toss to mix, and transfer to a serving bowl.

Cucumber Namul

Oi namul

SERVES *4 as a shared side dish*

3 cucumbers, thinly sliced
1 teaspoon salt
2 tablespoons sesame oil
½ teaspoon black pepper
2 tablespoons white sesame seeds, crushed
1 teaspoon red chili flakes
1 scallion, finely chopped
1 tablespoon rice vinegar
1 teaspoon castor sugar
1 clove garlic, grated

1. Sprinkle the cucumber with salt, and leave to stand for 30 minutes. Squeeze out the excess liquid.
2. Heat the sesame oil in a saucepan and sauté the cucumber briefly. Add all the other ingredients. Stir to mix, remove from heat, and transfer to a serving bowl.

Okra Namul

Okra namul

SERVES *4 as a shared side dish*

In a saucepan, boil the okra in the 2 cups water for 2–3 minutes, until soft. Drain and transfer to a bowl. Add the other ingredients. Toss to mix and transfer to a serving bowl.

12 okra, each sliced into 3 diagonally
2 cups (480ml) water
3 teaspoons white sesame powder
2 teaspoons sesame oil
Pinch of salt
½ teaspoon red chili flakes
1 teaspoon vinegar
2 teaspoons soy sauce

Zucchini Namul

Ho bak namul

SERVES *4 as a shared side dish*

Heat the vegetable oil and sesame oil in a frying pan and sauté the onion briefly. Add the other ingredients. Sauté for 2–3 minutes. Transfer to a serving bowl.

1 tablespoon vegetable oil
2 teaspoons sesame oil
½ onion, thinly sliced
2 medium zucchini, cut into thin rounds
½ teaspoon salt
2 tablespoons white sesame seeds
¼ teaspoon black pepper
½ teaspoon red chili flakes

Simmered Potato Chorim

Kamja chorim

SERVES *4 as a shared side dish*

Like namul, the simmered vegetable dishes known as *chorim* are an essential part of the main meal in Korea. Several chorim dishes will be placed on the table for everyone to share. Simmered vegetables are often served alongside soup, namul, and kimchi to make a complete meal.

1 pound (450g) baby potatoes
½ cup (120ml) soy sauce
2 cups (480ml) water
1 tablespoon sesame oil
1 tablespoon sake
½ cup (100g) castor sugar
½ tablespoon grated garlic
Fresh coriander leaves, for garnish

1. Boil the potatoes in their skins until tender. Drain and set aside.
2. In a saucepan, combine the soy sauce, water, sesame oil, sake, sugar, and garlic. Bring to a boil. Add the boiled potatoes and simmer for 12–15 minutes over medium heat, until most of the liquid has been absorbed.
3. Transfer to a serving bowl and garnish with coriander leaves.

Simmered Tofu Chorim

Tu bu chorim

SERVES *4 as a shared side dish*

Tofu is extremely popular in Korean cuisine. It is healthy, inexpensive and has a tremendous versatility as it absorbs the flavors of the seasoning sauce used with it.

1 block firm tofu, about 7 ounces (200g)
Pinch of salt
1 tablespoon vegetable oil
Chives, for garnish
1 fresh red chili, chopped, for garnish

SAUCE

- 2½ tablespoons soy sauce
- 1 tablespoon castor sugar
- 1 tablespoon mirin
- 1 teaspoon garlic, grated
- 1 teaspoon sesame oil
- ½ tablespoon white sesame seeds, toasted (see page 42)
- 2 tablespoons water

1. Drain the tofu and cut into 8 pieces. Sprinkle with the salt. Heat the oil in a saucepan and sauté the tofu until crisp on both sides. Set aside.
2. In a saucepan combine the sauce ingredients. Bring to a boil. Put in the tofu in the saucepan and bring the sauce to a simmer.
3. Transfer to a serving dish and garnish with the chives and red chilies.

Stuffed Eggplant Chorim
Kaji chorim

SERVES *4 as a shared side dish*

- 4 dried shiitake mushrooms, soaked in hot water for 10 minutes
- 1¾ ounces (50g) firm tofu
- 1 tablespoon scallions, chopped
- 1 tablespoon soy sauce
- 1 teaspoon sesame oil
- 4 small eggplants
- ½ cup (120ml) Shiitake Dashi (see page 40)
- 1 teaspoon kochijan
- 2 tablespoons soy sauce
- ½ tablespoon potato starch
- 1½ tablespoons water

1. Drain and mince the shiitake. Drain the tofu and mash. In a bowl, combine the mushrooms and tofu with the scallions, 1 tablespoon soy sauce, and the oil.
2. Remove the tops of the eggplants, and make a cross-shaped incision along the body of each eggplant, keeping both ends intact. Stuff the tofu mixture into the slits.
3. Put the shiitake dashi, kochijan, and 2 tablespoons soy sauce into a saucepan, add the eggplant, and simmer for 15 minutes. Mix the potato starch and the water together, and add to the saucepan. Bring to a simmer, remove from the heat, and serve.

Cabbage Radish Kimchi
Paechu mu kimchi

MAKES *4 cups*

PHOTOGRAPH ON PAGE 110

- 9 ounces (255g) white radish, julienned
- 1 medium carrot, julienned
- 11 cups (500g) Chinese cabbage, cut into bite-sized pieces
- 1 cup (50g) chives, cut into 1 inch (3-cm) lengths
- 1 tablespoon salt
- 4 cups (960ml) water

SEASONING

- 2 cloves garlic, minced
- Walnut-sized piece fresh ginger, peeled and finely chopped
- 1 tablespoon Korean red pepper powder
- 1 tablespoon hot water

Kimchi, the soul of Korean cuisine, is a spicy, fermented pickle which accompanies every Korean meal. Chinese cabbage, white radish, cucumber, carrot, and other seasonal vegetables are commonly used to make kimchi. The vegetables are salted and then seasoned with red chili powder, grated ginger, ginger juice, and garlic.

1. Place the radish, carrot, cabbage, and chives in a large bowl. Add the salt to the water. Pour the salted water over the vegetables and place a heavy weight, such as a plate, inside the bowl on top of the vegetables, so that the vegetables are completely immersed. Allow to stand for 4–5 hours.
2. Drain the vegetables and discard the brine. Rinse thoroughly under running water and drain again. Squeeze out any remaining liquid and set aside.

3. In a small bowl, mix the seasoning ingredients, and sprinkle over the vegetables. Toss the vegetables until they are evenly coated with the spices.

4. Place the spiced vegetables in a large jar, covered, and allow to ferment in a cool place for 2–3 days. During hot summer weather, kimchi can be ready within a day. Store in an airtight container. Kimchi will keep in the refrigerator for several weeks.

Chunky Radish Kimchi
Kkaktugi

MAKES **4 cups**

2 medium white radishes, cut into 1-inch (3-cm) dice
1½ tablespoons salt
2 heaping tablespoons Korean red pepper powder
4 cloves garlic, finely chopped
3 scallions cut into 1-inch (3-cm) lengths
1 tablespoon castor sugar
1 tablespoon red pepper threads

There are hundreds of variations of kimchi and each family has their personal favorite and their very own style of making it. White radish is readily and cheaply available all year round, making this dish one of the more popular kimchis. Delicious with hot, fluffy white rice.

1. Place the radish in a deep bowl and sprinkle with the salt and the red pepper powder. Wearing rubber gloves, rub the radish well to coat evenly with the salt and red pepper powder. Allow to stand for 20 minutes.

2. Mix in the garlic, scallions, sugar, and red pepper threads and place a weight, such as a plate, inside the bowl, so that it presses down on the vegetables. Leave for two hours. This will help the excess liquid to ooze out.

3. Leave to ferment in a covered jar in a cool place for 2 days, or 24 hours if the weather is hot. Will keep for several weeks in an airtight jar in the refrigerator.

Cucumber Kimchi

Oi kimchi

8 cucumbers
1 tablespoon salt
4 scallions, finely chopped
½ cup (50g) white radish, finely chopped
3 cloves garlic, finely chopped
3 tablespoons fresh ginger, peeled and finely chopped
1 tablespoon Korean red pepper powder
½ tablespoon red pepper threads
2 tablespoons rice vinegar
1 tablespoon salt
3 teaspoons castor sugar

MAKES *4 cups*

Traditionally, kimchi was made in large quantities to prepare for the long harsh winters when fresh vegetables were hard to come by. The ritual of kimchi making, called *kimjang*, usually started at the beginning of winter and the kimchi would be left to ferment for two to three months. Small portions of the kimchi would then be taken out as needed. The kimchi would last until the spring time, when fresh vegetables were available once again. Cucumber kimchi, however, can be eaten on the same day as it is prepared.

1. Cut the cucumbers into 1½-inch (4-cm) thick rounds. Score a deep cross on one side of each round, taking care not to slice through completely. Place the cucumber pieces in a bowl and rub with 1 tablespoon salt. Allow to stand for 45–50 minutes to soften. Rinse under running water and drain.
2. In a deep bowl, combine the cucumber with the scallions, radish, garlic, and ginger.
3. Add the red pepper powder, red pepper threads, rice vinegar, salt, and sugar and mix thoroughly. Allow to stand for 2–3 hours at room temperature before serving. Store in an airtight jar in the refrigerator. Keeps for several weeks.

Tofu Kimchi

Tu bu kimchi

1 tablespoon vegetable oil
½ onion, thinly sliced
1 leek, sliced diagonally
1 clove garlic, finely chopped
1 cup (225g) kimchi, any kind, chopped
1 teaspoon castor sugar
1 teaspoon soy sauce
1 teaspoon sesame oil
1 teaspoon white sesame seeds, toasted (see page 42)
11 ounces (310g) firm tofu, drained
2 cups (480ml) water
Chives, for garnish

MAKES *4 cups*

Tofu kimchi is a popular snack with beer or Korean liquor, and is often found on beer garden menus.

1. Heat the oil in a saucepan and sauté the onion, leek, and garlic over medium heat for 2–3 minutes.
2. Add the kimchi and stir briefly. Add the sugar and soy sauce and mix well.
3. Drizzle the sesame oil over the ingredients in the saucepan and sprinkle with the sesame seeds.
4. Cut the tofu into short thin strips, and place in a separate saucepan. Put in the 2 cups of water and bring to a boil. Drain well and set aside on a serving dish.
5. Arrange the tofu slices on a platter with the kimchi sauce mixture on the side. Serve garnished with chives.

PANCAKES AND MORE

Korean Wontons

Pyontse

MAKES **30**

The unusual combination of vegetables, pine nuts, and sesame seeds creates a delicious medley of flavors in this popular accompaniment to the Korean staple of white rice.

1. Keep the wonton wrappers covered until ready to use. Reconstitute the shiitake and cut into thin slices. Boil the bean sprouts and drain.
2. Heat the vegetable oil in a saucepan and sauté the shiitake and zucchini over high heat for 1 minute. Add the soy sauce, salt, and rice vinegar and stir briefly.
3. In a mixing bowl, combine the seasoned shiitake and zucchini with the bean sprouts, scallions, sesame seeds, sesame oil, black pepper, and pine nuts. Mix thoroughly.
4. Arrange the wonton wrappers on a dry surface and place a spoonful of the mixture in the center of each. Apply a little water to the edges, and fold over and press the edges together to seal.
5. Steam the wontons in small batches for 5–7 minutes, in a steamer, or over a pan of boiling water. Serve on a bed of lettuce leaves with Soy and Sesame Dipping Sauce.

30 wonton wrappers
3 dried shiitake mushrooms
1½ cups (150g) bean sprouts
1 tablespoon vegetable oil
1 medium zucchini, julienned
1 tablespoon soy sauce
Pinch of salt
2 tablespoons rice vinegar
2 tablespoons scallions, minced
½ tablespoon white sesame seeds
½ tablespoon sesame oil
¼ teaspoon black pepper
1 tablespoon pine nuts, crushed
Soy and Sesame Dipping Sauce, to serve (see below)
Lettuce leaves, to serve

Soy and Sesame Dipping Sauce
Yang nyom jang

MAKES **about 1 cup (240ml)**

5 tablespoons soy sauce
1 tablespoon Korean red pepper powder
2 tablespoons sake
3 tablespoons rice vinegar
4 tablespoons Konbu Stock (see page 40)
1 scallion, finely chopped

4 fresh hot green chilies, finely chopped
1 tablespoon ground white sesame seeds
1 tablespoon sesame oil
1 tablespoon white sesame seeds, toasted
1 teaspoon castor sugar

This colorful dipping sauce adds zest to any dish on the table. An excellent sauce to serve with pancakes and wontons.

Combine all the ingredients in a bowl and allow to stand for 10 minutes. Serve in individual dipping bowls with the meal. Keeps refrigerated for a week.

Mini Lotus Root Pancakes

Yon kun jeon

SERVES *4*

5 ounces (140g) lotus root, grated
½ teaspoon salt
3 tablespoons potato starch
¾ cup (90g) all-purpose flour
1 cup (240ml) water
5 shiso leaves, shredded
Vegetable oil for frying and drizzling

FOR THE DIPPING SAUCE

2 tablespoons soy sauce
1 tablespoon rice vinegar
1 teaspoon pine nuts, ground
1 tablespoon sesame oil
½ teaspoon Korean red pepper powder

Savory pancakes are a regular feature of Korean cuisine, and are always accompanied by at least one variety of dipping sauce.

1. In a mixing bowl, combine the grated lotus root, salt, potato starch, and flour. Add the water gradually and mix to make a smooth and fairly thin batter. Add the shiso leaves and mix.
2. In a small bowl, mix the dipping sauce ingredients together.
3. Place a greased frying pan over medium heat and pour in a heaping ladleful of the vegetable and batter mixture. Spread out the batter evenly to a circle about 2 inches (5 cm) in diameter. Cook over medium heat for 3–4 minutes on each side until crisp and golden, drizzling a little oil around the sides of the pan. Slide on to a serving plate. Repeat the process until all the batter has been used.
4. Place the bowl of dipping sauce in the center of a large plate with the mini pancakes all around it and serve.

Mushroom and Zucchini Fritters

Ho bak jeon

SERVES *4*

PHOTOGRAPH ON PAGE 112

FOR THE BATTER

¾ cup (90g) all-purpose flour
¼ cup (40g) rice flour
½ teaspoon salt
Pinch of baking soda
¾ cup (180ml) water

FOR THE SPICY DIPPING SAUCE

¼ cup (60ml) soy sauce
2 tablespoons vinegar
1 tablespoon Chili Oil (see page 67)
1 teaspoon white sesame seeds, toasted (see page 42)

Vegetable oil for deep frying
1 medium zucchini, thinly sliced
4 eringi mushrooms, each cut in half lengthwise

A delightful and appealing side dish. The eringi mushrooms and zucchini lend contrasting flavors and textures. Any variety of mushroom or squash may be used for an interesting variation.

1. In a mixing bowl, combine the ingredients for the batter. Mix to get a smooth consistency. The batter should not be too thick.
2. Mix the dipping sauce ingredients in a small bowl.
3. In a wok, heat the oil for deep frying to 350°F (180°C). Dip the vegetables in the batter, a few at a time, and deep-fry until crisp and golden brown. Drain on kitchen paper.
4. Place the dipping sauce on a serving plate and arrange the fritters around it.

Potato and Onion Pancakes

Kamja chijimi

SERVES *4*

1 medium potato, grated
1 onion, grated
1 cup (50g) chives, finely chopped
1½ cups (185g) all-purpose flour
½ teaspoon salt
1 cup (240ml) water
Vegetable oil for frying and drizzling
Soy and Sesame Dipping Sauce, to serve (see opposite)

These savory pancakes—often referred to as the Korean pizza—make great appetizers, or a tasty light meal served with namul and salad. The chewy texture of the crispy pancake and the tangy Soy and Sesame Dipping Sauce make it one of my favorite Korean dishes.

1. In a mixing bowl, combine the grated potato, grated onion, chives, flour, and salt. Add the water gradually, mixing continuously to make a smooth batter.
2. Place a greased frying pan over medium heat and pour in a heaping ladleful of the vegetable and batter mixture. Spread the batter evenly to make a thin pancake, about 3 inches (8 cm) in diameter. Cook for 3–4 minutes on each side over medium heat, until firm and slightly browned, drizzling a little oil around the sides of the frying pan. When both sides are evenly browned, slide on to a serving plate. Repeat this process with the remaining batter.
3. Serve with individual dipping bowls of Soy and Sesame Dipping Sauce.

Vegetable Pancakes   *Chijimi*

SERVES *4*   PHOTOGRAPH ON PAGE 111

Chijimi, a colorful pancake with leeks and red bell pepper, is served in Korean homes as an appetizer or as part of the main meal, with a variety of dipping sauces. For my Korean party menu, I usually include chijimi with Korean Noodles (see page 178) and Korean Wok-seared Spicy Rice with Vegetables (page 179), accompanied by a variety of kimchi, namul, and chorim.

1. Heat the sesame oil in a saucepan and sauté the vegetables for 1 minute over medium heat. Transfer to a dish to cool.
2. Combine the batter ingredients in a mixing bowl and whisk until smooth. The batter should be of pouring consistency and not too thick.
3. Heat a frying pan and grease it with a little oil. Pour a ladleful of the batter into the pan and spread to make a thin crepe.
4. Sprinkle a quarter of the vegetables evenly over the crepe and press gently with a spatula.
5. Drizzle a little oil around the sides of the crepe and cook over medium heat for one minute. Flip over and cook the other side for a further minute, then slide onto a serving dish. Repeat this process with the remaining batter and vegetables. Serve with the dipping sauces.

2 teaspoons sesame oil
2 leeks, sliced into bite-sized pieces
3 scallions, cut into bite-sized pieces
1 red bell pepper, thinly sliced
Vegetable oil for frying and drizzling
Soy and Sesame Dipping Sauce (see page 174), to serve
Kochijan Sauce (see below), to serve

FOR THE BATTER
1 cup (125g) all-purpose flour
2 tablespoons rice flour
2 tablespoons potato starch
½ teaspoon salt
1 teaspoon sesame seeds, toasted (see page 42)
1 cup (240ml) water

Kochijan Sauce   *Chogochujang*   MAKES *about 1 cup (240ml)*

½ cup (100ml) Kochijan paste
3 tablespoons castor sugar
3 tablespoons water
2 tablespoons mirin

3 tablespoons rice vinegar
1 tablespoon white sesame seeds, toasted (see page 42) and ground
1 tablespoon sesame oil

Combine all the ingredients in a bowl and mix until smooth. Store in an airtight jar in the refrigerator.

RICE AND NOODLE DISHES

Chilled Noodles

Bibim naeng myeon

SERVES *4*

10 dried shiitake mushrooms, soaked in hot water for 10 minutes, drained, and sliced
2 pears or apples, peeled and grated
3 tablespoons vegetable oil
4 tablespoons red chili flakes
3 tablespoons soy sauce
4 tablespoons rice vinegar
1 tablespoon castor sugar
Pinch of salt
2 tablespoons white sesame seeds, toasted (see page 42)
6 cups (1.5 L) water
1 pound (450g) sweet potato noodles or harusame noodles
Cucumber, julienned, for garnish
Kochijan Sauce, to serve (see opposite)
Multipurpose Sauce, to serve (see page 178)

These sweet and spicy noodles appear on the menus of most restaurants, popular with the tourists and locals alike, especially during the hot Korean summer.

1. Heat the vegetable oil in a frying pan and sauté the mushrooms. Add the chili flakes and soy sauce and mix. Transfer to a bowl, and add the grated pear, vinegar, sugar, salt, and sesame seeds and mix. Place in the refrigerator to cool.
2. In a large saucepan, bring the 6 cups water to a boil. Add the noodles and cook for 5–7 minutes over medium heat, until tender. Drain and rinse under running cold water.
3. Before serving, place an ice-cube in each individual serving bowl. Divide the noodles between the bowls and top with the chilled seasoned vegetables. Garnish with julienned cucumber, and serve with Kochijan Sauce and Multipurpose Sauce.

Kimchi Rice

Pokkunbap

SERVES *4*

1 tablespoon sesame oil
⅔ cup (150g) kimchi, any kind, chopped
7 ounces (200g) white radish, julienned
2 cups (200g) bean sprouts
3 cups (550g) cooked short-grain rice
½ teaspoon salt
Multipurpose Sauce, to serve (see page 178)

The versatile kimchi is tossed with crunchy bean sprouts and white radish in fragrant sesame oil—all basic ingredients in the Korean pantry—and mixed with cooked rice to make a spicy and delicious dish, ready in minutes.

1. Heat the oil in a saucepan and sauté the kimchi over high heat for 1 minute.
2. Add the radish and bean sprouts, turn the heat to medium, and sauté for a further 2–3 minutes.
3. Add the cooked rice and salt. Mix well. Transfer to a serving bowl. Can be sprinkled with Multipurpose Sauce, according to individual taste.

Korean Noodles

Jap chae

PHOTOGRAPH ON PAGE 112

5 cups (1.2 L) water
7 ounces (200g) sweet potato noodles
1 tablespoon Chili Sesame Oil (see below)
2 cloves garlic, finely chopped
½ onion, thinly sliced
1 red bell pepper, thinly sliced
½ medium carrot, julienned
1 scallion, thinly sliced
½ cup (50g) garlic stems, cut into bite-sized pieces
2 dried wood ear mushrooms, reconstituted and chopped
1 cup (100g) bean sprouts
¼ teaspoon salt
¼ teaspoon pepper
1 teaspoon castor sugar
3 tablespoons soy sauce
2 teaspoons white sesame seeds, toasted (see page 42)
Red chili threads, for garnish

This colorful noodle dish is usually reserved for special occasions and guests. The transparent gray noodles made from sweet potato are best suited to this dish as they retain their elasticity even after cooking, but cellophane noodles make a good substitute.

1. Bring the water to a boil in a large pan. Add the noodles and cook for 5–6 minutes until soft. Drain and rinse under running water.
2. Heat the Chili Sesame Oil in a wok and sauté the garlic and onion briefly over medium heat. Add the bell pepper, carrot, scallions, garlic stems, and wood ear mushrooms, turn the heat to high, and stir-fry for 2–3 minutes.
3. Add the bean sprouts, salt, pepper, sugar, and soy sauce. Toss the vegetables and reduce the heat to medium. Sprinkle with sesame seeds.
4. Mix in the cooked noodles and sauté for 1 minute. Transfer to a serving dish and garnish with red chili threads.

Chili Sesame Oil

Kotchu chamgirum

MAKES **5 tablespoons**

3 tablespoons sesame oil
2 tablespoons chili oil

Combine the sesame oil and chili oil, and heat until smoky. Allow to cool before using.

Multipurpose Sauce

Man nung kanjang

MAKES **about 1 cup (240ml)**

½ cup (120ml) soy sauce
¼ cup (60ml) water
¼ cup (50g) castor sugar
1 tablespoon ground black pepper
4 tablespoons mirin

4 tablespoons sake
Walnut-sized piece fresh ginger, peeled and sliced
2 cloves garlic, sliced
¼ onion, sliced
1 scallion, sliced

This is a basic dipping sauce seasoning for a noodle or rice dish.

In a saucepan, combine all the ingredients and bring to a boil. Simmer for 5 minutes and remove from heat. Set aside for 10 minutes and strain before use. Keeps refrigerated for 2–3 days.

Korean Wok-seared Spicy Rice with Vegetables

Bibimbap

SERVED *1*

2 dried shiitake mushrooms
3½ ounces (100g) atsuage deep-fried tofu, cut into strips
1 cup (240ml) Konbu Dashi (see page 40)
1 tablespoon soy sauce
1 tablespoon mirin
1 teaspoon castor sugar
1 tablespoon sesame oil
2 tablespoons kochijan paste
4 cups (720g) cooked short-grain rice
1¾ ounces (50g) white radish, julienned
½ medium carrot, julienned
½ cucumber, julienned
½ red bell pepper
5 green beans
Beni shoga pickled ginger, to serve

Bibimbap is one of the most famous Korean dishes in the world and can be made with a variety of vegetables. Feel free to add red cabbage, shiso leaves, baby greens, green chilies, or shredded nori seaweed to the vegetables suggested in this recipe.

1. Place the mushrooms and tofu strips in a saucepan. Pour in the dashi and bring to a boil. Add the soy sauce, mirin, and sugar. Simmer for 5–6 minutes and remove from heat. Use a slotted spoon to transfer the mushrooms and tofu to a bowl. Discard any remaining liquid.
2. Heat 1 tablespoon sesame oil in an iron wok or a frying pan and sauté the kochijan paste. Add the cooked rice and stir to mix over high heat. Transfer to a serving platter, and arrange the mushrooms, tofu, and other vegetables in groups over the rice. Mix well, and serve garnished with pickled ginger.

Tofu Fried Rice

Tubu noun pokkunbop

SERVES *4*

7 ounces (200g) atsuage deep-fried tofu
2 tablespoons vegetable oil
1 medium potato, peeled
½ medium carrot
1 medium zucchini
1 green bell pepper
1 cucumber
½ small eggplant
4 fresh shiitake mushroom caps
½ teaspoon salt
3 cups (550g) cooked short-grain rice
½ cup (120ml) Multipurpose Sauce (see opposite)
Chives, chopped, for garnish
½ teaspoon white sesame seeds, for garnish

Quick and colorful, this stir-fried rice makes a substantial addition to a dinner menu.

1. Cut the tofu into small dice. Dice all the vegetables finely.
2. Heat the vegetable oil in a saucepan and sauté the tofu and vegetables over high heat for 3–4 minutes. Add the salt and mix in the rice.
3. Pour the Multipurpose Sauce over the rice and quickly mix over high heat for 2–3 minutes. Transfer to a serving dish and serve garnished with chives and sesame seeds.

Glossary of ingredients

abura-age tofu
Deep-fried tofu sold in thin sheets, which can be slit open along one end to make pouches. Rinse in hot water before using to remove excess oil.

ajwain seeds
Also known as carom and bishop's weed, this spice goes well with green beans and potatoes, and is widely used in Indian cooking.

angel mushrooms
Many types of fresh mushrooms are used in Thai cooking, including angel mushrooms, straw mushrooms, and oyster mushrooms. They can be substituted for one another if necessary.

asafetida
A seasoning that can be bought from Indian groceries, in resin or powder form. A tiny pinch goes a long way, so buy the smallest quantity available.

atsuage deep-fried tofu
Blocks of atsuage deep-fried tofu can be bought ready-made from Asian supermarkets. Before using, rinse in hot water, and lightly press between sheets of kitchen towel to remove excess oil.

bamboo shoots
These crisply textured shoots of the bamboo plant are widely available in canned form from Asian supermarkets.

bean thread noodles
Thin noodles made from mung beans. Also know as transparent or cellophane noodles.

beni shoga pickled ginger
The Japanese pickled ginger known as *beni shoga* is made of ginger that has been colored bright red and cut into thin strips. It is used as a garnish for a variety of dishes. Do not confuse with *gari*, which is the pale pink thinly sliced pickled ginger that accompanies sushi.

bird's eye chilies
Extremely hot Thai chilies, available fresh or dried.

bitter gourd
Also known as bitter melon. A bitter tasting, cucumber-like squash.

black Chinese miso
Also known as Chinese black bean paste. Available from Asian supermarkets.

burdock
Burdock root is about 1 inch (2–3 cm) in diameter and 15–20 inches long. Before cooking, scrub gently under running water, taking care not to scrape off all the skin, as the skin contains the flavor. Slice, and soak in vinegared water for 5 minutes to remove any bitterness.

candlenut
A round, oily nut, often used to give texture to dishes. Macadamia or cashew nuts make a good substitute.

castor sugar
Finely granulated white sugar. Use regular granulated sugar if castor sugar is unavailable.

chickpea flour
Also known as Bengal gram and besan. An Indian staple, which is gluten-free.

Chinese chives
Also known as garlic chives. Sold fresh in Asian supermarkets.

Chinese kale
Also known as Chinese broccoli. Has blue-green leaves and thick, cripsy stems.

Chinese radish
See *white radish*.

Chinese red chili paste
Sold in jars, and widely available from Asian supermarkets.

Chinese yam
A tuber that is viscous when grated. Also known as Japanese mountain yam and Korean yam.

coconut cream
The thick, creamy part of canned coconut milk.

coconut milk
The thin, watery part of canned coconut milk.

coriander root
Can be bought fresh from Asian supermarkets. If you cannot find it, use coriander stems and leaves instead.

cucumber
The cucumber used in these recipes is the Asian variety, about 8 inches (20 cm) long and 1 inch (2–3 cm) in diameter.

curry leaves
Small highly aromatic leaves, easily obtainable dried from Asian supermarkets.

daikon radish
Daikon radish is a winter root vegetable about 16 inches (40 cm) long. When buying, choose a daikon that is firm and glossy. If you purchase a whole daikon, cut off the leaves, wrap the radish in paper, and refrigerate. Wrap the leaves in wet paper, place in a plastic bag, and refrigerate.

edamame beans
Edamame beans are soybeans harvested while they are still green, and are rich in protein and Vitamin C. They can be bought fresh or frozen.

eggplant
The eggplant used in these recipes is the small, long, purple variety, about 6 inches (15 cm) long.

enoki mushrooms
Sold in clusters about 4 inches (10 cm) long. Cut off the spongy root about 1 inch (2–3 cm) from the bottom before using.

eringi mushrooms
Plump, milky white mushrooms with a crunchy texture. When buying, choose eringi that are firm and white with an elastic texture.

fenugreek leaves
Fresh or dried leaves can be found in Indian stores. Their Indian name is kasuri methi. Celery leaves can be used as a substitute.

fruit salt
Fruit salt, made of sodium bicarbonate and citric acid, is used in Indian cooking to give a porous texture to dishes such as sponge cakes. Available in Indian stores, most commonly under the brand name Eno Fruit Salts.

fu
The Japanese name for wheat gluten, most commonly sold in dried breadlike discs. Wheat gluten is often known as seitan in the West, is widely used by those who follow a macrobiotic diet, and can be found in health food stores.

galangal
A type of ginger, with a mild taste and reddish skin. Can be bought dried or fresh.

garlic chives
Sweet, pungent garlic greens, sold fresh in thick bunches that resemble grass. Available from Asian supermarkets.

garlic stem
A long green shoot, sturdier than the garlic chive, available in bunches from Asian supermarkets.

glutinous rice flour
Made from short-grain rice, this flour gives dishes a chewy texture, and is widely used in Southeast Asian cuisine.

harusame noodles
Thin, translucent Japanese noodles, very similar to *bean thread noodles*.

jackfruit
Fresh jackfruit is a very large fruit, with flesh similar to pineapple. It is also widely available canned in syrup, which is more convenient when only small quanitities are required.

jasmine rice
A variety of long-grain rice, popular in Thailand, with a nutty aroma.

kaffir lime leaves
Can be bought fresh, dried, or frozen from Asian super markets.

kaiware radish sprouts
Peppery sprouts of the daikon radish.

karashi mustard
This Japanese mustard is available in powder or paste form. If using powder, mix a small amount with warm water, cover the bowl, and leave to stand for 10 minutes before using.

Kashmiri chilies
Usually sold dried in Asian supermarkets. They impart a deep red color to the dish.

kecap manis
A thick dark sweetened soy sauce, widely used in Indonesian cooking, as a dip or as a seasoning in various dishes. Can

be bought ready-made from Asian supermarkets. It can be substituted with dark Chinese soy sauce mixed with brown sugar.

kenari nuts
Also known as molucca nuts, they grow on the kenari tree in the Indonesian rainforest.

kochijan paste
A Korean chili paste, available ready-made in jars from Asian supermarkets.

komatsuna
A Japanese leafy vegetable, also known as Japanese mustard spinach.

konbu
A dried seaweed, often used to make stock. When buying, choose konbu that that is almost black in color, thick, and has a fine white powder on the surface.

konbu powder
Ready-made powdered konbu is available from Japanese stores and is a simple way to add seasoning to dishes.

Korean red pepper powder
A spicy seasoning widely used in Korean cuisine, and available from Korean stores.

koyadofu
Freeze-dried tofu. Soak in water for 2–3 minutes to reconstitute, then squeeze gently to remove excess moisture before using.

krupuk
A popular snack in Southeast Asia, these deep-fried crackers are made from tapioca or potato flour. Although they are commonly flavored with fish or prawns, there are many varieties available, some of which are flavored with vegetables and do not use any fish products.

kuko seeds
Small red seeds, available dried from Asian supermarkets. Also known as kukoshi, lycium wolfberry, and goji berry.

lemongrass
A fragrant stalk, usually added to dishes during cooking to impart a lemony flavor.

long beans
These Asian beans are also known as yardlong beans, so called because their pods can be up to 25 inches (60 cm) long. They are eaten raw or cooked, and taste best when young and slender.

lotus root
Lotus root has crunchy grayish-white or cream-colored flesh, and holes that run the length of the tuber. Wash thoroughly to remove all mud from the holes, and pare off the skin. If not using immediately, soak in water to which a few drops of vinegar have been added. This will prevent discoloring.

lotus stem
Can be bought fresh, but is easier to find preserved in brine.

maitake mushrooms
Also known as sheep's head, ram's head, and hen of the woods. Grow in a cluster of wavy brown caps, and have a nutty flavor and crisp texture.

mango powder
Also known as amchur. A beige powder made from dried green mango, used as a sweet and sour flavoring in Indian curries. Lemon juice may be used as a substitute.

matcha green tea powder
Powdered green tea used in the tea ceremony and sometimes as an ingredient in Japanese desserts. A little can be mixed with salt to accompany dishes such as tempura.

mirin
A liqueur used for cooking, made from rice, that adds sweetness, flavor, and a glaze to a dish. Dry sherry can be used as a substitute.

miso
Fermented soybean paste used as a seasoning for soups and stews. Red miso and white miso are the two most common types. Red miso has the stronger flavor.

mizuna leaves
A leafy green of the mustard family, popular in Japan, with a mild, peppery flavor.

myoga
An Asian variety of ginger grown for its edible buds.

nigella
Widely used as a spice in Indian cooking, nigella resembles the poppy seed but has a peppery taste.

nori
Thin, flat sheets of seaweed, usually sold in packs of ten, and most commonly used as the wrapping for sushi rolls. Once opened, store in an airtight container.

palm sugar
This dark sugar is made from the sap of the coconut palm and has a deep, caramel flavor. Brown sugar can be used as a substitute.

palm syrup
The boiled-down sap of the date palm tree, this thick dark syrup is used as a sweetener in a variety of Asian dishes.

pandan leaves
Sweet-flavored tropical leaves that add a bright green color to dishes. Can be bought fresh or frozen.

peanut oil
Widely used in Southeast Asian cooking, peanut oil will give your dishes an authentic Asian taste. Vegetable oil can be substituted for peanut oil in any of the recipes.

peppermint leaves
Fresh peppermint leaves are greenish purple in color and have a stronger taste than spearmint leaves.

pigeon pea dal
A pulse widely used in Indian cuisine, available dried from Asian supermarkets.

plum sauce
A sweet and sour sauce often used as a dip in Chinese cuisine, available from Asian supermarkets.

pumpkin
The pumpkin used in these recipes is the Japanese kabocha variety, which has a smooth, dense texture and sweet taste. Acorn squash is a good substitute.

red pepper threads
About 2 inches (4 cm) long, these dried red chili pepper threads have a smoky flavor. Often used in Korean cuisine to add spice to kimchi dishes, or simply as a garnish. Not as hot as chili powder, they can be used to get the exact degree of desired heat in a dish.

rice flour
Also known as rice powder, or rice starch, this type of flour is widely used in Asian cuisine.

rice noodles
Rice noodles of many different thick and thin varieties are widely used in Asian cooking. Dried rice noodles can be found in many Western supermarkets. Fresh rice noodles can be found in Asian stores.

rice vinegar
Rice vinegar is distilled vinegar made from rice wine.

sake
Sake is wine made from rice, and is often used as a seasoning in Japanese cuisine. Bottles of cooking sake can be found in Japanese supermarkets.

salam leaves
Often thought of as the Indonesian equivalent of bay leaves. Bay leaves can be substituted if salam leaves are unavailable.

sesame paste
Sesame paste can be bought ready-made in Asian supermarkets.

shichimi pepper
This Japanese pepper contains seven spices, and is often used to flavor noodles and stews.

shiitake mushrooms
Shiitake can be bought fresh or dried. Two types of dried shiitake are available in stores: the thick-capped shiitake called *donko shiitake* in Japanese have more flavor than the flat-capped *koshin shiitake*. Keep fresh shiitake in the refrigerator, wrapped in paper. Do not keep in a polythene bag, as this will make them slimy.

shimeji mushrooms
Shimeji mushrooms have gray caps and short, fat stems. Their flavor disappears if washed too well before use. Cut off the spongy part of the stem about 1 inch (2–3 cm) from the bottom, and quickly rinse.

shirataki noodles
Transparent, gelatinous noodles, made from *konnyaku*, a type of tuber. They are sold in water filled bags and can be found in Japanese supermarkets and health food stores.

shishito peppers
Small green sweet hot peppers, popular in Japan. Sold fresh

shiso leaves
Shiso, also known as perilla, Japanese basil, and oba, is a fragrant herb, whose fresh leaves are widely used in Japanese cuisine as a garnish for sashimi or soup.

soba noodles
Thin brown buckwheat noodles, available dried from Japanese stores.

soy sauce
Soy sauces vary from country to country, and it may not be appropriate to substitute one type for another. Japanese soy sauce is lighter and more refined than the darker and thicker Chinese soy sauce. The soy sauce used in Thai, Vietnamese, Burmese, Indonesian, and Malaysian cooking is closer to the Chinese type. The soy sauce used in Korea is closer to the Japanese type.

soybean gluten

Minced soybean gluten can be found in canned form at Asian supermarkets. Seitan (see *fu*) is an acceptable substitute.

spearmint leaves

Fresh spearmint leaves have a cooler, subtler taste than peppermint leaves.

split black gram

These white lentils are black lentils (urad dal) that have been skinned and split.

split mung beans

A yellow pulse widely used in Indian cuisine, available dried from Asian supermarkets.

split yellow lentils

Widely used in Indian cuisine for their nutty, grainy taste. Also known as Bengal gram, chana dal, and yellow split peas.

spring chrysanthemum leaves

Popular in Japan (where they are known as *shungiku* leaves) and other Asian countries as an ingredient in soups and hotpots. Spinach can be used as a substitute.

straw mushrooms

This Thai variety of mushroom is highly perishable raw. Canned straw mushrooms can be found in Asian supermarkets.

sweet potato noodles

Dried gray-colored noodles which are good at absorbing the flavors of whatever they are cooked in. Widely used in Korean cuisine. Sold in packets in Asian supermarkets, each packet usually holding three large bundles of noodles.

sweet soy sauce

Soy sauce to which palm sugar has been added. A variety of bottled brands are available in Asian supermarkets.

tamarind

A commonly used souring agent in Asian cuisine. Use lemon juice if you can't get hold of tamarind. Commonly available in paste, or in solid pulpy form, which can be mashed and strained and then diluted with water to make juice.

taro

An egg-shaped potato with a sticky texture. Rub with salt and rinse before using, to remove bitterness.

tempeh

A cake of fermented soybeans, often used in Asian cooking, and widely available in health food stores in the West. Tempeh is versatile but bland, and is tastier if soaked in 2 cups (480ml) water with 1 tablespoon of sliced garlic for 30 minutes prior to using. Keep refrigerated.

udon noodles

Thick white Japanese noodles made from wheat flour and usually sold dried.

urad dal

Also known as black gram, or black lentils. Ural dal is black. Split black gram—urad dal with the skin removed—is white.

wakame

A variety of Japanese seaweed, usually bought dried. Soak in cold water for 10 minutes before using.

wasabi

Also known as Japanese horseradish. The fresh root of the wasabi plant can be grated and used as a spice. It is also available as a ready-made paste from Japanese stores.

water chestnuts

Available canned from Asian supermarkets.

water spinach

An Asian vegetable similar to spinach, and often used as a stir-fry ingredient.

white radish

The long, thick white radish is used widely in Asian cooking. Also known as Chinese radish or daikon. See *daikon radish* for further information.

wood ear mushrooms

Brown ear-shaped mushrooms that have a crispy texture when cooked. Available dried or fresh from Asian supermarkets.

yakisoba noodles

Made from wheat flour, available dried from Asian supermarkets.

yuzu

A citrus fruit with a fresh aroma, about 2–3 inches (5–8 cm) in diameter. Yuzu is not edible, but the grated zest is often added to soups, salads, and hotpots to provide fragrance.

INDEX OF MAIN INGREDIENTS

A

abura age—*see* tofu

almonds
- Almond Gravy 21
- Biryani 26, 83
- Mushroom and Green Pea Curry 21
- Saffron Rice with Almonds and Cashews 27
- Sesame Almond Green Beans 44
- Spicy Basmati Rice with Whole Spices 162
- Vegetable Salad with Sesame Almond Dressing 168

angel mushrooms—*see* mushrooms

apple
- Chilled Noodles 177
- Fruit in Coconut Milk 158
- Sprouted Mung Bean and Fruit Salad 17

arugula
- Fried Vegetable Salad 66
- Tomato Salad 141

asparagus
- Asparagus, Baby Corn, Pepper, and Tofu Satay 100, 118
- Asparagus Namul 169
- Asparagus Soup 130
- Green Asparagus with Black Sesame Dressing 59
- Stir-fried Asparagus 137
- Szechuan Asparagus, Baby Corn, Water Chestnuts, and Eggplant 73
- Tofu Teriyaki Steak with Sautéed Asparagus and Mushrooms 50, 93
- Vegetable Salad with Sesame Almond Dressing 168

atsuage *see* tofu

avocado
- Avocado Espresso Shake 158
- Sprouted Mung Bean and Avocado Salad 16, 84
- Tomato Salad 141

B

baby corn
- Asparagus, Baby Corn, Pepper, and Tofu Satay, 100, 118
- Drunkard's Noodles 123
- Mixed Vegetable Coconut Curry 107, 152
- Red Curry with Vegetables 120
- Stir-fried Sugar Snap Peas and Baby Corn 161
- Sweet and Sour Vegetables 73
- Szechuan Asparagus, Baby Corn, Water Chestnuts, and Eggplant 73
- Vegetable Soup from Jakarta 151

bamboo shoots
- in glossary 180
- Aromatic Vegetable Fried Rice 75
- Bamboo Shoot and Green Pea Stir-fry 145
- Bamboo Shoot Salad 130
- Fried Noodles 54
- Green Curry with Eggplant and Bamboo Shoot 119
- Red Curry with Vegetables 120
- Simmered Mixed Vegetables 62
- Sour and Spicy Soup 67
- Spicy Fried Vegetables 71
- Stir-fried Bean Thread Noodles with Bok Choy 77
- Stir-fried Rice Noodles with Vegetables 77
- Sweet and Sour Vegetables 73

banana
- Deep-fried Banana 158
- Deep-fried Winter Squash 117
- Fruit in Coconut Milk 158
- Sprouted Mung Bean and Fruit Salad 17
- Tofu Shake with Blueberries and Banana 64

bean sprouts (*see also* mung bean sprouts)
- Aromatic Vegetable Fried Rice 75
- Bean Sprout Namul 169
- Bean Thread Noodle Salad with Potatoes 140

- Chinese Spring Rolls 79
- Coriander Soup 132
- Crispy Noodles with Spicy Sauce 163
- Fried Noodles 54
- Indonesian Fried Rice 155
- Kimchi Rice 177
- Korean Noodles 112, 178
- Korean Wontons 174
- Manado Sambal 157
- Mixed Vegetable Salad with Peanut Sauce 106, 150
- Noodles in Spicy Coconut Soup 163
- Pancakes Rolled with Vegetables 133
- Penang Noodles with Sour Soup 164
- Rice Noodle Soup 134
- Shanghai-style Chow Mein 76, 97
- Stir-fried Bean Thread Noodles with Bok Choy 77
- Stir-fried Noodles with Vegetables 109, 164
- Stir-fried Rice Noodles with Vegetables 77
- Szechuan Noodles with Vegetables 70
- Tamarind Soup with Pineapple and Okra 103, 132
- Thai Stir-fried Noodles with Tofu 101, 124
- Vegetable Soup 107, 151
- Vietnamese Transparent Spring Rolls 102, 137

bean thread noodles—*see* noodles

bell peppers
- Aromatic Vegetable Fried Rice 75
- Asparagus, Baby Corn, Pepper, and Tofu Satay 100, 118
- Cabbage and Potato Dry Curry 28
- Crispy Noodles 122
- Deep-fried Vegetables in Batter 146
- Drunkard's Noodles 123
- Fried Noodles 54
- Fried Rice with Basil 123

Green Curry with Eggplant and Bamboo Shoot   119
Indonesian Fried Rice   155
Korean Noodles   112, 178
Korean Wok-seared Spicy Rice with Vegetables   110, 179
Marinated Eggplant and Bell Peppers   60
Mint and Coriander Chutney   34
Pineapple Fried Rice   124
Red Curry with Vegetables   120
Scrambled Tofu   61, 93
Shanghai-style Chow Mein   76, 97
Spicy Fried Vegetables   72
Stir-fried Eggplant and Green Peppers   63
Stir-fried Rice Noodles with Vegetables   77
Stir-fried Spinach with Mushrooms   143
Sweet and Sour Vegetables   73
Szechuan Noodles with Vegetables   78
Tofu Fried Rice   179
Vegetable Curry with Bread Rolls   25
Vegetable Pancakes   111, 176
Vegetable Salad with Sesame Almond Dressing   168
Vegetable Tempura   52, 94
bitter gourd
    in glossary   180
    Bitter Gourd and Tofu Stir-fry   47
    Braised Bitter Gourd   145
blueberries
    Tofu Shake with Blueberries and Banana   64
bok choy
    Stir-fried Bean Thread Noodles with Bok Choy   77
    Stir-fried Noodles   144
bottle gourd
    Deep-fried Winter Squash   147
broccoli
    Broccoli with Tofu Dressing   42, 90
    Spicy Coconut and Vegetable Soup   141
    Vegetable Salad with Sesame Almond Dressing   168
burdock
    in glossary   180
    Burdock and Carrot Kimpira   58, 91
    Mixed Vegetable Fritters   48
    Mushroom Rice Balls   56, 94
    Mushroom Soup   168
    Mizuna Salad with Fried Burdock and Garlic   43, 92

Simmered Mixed Vegetables   62
Tofu and Vegetable Soup   45, 89

C
cabbage
    Chinese cabbage
        Cabbage Radish Kimchi   110, 171
        Crispy Noodles with Spicy Sauce   163
        Fried Noodles   54
        Gyoza   70, 96
        Spicy Vegetable Soup with Coconut   116
        Stir-fried Bean Thread Noodles with Bok Choy   77
        Stir-fried Noodles   144
        Stir-fried Rice Noodles with Vegetables   77
        Sukiyaki   49
        Tofu and Vegetable Sukiyaki   49
        Vegetable Pancake   51
    red cabbage
        Crispy Noodle Salad   66, 98
        Crunchy Red Cabbage Kachumber   14, 85
        Crunchy Vegetable Salad with Japanese-style Dressing   42
    white cabbage
        Assorted Vegetable Fritters   156
        Bean Thread Noodle Salad with Potatoes   140
        Cabbage and Potato Dry Curry   28
        Chinese Spring Rolls   79
        Clear Vegetable Stock   67
        Crunchy Red Cabbage Kachumber   14, 85
        Ginger Salad   140
        Mixed Vegetable Coconut Curry   107, 152
        Mixed Vegetable Salad with Peanut Sauce   106, 150
        Oriental Vegetable Crepes   147
        Shanghai-style Chow Mein   76, 97
        Stir-fried Noodles   144
        Stir-fried Noodles with Vegetables   109, 164
        Szechuan Noodles with Vegetables   78
        Thai Vegetable Stock   117
        Tomato Salad   141
        Vegetable Manchurian   74
        Vegetable Soup   107, 151
        Vegetable Soup with Mung Beans   17
carrot
    Aromatic Vegetable Fried Rice   75

Assorted Vegetables in Cashew Gravy   18, 81
Assorted Vegetable Fritters   156
Bamboo Shoot Salad   130
Biryani   26, 83
Braised Onions and Potatoes   58
Burdock and Carrot Kimpira   58, 91
Cabbage Radish Kimchi   110, 171
Cauliflower Coconut Curry with Noodles   104, 142
Chinese Spring Rolls   79
Crunchy Vegetable Salad with Japanese-style Dressing   42
Cucumber Relish   127
Cucumber Salad with Sesame Seeds   131
Fine noodles   54
Fried Noodles   54
Fried Vegetable Salad   66
Gold Bags   101, 125
Indian Vegetable Curry   161
Korean Noodles   112, 178
Korean Wok-seared Spicy Rice with Vegetables   110, 179
Lettuce Wrap with Spicy Lotus Root   71
Mixed Vegetable Coconut Curry   107, 152
Mixed Vegetable Fritters   48
Mixed Vegetable Salad with Peanut Sauce   106, 150
Mushroom Balls with Plum Sauce   136
Mushroom Rice Balls   56, 94
Pancakes Rolled with Vegetables   133
Pickled Radish and Carrot   133
Pickled Vegetable Salad   150
Rice Noodle Soup   134
Scattered Sushi   57, 95
Shanghai-style Chow Mein   76, 97
Simmered Mixed Vegetables   62
Sindhi Vegetable and Lentil Curry   23
Sour and Spicy Soup   67
South Indian Salad   15
Spicy Fried Vegetables   72
Spicy Green Papaya Salad   117
Spinach with Sesame Dressing   45, 90
Stir-fried Bean Thread Noodles with Bok Choy   77
Stir-fried Noodles   144
Stir-fried Rice Noodles with Vegetables   77
Sweet and Sour Vegetables   73

Szechuan Noodles with Vegetables 78
Tofu Fried Rice 179
Tofu and Vegetable Soup 45, 89
Vegetable Manchurian 74
Vegetable Salad with Sesame Almond Dressing 168
Vegetable Soup with Mung Beans 17
Vegetable Sweet Corn Soup 68
Vietnamese Fried Rice 103, 135
Vietnamese Transparent Spring Rolls 102, 137
Vietnamese Vegetable Stock 130

cashew nuts
Assorted Vegetables in Cashew Gravy 18, 81
Cucumber Salad with Roasted Cashews 100, 114
Kung Pao Tofu 71
Pineapple Fried Rice 124
Stir-fried Eggplant and Tofu in Spicy Sauce 103, 135

cauliflower
Assorted Vegetables in Cashew Gravy 18, 81
Biryani 26, 83
Cauliflower Coconut Curry with Noodles 104, 142
Cauliflower and Potato with Spices 19, 82
Clear Vegetable Stock 67
Red Curry with Vegetables 120
Spicy Coconut and Vegetable Soup 141
Spicy Vegetable Soup with Coconut 117
Vegetable Curry with Bread Rolls 25
Vegetable Fritters 33
Vegetable Manchurian 74
Vegetable Soup with Mung Beans 17
Vegetable Sweet Corn Soup 68

celery
Aromatic Vegetable Fried Rice 75
Clear Vegetable Stock 67
Spicy Fried Vegetables 72
Szechuan Sauce 78
Tamarind Soup with Pineapple and Okra 103, 132
Thai Vegetable Stock 117
Vegetable Soup 107, 151
Vietnamese Vegetable Stock 130

chickpeas
Bamboo Shoot and Green Pea Stir-fry 145

Chickpea Curry 19, 82
Chinese cabbage—see cabbage
Chinese kale
in glossary 180
Drunkard's Noodles 123
Chinese yam
in glossary 180
Chinese Yam Cakes 80
coconut
coconut cream
in glossary 180
Mango with Sticky Rice 128
Pumpkin in Coconut Cream 101, 128
coconut milk
in glossary 180
Almond Gravy 19
Cauliflower Coconut Curry with Noodles 104, 142
Corn in Coconut Milk 138
Deep-fried Banana 158
Fragrant Lemongrass Rice 108, 162
Fruit in Coconut Milk 158
Green Curry with Eggplant and Bamboo Shoot 119
Mango with Sticky Rice 128
Massaman Curry 119
Mixed Vegetable Coconut Curry 107, 152
Noodles in Spicy Coconut Soup 109, 163
Pancakes Rolled with Vegetables 133
Pumpkin in Coconut Cream 101, 128
Red Curry with Vegetables 120
Satay Sauce 154
Spicy Coconut and Vegetable Soup 141
Spicy Vegetable Soup with Coconut 117
Stir-fried Asparagus 137
Stir-fried Tempeh in Coconut Milk 153
Sweet Peanut Sauce 118
Tapioca with Mung Beans 128
Tempeh in Coconut Milk 153
Yellow Rice 155
desiccated coconut
Stuffed Eggplant, Squash, and Potato Curry 24
Stuffed Okra with Coriander 30
fresh coconut
Red Lentil Fritters 166
Stuffed Eggplant, Squash, and Potato Curry 24

cucumber
in glossary 181
Bamboo Shoot Salad 130
Crispy Noodle Salad 66, 98
Crunchy Vegetable Salad with Japanese-style Dressing 42
Cucumber Kimchi 173
Cucumber Namul 169
Cucumber Relish 127
Cucumber Salad with Roasted Cashews 100, 114
Cucumber Salad with Sesame Seeds 131
Hot and Sour Dip 125
Korean Wok-seared Spicy Rice with Vegetables 110, 179
Manado Sambal 157
Mixed Vegetable Salad with Peanut Sauce 106, 150
Noodles in Sesame Sauce 75
Pickled Radish and Carrot 133
Pickled Vegetable Salad 150
South Indian Salad 15
Sprouted Mung Bean and Avocado Salad 16, 84
Sweet and Sour Cucumber 68
Tofu Fried Rice 179
Vinegared Cucumber and Wakame 46

D
daikon—see radish

E
eggplant
in glossary 181
Chili Eggplants with Fresh Basil 160
Deep-fried Vegetables in Batter 146
Eggplant in Chili Garlic Sauce 69
Eggplant with Ginger and Garlic 69
Eggplant in Tomato Gravy 20
Green Curry with Eggplant and Bamboo Shoot 119
Indian Vegetable Curry 161
Marinated Eggplant and Bell Peppers 60
Mixed Vegetable Coconut Curry 107, 152
Parsee Lentil and Vegetable Curry 22
Red Curry with Vegetables 120
Roasted Eggplant Salad 116
Sindhi Vegetable and Lentil Curry 23

Spicy Coconut and Vegetable Soup 141

Spicy Eggplant 152

Spicy Roasted Eggplant Curry 23

Spicy Tofu 72, 99

Stir-fried Eggplant and Green Peppers 63

Stir-fried Eggplant and Tofu in Spicy Sauce 103, 135

Stuffed Eggplant Chorim 171

Stuffed Eggplant, Squash, and Potato Curry 24

Szechuan Asparagus, Baby Corn, Water Chestnuts, and Eggplant 73

Tofu Fried Rice 179

Vegetable Fritters 33

Vegetable Tempura 52, 94

enoki—*see* mushrooms

G

green beans

Aromatic Vegetable Fried Rice 75

Assorted Vegetables in Cashew Gravy 18, 81

Biryani 26, 83

Korean Wok-seared Spicy Rice with Vegetables 110, 179

Massaman Curry 119

Mixed Vegetable Coconut Curry 107, 152

Mixed Vegetable Salad with Peanut Sauce 106, 150

Pickled Vegetable Salad 150

Red Curry with Vegetables 120

Sesame Almond Green Beans 44

Spicy Green Papaya Salad 116

Vegetable Soup from Jakarta 151

Vegetable Sweet Corn Soup 68

green mango—*see* mango

green papaya—*see* papaya

green peas

Assorted Vegetables in Cashew Gravy 18, 81

Bamboo Shoot and Green Pea Stir-fry 145

Biryani 26, 83

Cauliflower Coconut Curry with Noodles 104, 142

Curry Puffs 165

Mushroom and Green Pea Curry 21

Saffron Rice with Almonds and Cashews 27

Spicy Roasted Eggplant Curry 23

Stuffed Eggplant, Squash, and Potato Curry 24

Stuffed Potato Cakes 32, 86

Vietnamese Fried Rice 103, 135

H

harusame noodles—*see* noodles

hatcho miso—*see* miso

J

jasmine rice—*see* rice

K

kale—*see* Chinese kale

koyadofu—*see* tofu

L

leeks

Crispy Noodles with Spicy Sauce 163

Penang Noodles with Sour Soup 164

Red Lentil Fritters 166

Spicy Fried Vegetables 72

Stir-fried Noodles with Vegetables 109, 164

Sukiyaki 49

Tofu Kimchi 173

Tofu and Vegetable Soup 45, 89

Vegetable Pancakes 111, 176

Vietnamese Vegetable Stock 130

lentils

pigeon pea dal

in glossary 183

Parsee Lentil and Vegetable Curry 22

red lentils

Red Lentils with Coriander 15

Red Lentil Fritters 166

split black gram

in glossary 185

Spicy White Lentil Soup 16

split yellow lentils

in glossary 184

Cumin Seed and Pepper Soup 14

Sindhi Vegetable and Lentil Curry 23

Split Pea Fritters 105, 148

lettuce

Crispy Noodle Salad 66, 98

Lettuce Wrap with Spicy Lotus Root 71, 99

lotus root

in glossary 182

Fried Vegetable Salad 66

Lettuce Wrap with Spicy Lotus Root 71, 99

Mini Lotus Root Pancakes 175

Scattered Sushi 57, 95

Simmered Mixed Vegetables 62

Spicy Vegetable Soup with Coconut 116

Stir-fried Lotus Root 63, 91

M

mango

Green Mango Salad 114

Mango Sambal 157

Mango with Sticky Rice 128

Sweet Mango Chutney 146

miso

black Chinese miso

in glossary 180

Spicy Fried Vegetables 73

hatcho miso

Stir-fried Eggplant and Green Peppers 63

Tofu and Vegetable Soup 45

red miso

Tofu and Vegetable Soup 45

white miso

Eggplant in Chili Garlic Sauce 69

Kung Pao Tofu 71

Miso Soup with Tofu and Wakame 43

Simmered Daikon with Miso 61

Spicy Peanut Sauce 102, 137

Spicy Tofu 72

Tofu and Vegetable Soup 45

Vegetable Pancakes 51

Vietnamese Transparent Spring Rolls 137

mung bean sprouts

How to sprout mung beans 17

Sprouted Mung Bean and Avocado Salad 16, 84

mushrooms

angel mushrooms

in glossary 180

Mushroom Balls 126

button mushrooms

Asparagus, Baby Corn, Pepper, and Tofu Satay 100, 118

Chili Fried Rice 122

Coriander Soup 132

Fried Rice with Basil 123

Green Curry with Eggplant and Bamboo Shoot 119

Hot and Sour Mushroom Soup 115

Mushroom and Green Pea Curry 21

Mushroom Soup 168

Spicy Vegetable Soup with Coconut 117

Stir-fried Rice Noodles with Vegetables 77

Vegetable Sweet Corn Soup   68
enoki
    in glossary   181
    Grilled Tofu with Mushroom
        Sauce   60
    Mushroom Rice Balls   56, 84
    Stir-fried Spinach with Mush-
        rooms   105, 143
    Sukiyaki   49
eringi
    Deep-fried Vegetables in Batter
        146
    Mushroom and Zucchini Fritters
        112, 175
    Tofu Satay   154
maitake
    in glossary   182
    Mushroom Rice Balls   56, 94
shiitake, dried
    in glossary   183
    Chilled Noodles   177
    Deep-fried Mushroom Balls   80
    Fried Noodles   54
    Korean Wok-seared Spicy Veg
        etables   110, 179
    Korean Wontons   174
    Mushroom Balls   126
    Mushroom Balls with Plum Sauce
        136
    Mushroom Rice Balls   56, 94
    Mushroom Soup   168
    Scattered Sushi   57, 95
    Shiitake Mushroom Dashi   40
    Stir-fried Eggplant and Tofu in
        Spicy Sauce   103, 135
    Stuffed Eggplant Chorim   171
    Vietnamese Fried Rice   103, 135
    Vietnamese Transparent Spring
        Rolls   102, 137
    Wheat Noodles in Soup   55
shiitake, fresh
    in glossary   183
    Chinese Spring Rolls   79
    Deep-fried Mushroom Balls   80
    Fried Vegetable Salad   66
    Gold Bags   101, 125
    Grilled Tofu with Mushroom
        Sauce   60
    Gyoza   70, 96
    Hot and Sour Mushroom Soup   115
    Roasted Eggplant Salad   116
    Scrambled Tofu   61, 93
    Shanghai-style Chow Mein   76, 97
    Simmered Mixed Vegetables   62
    Sour and Spicy Soup   67
    Spicy Tofu   72, 99

Stir-fried Bean Thread Noodles
    with Bok Choy   77
Sukiyaki   49
Szechuan Noodles with Vegetables
    78
Tofu Fried Rice   179
Tofu Teriyaki Steak with Sautéed
    Asparagus and Mushrooms   50,
    93
Tofu and Vegetable Soup   45, 89
Vegetable Pancakes   51
Vegetable Tempura   52, 94
shimeji
    in glossary   184
    Grilled Tofu with Mushroom
        Sauce   60
    Mushroom Rice Balls   56, 94
straw mushrooms
    in glossary   184
    Mushroom Balls   126
    Mushroom Balls with Plum Sauce
        136
    Spicy Coconut and Vegetable Soup
        141
wood ear mushrooms
    in glossary   185
    Bean Thread Noodle Salad with
        Potatoes   140
    Chinese Yam Cakes   80
    Korean Noodles   112, 178
    Kung Pao Tofu   71
    Mushroom Balls   126
    Mushroom Balls with Plum Sauce
        136
    Mushroom Soup   168
    Pineapple Fried Rice   124
    Sour and Spicy Soup   67

N
noodles
    bean thread
        in glossary   180
        Bean Thread Noodle Salad with
            Potatoes   140
        Stir-fried Bean Thread Noodles
            with Bok Choy   77
        Vegetable Soup   107, 151
    harusame
        in glossary   181
        Chilled Noodles   177
        Sukiyaki   49
    ramen
        Crispy Noodles with Spicy Sauce
            163
    rice noodles
        Penang Noodles with Sour Soup
            164

Rice Noodle Soup   134
Stir-fried Noodles   144
Stir-fried Rice Noodles with Veg-
    etables   77
Vietnamese Transparent Spring
    Rolls   102, 137
sen lek
    definition   121
    Thai Stir-fried Noodles with Tofu
        101, 124
sen mee
    definition   121
    Crispy Noodles   122
sen yai
    definition   121
    Drunkard's Noodles   123
shirataki
    Sukiyaki   49
soba
    Chilled Buckwheat Noodles   53
somen
    Fine noodles   54
sweet potato noodles
    in glossary   184
    Chilled Noodles   177
    Korean Noodles   112, 178
udon
    in glossary   184
    Noodles in Sesame Sauce   75
    Spicy Noodles   76
    Wheat Noodles in Soup   55
wheat flour noodles
    Cauliflower Coconut Curry with
        Noodles   104, 142
    Crispy Noodle Salad   66, 98
    Noodles in Spicy Coconut Soup
        109, 163
    Shanghai-style Chow Mein   76, 97
wun sen
    definition   121
yakisoba
    in glossary   185
    Fried Noodles   54
    Stir-fried Noodles with Vegetables
        109, 164
    Szechuan Noodles with Vegetables
        78

O
okra
    Indian Vegetable Curry   161
    Okra Namul   170
    Stuffed Okra with Coriander   30
    Tamarind Soup with Pineapple
        and Okra   103, 132
    Tomato, Okra, and Tofu Salad
        with Yuzu Dressing   46

P

papaya
    Green Papaya Pickle   165
    Spicy Green Papaya Salad   116
peanuts
    Bean Thread Noodle Salad with Potatoes   140
    Braised Bitter Gourd   145
    Chili Rice   144
    Chilies in Oil   148
    Cucumber Salad with Sesame Seeds   131
    Fried Peanuts   136
    Gold Bags   101, 125
    Mixed Vegetable Salad with Peanut Sauce   106, 150
    Pickled Vegetable Salad   150
    Satay Sauce   154
    Spicy Fried Tempeh   106, 153
    Spicy Green Papaya Salad   116
    Spicy Peanut Sauce   102, 137
    Sweet Peanut Sauce   118
    Tapioca and Potato Patties   33
    Thai Stir-fried Noodles with Tofu   101, 124
    Tomato Salad   141
    Vegetable Soup from Jakarta   151
pear
    Chilled Noodles   177
peas—see green peas
persimmon
    Persimmon with Walnut Dressing   44
pigeon pea dal—see lentils
pineapple
    Penang Noodles with Sour Soup   164
    Pineapple Fried Rice   124
    Sweet and Sour Vegetables   73
    Tamarind Soup with Pineapple and Okra   103, 132
potatoes (see also sweet potatoes)
    Assorted Vegetables in Cashew Gravy   18, 81
    Bean Thread Noodle Salad with Potatoes   140
    Biryani   26, 83
    Braised Onions and Potatoes   58
    Cabbage and Potato Dry Curry   28
    Cauliflower and Potato with Spices   19, 82
    Curry Puffs   165
    Fiery Potato Curry   160
    Indian Vegetable Curry   161
    Massaman Curry   119
    Mixed Vegetable Salad with Peanut Sauce   106, 150

North Indian Potato Curry   22
Potato and Onion Pancakes   175
Sesame Potatoes   29
Simmered Potato Chorim   170
Sindhi Vegetable and Lentil Curry   23
Spiced Zucchini and Potato   29, 86
Stuffed Eggplant, Squash, and Potato Curry   24
Stuffed Potato Cakes   32, 86
Tapioca and Potato Patties   33
Tofu Fried Rice   179
Vegetable Curry with Bread Rolls   25
Vegetable Soup   107, 151
pumpkin
    in glossary   183
    Crispy Pumpkin Turnovers   31, 87
    Parsee Lentil and Vegetable Curry   22
    Pumpkin in Coconut Cream   101, 128
    Simmered Pumpkin   62, 91

R

radish
    daikon
        in glossary   181
        Bamboo Shoot Salad   130
        Crunchy Vegetable Salad with Japanese-style Dressing   42
        Pancakes rolled with Vegetables   133
        Simmered Daikon with Miso   61
        Tofu and Vegetable Soup   45, 89
        Vietnamese Transparent Spring Rolls   102, 137
    red radish
        Radish, Ginger, and Cabbage Pickle   57
    white radish
        in glossary   185
        Cabbage Radish Kimchi   110, 171
        Chunky Radish Kimchi   172
        Cucumber Kimchi   173
        Kimchi Rice   177
        Korean Wok-seared Spicy Rice with Vegetables   110, 179
        Mixed Vegetable Coconut Curry   107, 152
        Thai Stir-fried Noodles with Tofu   101, 124
        Thai Vegetable Stock   117
ramen—see noodles
red cabbage—see cabbage
red lentils—see lentils

rice
    basmati rice
        Biryani   26, 83
        Browned Rice   26
        Spiced Rice with Mung Beans and Vegetables   27
        Spicy Basmati Rice with Whole Spices   162
    jasmine rice
        in glossary   181
        Chili Fried Rice   122
        Fried Rice with Basil   123
        Pineapple Fried Rice   124
    long-grain rice
        Aromatic Vegetable Fried Rice   75
        Fragrant Lemongrass Rice   108, 162
        Indonesian Fried Rice   155
        Vietnamese Fried Rice   103, 135
        Yellow Rice   155
    short-grain rice
        how to cook   41
        Chili Rice   144
        Fried Rice with Pickled Mustard Greens   56
        Kimchi Rice   177
        Korean Wok-seared Spicy Rice   110, 179
        Mushroom Rice Balls   56, 94
        Scattered Sushi   57, 95
        Sushi Rice   41
        Tofu Fried Rice   179
rice noodles—see noodles
rice vermicelli—see rice noodles

S

sen lek noodles—see noodles
sen mee noodles—see noodles
sen yai noodles—see noodles
shiitake—see mushrooms
shimeji—see mushrooms
shirataki noodles—see noodles
soba noodles—see noodles
spinach
    Bengal Gram and Spinach Kebabs   31
    Crispy Noodles with Spicy Sauce   163
    Mixed Vegetable Salad with Peanut Sauce   106, 150
    Sindhi Vegetable and Lentil Curry   23
    Spinach with Sesame Dressing   45, 90
    Stir-fried Spinach with Mushrooms   105, 143
split black gram—see lentils
split yellow lentils—see lentils

sweet potato noodles—*see* noodles
sweet potatoes
    Stuffed Eggplant, Squash, and
        Potato Curry   24
    Vegetable Tempura   52, 94

T
tapioca
    Tapioca with Mung Beans   138
    Tapioca and Potato Patties   33
tempeh
    in glossary   184
    Mixed Vegetable Coconut Curry
        107, 152
    Spicy Fried Tempeh   106, 153
    Stir-fried Tempeh in Coconut
        Milk   153
    Tempeh Fritters   157
tofu
  abura-age
    in glossary   180
    Mushroom Rice Balls   56, 94
    Pineapple Fried Rice   124
  atsuage
    in glossary   180
    Asparagus, Baby Corn, Pepper,
        and Tofu Satay   100, 118
    Hot and Sour Mushroom Soup   115
    Korean Wok-seared Spicy Rice
        with Vegetables   110, 179
    Kung Pao Tofu   71
    Massaman Curry   119
    Mixed Vegetable Coconut Curry
        107, 152
    Mixed Vegetable Salad with Pea-
        nut Sauce   106, 150
    Noodles in Spicy Coconut Soup
        109, 163
    Pineapple Fried Rice   124
    Rice Noodle Soup   134
    Sour and Spicy Soup   67
    Stir-fried Eggplant and Tofu in
        Spicy Sauce   103, 135
    Stir-fried Noodles with Vegetables
        109, 164
    Sweet and Sour Vegetables   73
    Thai Stir-fried Noodles with Tofu
        101, 124
    Tofu Fried Rice   179
    Tofu Satay   154
    Vietnamese Transparent Spring
        Rolls   102, 137
  koyadofu
    in glossary   182
    Fried Tofu Cutlets   48
tofu, firm
    Bitter Gourd and Tofu Stir-fry   47

Chili Fried Rice   122
Crispy Noodles   122
Deep-fried Battered Tofu   156
Grilled Tofu with Mushroom
    Sauce   60
Gold Bags   101, 125
Gyoza   70, 97
Scrambled Tofu   61, 93
Simmered Tofu Chorim   170
Spicy Tofu   72, 99
Stir-fried Morning Glory   126
Sukiyaki   49
Tofu Kimchi   173
Tofu and Pickled Mustard Stir-fry
    43
Tofu Teriyaki Steak with Sautéed
    Asparagus and Mushrooms   50,
    93
Tofu and Vegetable Soup   45, 89
tofu, silken
    Broccoli with Tofu Dressing   42, 90
    Deep-fried Tofu   59
    Miso Soup with Tofu and Wakame
        43
    Tofu Mayonnaise   51
    Tofu Shake with Blueberries and
        Banana   64
    Tomato, Okra, and Tofu Salad
        with Yuzu Dressing   46
tomatoes
    Assorted Vegetables in Cashew
        Gravy   18, 81
    Basic Curry Sauce   25
    Biryani   26, 83
    Chickpea Curry   20, 82
    Curry with Split Pea Fritters   142
    Drunkard's Noodles   123
    Eggplant in Chili Garlic Sauce   69
    Indian Vegetable Curry   161
    Marinated Eggplant and Bell Pep-
        pers   60
    Noodles in Spicy Coconut Soup
        109, 163
    North Indian Potato Curry   22
    Parsee Lentil and Vegetable Curry
        22
    Sindhi Vegetable and Lentil Curry
        23
    Sour and Spicy Soup   67
    Spicy Fried Tempeh   106, 153
    Spicy Green Papaya Salad   116
    Spicy Roasted Eggplant Curry   23
    Spicy White Lentil Soup   16
    Sprouted Mung Bean and Avocado
        Salad   16, 84
    Stir-fried Noodles with Vegetables
        109, 164

    Stir-fried Tempeh in Coconut
        Milk   153
    Tamarind Soup with Pineapple
        and Okra   103, 132
    Tomato Chutney   34
    Tomato Gravy   20
    Tomato, Okra, and Tofu Salad
        with Yuzu Dressing   46
    Tomato Salad   141
    Tomato Sambal   157
    Vegetable Soup   107, 151
    Vegetable Soup with Mung Beans
        17

U
udon noodles—*see* noodles

W
white cabbage—*see* cabbage
white miso—*see* miso
white radish—*see* radish
wood ear mushrooms—*see* mushrooms
wun sen noodles—*see* noodles

Y
yakisoba—*see* noodles
yam—*see* Chinese yam

Z
zucchini
    Korean Wontons   174
    Kung Pao Tofu   71
    Mushroom and Zucchini Fritters
        112, 175
    Spiced Zucchini and Potato   29, 86
    Stuffed Eggplant, Squash, and
        Potato Curry   24
    Tofu Fried Rice   179
    Vegetable Salad with Sesame
        Almond Dressing   168
    Zucchini Namul   170

Acknowledgments

I am very fortunate to have parents who have given so generously of themselves. Thank you for all the warmth and love. My brother Ketan's passion for food has been inspiring and my sisters, Kalpana, Rina, and Shilpa have been the calming force in my life. Thank you for always being just a phone call away.

I would like to thank my children, Ayesha and Alok, without whose unflinching support and conviction this book would not have happened. They sparked my interest in cooking dishes from various cuisines and with their sheer energy, admiration, and innocent belief that I am the best cook in the world, encouraged me to move on in this journey. They tirelessly listened to my ideas, went through my writing, and stayed up with me on many nights as I tried to put my thoughts into words. Thanks for braving my experiments and being patient in my exploration of new recipes. You are my most ardent fans and my harshest critics. Just the thought of you is enough to brighten my day! And thanks to all their friends. Every evening you spent at our home was special as we laughed and shared stories. Thank you for those happy moments.

A special thanks to all my family and friends around the world, who have touched my life and given me moments to cherish.

I would like to thank my teachers, Ishida sensei and Ishii sensei who have enriched my life with the arts of bonseki and ikebana.

I am indebted to all my friends and cooking students in Tokyo for making this place a home away from home for me.

My sincere thanks to Dilly Daver, Pushkala Mani, Emiko Kothari, Ayesha Bhattal, Chitra Rajashekaran, Preethy Rao, Kimiko Ogawa, Mayumi Rakyan, Eri Tsutsumi, Akiko Trohan, Tomoko Masui, and Kazue Ozeki for sharing their time and knowledge of recipes. And to those who kindly gave their time to ensure the authenticity of all the recipes—Nancy Menayang, Rumini, Bui Eva, Helene Fournier, Marsita Yunous, Hiroko Maeda, Choi Yeonhee, Chae, Mo Ko Ko, Joseph Transg, and Piya Maneewas.

A million thanks to Miho Takaki, Yuki Itoh, Rie Suzuki, and Preethy Rao for the endless hours spent at my home preparing for the photo shoots and editing my recipes.

My sincere gratitude goes to those restaurants that opened their kitchens to me: Burma No Tate Goto, Erawan, Bangkok Kitchen, Sousian, Zassoya, Vietnam Garden, and Kenpuku.

And, finally, I would like to thank my husband for sharing his world with me and for being my pillar of strength. Atul, I could never have done this without you!

（英文版）究極のエイジャン・ベジタリアン・レシピ
The Asian Vegan Kitchen

2007年12月28月　第1刷発行

著　者　ヘーマ・パレック
撮　影　浜村多恵
発行者　富田　充
発行所　講談社インターナショナル株式会社
　　　　〒112-8652 東京都文京区音羽1-17-14
　　　　電話　03-3944-6493（編集部）
　　　　　　　03-3944-6492（営業部・業務部）
　　　　ホームページ www.kodansha-intl.com
印刷・製本所　大日本印刷株式会社

落丁本・乱丁本は購入書店名を明記のうえ、講談社インターナショナル業務部宛にお送りください。送料小社負担にてお取替えします。なお、この本についてのお問い合わせは、編集部宛にお願いいたします。本書の無断複写（コピー）、転載は著作権法の例外を除き、禁じられています。

定価はカバーに表示してあります。

© ヘーマ・パレック 2007
写真 © 浜村多恵 2007
Printed in Japan
ISBN 978-4-7700-3069-6